EMOTIONAL VICTORY
A Biblical View of Feelings and Relationships

*The key to emotional stability is to
let God sit on the throne of our heart and will*

Deb Molder

Copyright © 2021 by Deb Molder. All scripture quotations are taken from the King James Authorized Version.

First published in 2021 by Living Faith Books.

All rights reserved. This book or parts thereof may not be reproduced in any form, stored in any retrieval system, or transmitted in any form by any means—electronic, mechanical, photocopy, recording, or otherwise—without prior written permission of the publisher and/or author, except as provided by United States of America copyright law.

Living Faith Books
3953 Walnut St
Kansas City, MO 64111

Cover Design and Illustrations: Victoria Khan
Compiled by: Charity Fluharty, Havilah Guenther, Tiffini Fyffe
Creative Director: Joel Springer
Revised by: Connor Muolo
Page Design: Lynnsie Hudson
Page Editing: Anna Ryan and Melissa Wharton

ISBN: 978-1-950004-08-9
Printed in the United States of America

Dedication

This book is dedicated to the greatest Father in the universe and His Son, my bridegroom, the Lord Jesus Christ, (and the Comforter who revealed them to me through His Word).

Psalm 73:25-26
Whom have I in heaven but thee? and there is none upon earth that I desire beside thee. My flesh and my heart faileth: but God is the strength of my heart, and my portion for ever.

This book has been 20 years in the making. Despite many starts and stops, I am amazed by how the Lord put a fabulous team together this past year to accomplish His work in His perfect timing. Thank you Connor Muolo, Charity Fluharty, Havilah Guenther, Melissa Wharton, Victoria Khan, Anna Ryan, and Tiffini Fyffe for all of your awesome help!

Table of Contents

Chapter 1:	Introduction	1
Chapter 2:	The Real Problem	23
Chapter 3:	Developing Confidence and Security	47
Chapter 4:	Making God the Center	73
Chapter 5:	Running Your Emotions Through the Word of God	95
Chapter 6:	Grace - Life's Most Important Commodity	115
Chapter 7:	Dealing with Anger (or Any Emotion that Becomes Sin)	133
Chapter 8:	How to Love and Forgive	149
Chapter 9:	Job's Example of Overcoming Fear (An Application of Love and Forgiveness)	167
Chapter 10:	Conquering Fear and Finding the Secret Place	181
Chapter 11:	How to Keep from Being Deceived	205
Chapter 12:	Romantic Relationships	229
Chapter 13:	Depression	249
Chapter 14:	Developing and Keeping a Positive Attitude	269
Chapter 15:	A Meek and Quiet Spirit	287
Chapter 16:	Learning from Failure	303
Chapter 17:	Suffering	319
Chapter 18:	The Joy of the Lord	345
Chapter 19:	Mentorship	361
Chapter 20:	Closing Principles	367
Appendix:	Biblical Discipleship Overview	379

1

Introduction

When the Bible mentions the heart, it isn't usually referring to the literal, beating presence in the center of our chest. Rather, it is referring to the attitude of our "heart," the seat of our emotions. That is why the original cover of this book — for many years called "The Emotions Study" — though corny, was the way that it was. I put it together nearly 25 years ago with various clipart images: a throne, a crown, and a key. This simple picture shows us a lot about our emotions and our relationships, and it can even be a visual explanation of why we, as women, have so many difficulties with the issues of our heart. Each one of us has a heart with a throne, a crown, and a key. Our physical heart keeps our physical body alive, but our actual heart — the one made of spiritual tissue and substance — is so much more important. It defines our spiritual life — the life that will shape how we interact with God and others. Our physical heart will fail and be buried in the ground, but our spiritual heart is eternal.

The intent of the first couple of chapters is to cause us to ask ourselves a very simple question: Who (or what) is sitting on the throne of my heart and wearing the crown of authority and influence? The answer to this question is paramount because it governs all the decisions that we make. It is the sail on the sailboat pulling us at every whim of the wind. As we continue through this study, we will see that our greatest need is for the Lord Jesus Christ to be the One on that throne with all idols toppled over and broken, like Dagon bowed down and broken before the ark of the LORD in 1 Samuel 5:4. To have and keep God on the throne of our heart as God the Father, God the Son, and God the Holy Spirit is, in a nutshell, the key to life. It's the key to your emotions and relationships as well.

While we as humans look at the outward appearance, the Lord says in 1 Samuel 16:7 that He looks on the heart. It is our internal heart attitude that actually propels us forward in life. It is what moves us. And behind that internal attitude of the heart, there is a throne upon which we, through our thoughts, place the things which control us. It is where we bow the knee and place a crown on every pursuit, desire, and idol.

We will see that the key to all emotional stability is for God to be and stay on the throne of our hearts, and that He also needs to stay on the throne of our personal will, for God gave each of us free will, even limiting Himself by it. If we're not careful, the thoughts we allow to creep onto that throne can become patterns that stubbornly refuse to be unseated. Though the issues of our life seem to be so tied to this world and the things contained therein, the battle we face is always one of the mind and the emotions we allow to govern it. It's a battle over the throne and, in the big picture, over a spiritual kingdom that extends far beyond our individual selves. We all have the amazing ability to choose how that battle will end: with God on the throne or with something or someone else there instead. So, ask yourself: Who is on top? Who (or what) is number one in your life? All the distractions of life are truly just noise from different entities competing for that crown.

The table of contents shows many different subjects, all of which are centered around different emotions and states. While there are far more emotions than what we could cover in one book, the purpose of this book is to establish a framework for identifying and addressing any emotion by which a person might be swept away. It is a book of how to run all of our strong emotions through the boundaries of the Word of God, looking at the clear lines that God has given us for our emotions, and why He has given us these bounds. In addition to the "how," we will also look at some of the "whys" behind many of the problems in the area of our emotions, such as why our relationships so often defeat us and why we as ladies often have more difficulty in the area of our emotions than men do.

Because no person is exempt from emotions, this study is good for women of all ages and seasons of life, whether they be young or old, married or single, childless or facing motherhood. We all have a heart and a throne on that heart, and we each must choose to whom we will give the crown for that throne. This simple thought is the key to dealing with our emotions and relationships.

My Beginning and How This Study Came to Be

I was not raised in a Christian home. We really had no religion of any kind, good or bad. When I was one year old, my mom and dad separated, and that was the last time I saw my biological father. He had been diagnosed with catatonic schizophrenia, and at that time, my mom was told that if she remained married to him, my little brother and I had much greater chances of developing schizophrenia. She loved him very much, and it was a very hard decision for her to make. Sometimes he hit her, and the day she saw him shake my three-week-old brother, she finally decided to leave him. She took me and my brother to live with her parents, my grandparents. We stayed with them until I was six years old and my mom met an awesome man. They married, and he adopted me and my little brother. He had two children of his own who were a couple years older than we were. Mom and Dad were decent, moral people, but they didn't have Jesus.

He was a good man. I wasn't abused or neglected. I knew that he loved me. However, though I called him "Daddy," there was still a desire in my heart to know my real dad. Daddy had a son and a daughter before he married mom, and these were the children that he had known and raised since their births. Though I don't fully understand how this developed in me, as I grew up, the way I always perceived my relationship with him was as my sister's dad and my stepdad. Consequently, I grew up desperately wanting my own dad.

I was so desperate in this desire that I used to have dreams about it. I remember this recurring dream in which I was seeking to discover who my real father was. I was standing on a hill next to my home, and my real, biological father came running to grab me, calling out my name. I just knew that someday I was going to get to meet him, and that someday he was going to come back and rescue me. Yet looking back, my life was good, and I'm not sure what I thought I needed rescuing from.

When I was 13, I started asking lots of questions about my real father and expressing my desire to meet him. One day, after my family and I watched a movie about a man with mental illness, my mom decided to take me aside and tell me about my biological father. She explained that I could see him if I would like, but it may not be the best idea due to his condition. After thinking about it, I chose to take her advice. Looking back, I wish I had decided to meet him, because that day, my dreams of my real father coming to rescue me were shattered.

It was shortly thereafter that I began dating, and I was boy crazy — definitely in love with love. As soon as I began dating at the young age of 14, I was never without a boyfriend. I became very co-dependent and began this desperate search for the perfect man. I thought, "He's out there somewhere! He's going to complete me, and he's going to take care of all my problems. Everything is going to be solved because of this guy, this knight in shining armor." I was convinced that I was going to find him and be 100% fulfilled, and we would live happily ever after! Snow White, Cinderella, all of these fairytales fed into this obsession of living "happily ever after" with the prince of my dreams.

And oh yes, all of the songs about love fed my search. Songs became like my "Bible" and foundation, and I memorized them all! There were so many songs about how this man was my soulmate, the answer to my life, that he was somewhere out there, and that he would complete me. All I had to do was find him! And to find him I tried. My first marriage was at 21. He was a great guy by all normal standards. Within three years of marriage we both had good jobs and had purchased a nice home. Someone from the outside looking in would think we had it made, but I was drinking more and kept thinking, "Something is wrong. I don't know what it is, but I am not 100% fulfilled and he hasn't completed me." All of the dreams of him being my knight in shining armor simply weren't coming true. And so, based on my philosophy of life, I chose to leave him. He wanted children, and I just couldn't move forward on that. Now, looking back, I know that if we had just gotten saved at that point and began growing in Christ, things would have been totally different. But I left. It was very wrong and brought about many heartbreaking consequences; nevertheless, I left.

Within a week or two, I was already dating the man who would become my next husband, and I fell head over heels in love. Little did I know, he was an abuser, both physically and emotionally. He had grown up in a family of abusers, and this was his way of life. To make matters worse, I later found out that he had been married six times before. So began a really rough couple of years of physical and emotional abuse. By the time I was 26, I was a heavy smoker and a big partier. I was deep into the occult — I could chart your astrological natal charts, and believe me, there is more to that stuff than just a sun sign. I was tormented by fear and insecurity, and though I constantly felt like my insides were crumbling, I had learned how to keep up a "happy" facade.

Looking back, I have no doubt that without God, if I had stayed on that path, none of its destinations would have been good. I probably would have been committed to an insane asylum — this was back in the early '80s when there was no doctor with magic pills for your mind, and my mom even tried to get me committed to a mental home at one point. If not the insane asylum, death was a very real option, either at my hands or my husband's. I once tried to kill myself with a bottle of pills, and my husband almost succeeded in killing me on two separate occasions.

My husband and I were in a horrible cycle, which I later came to learn is very common in abusive relationships — the good is totally awesome and the bad is utterly horrific. I kept trying to stay on the "good" side of our relationship by walking on eggshells, but it never lasted. The common abusive pattern goes like this: he would beat me up (for reasons I didn't always understand), and then he would try to make it up to me by showering me with love, gifts, and promises. Looking back, the "good" that I thought was true was really just a lie. I thought that I loved him and that I could help him, but that was just not the reality. Neither one of us were saved and we knew nothing about the Lord Jesus Christ.

That was the state of my life in 1984 when a girl from Kansas City Baptist Temple (KCBT) came to work at my job. Her name was Karen, and she carried her Bible every day and would even read it at lunch. This intrigued me; I had never seen anything like it before. She would often say things like, "This Book has all the answers to life! It can solve all our problems!" She, of course, had no idea what I was going through at the time, and she didn't realize that I was listening to her words in complete desperation. I so wanted answers. I was about at the end of my rope and was overwhelmed with panic attacks, constantly wondering how I would ever move forward and make any sense out of life. She began bringing in cassette tapes and booklets from her church, which gave me a glimpse into her life: a life with Jesus. My husband rarely let me out of his sight, so church was out of the question, but Karen and I managed to become good friends at work.

After nearly two months of friendship, I remember waking up on a Monday morning and realizing, "I am going to die and go to hell." After listening to and reading some of the materials she had been giving me, I knew that I needed a Savior to save me from my sin. I went into work that morning, and

I immediately walked right to her desk and said, "Karen, how do I get saved? I need to be saved." Can you imagine? I'd never even been to church yet! Think about someone coming up to you and asking, "How can I get saved?" first thing at work on a Monday morning. She looked at me with surprise and, smiling ear to ear, said, "Of course, let me write this down."

She wrote down the Romans Road along with a simple prayer. She handed the paper to me and said, "We can talk about this when we get together later at lunch." I went back to my desk, staring at that piece of paper. I just couldn't wait any longer. I got up and walked to the bathroom. As I closed the restroom door, I said, "Lord, if you hear me, please don't let anyone come in here." And there, right there in the bathroom, I repented of my sin and accepted the Lord Jesus Christ as my personal Lord and Savior! It was the greatest decision of my life. I was on my way to Heaven! I was born again, and nothing could change that fact.

However, I had lived close to 27 years in this world — never reading the Bible, never understanding biblical principles — and I had developed a lot of bad habits and patterns. My foundation, or philosophy of life, had been built without the Bible. I had learned to run my whole life completely based on my feelings and emotions. God had fixed all of my eternal problems, but my life was in need of major renovation. I still had many, many problems and strongholds in the flesh.

That next year was a really rough year. My husband began taking me to church once in a while, and my prayer was for him to get saved too. I knew God could rescue him like He had me, but he continued beating me up after I was saved. I went in for biblical counseling and was advised to move in with my parents while the two of us came in for counseling. The abuse had gotten bad, and they didn't want him to kill me. That went on for a while, but eventually he came to the decision that he didn't want any part of my Jesus. He had faked it for a while, but it finally became clear that all he wanted was out. God could have changed his life as He had changed mine, but God had limited Himself to my husband's own will, and his will was to have nothing to do with his Creator.

Though this was heartbreaking, it finally gave me the opportunity to start going to church regularly and begin growing. As soon as possible, I was baptized and began discipleship. It's important to note that the term "discipleship" will be used frequently throughout this book. If you're not familiar with the philosophy of biblical discipleship, refer to the Appendix. There you'll find an overview of what it means to be a disciple of Jesus Christ and a summary of the material published by Living Faith Fellowship *Biblical Discipleship*.

At its core, biblical discipleship is when a young Christian gets paired up with an older Christian as they walk through some of the basics of the Word of God and are taught how to grow in their relationship with Christ. As I continued in the process of discipleship and learned how to order my life through biblical principles, my life began to change radically. A few years later, God gave me a burden to help others the same way that He had helped me, so I began mentoring and counseling ladies. While I was investing in other women, I was growing and healing through the ministries of my local church. There was a counseling assignment in the Bible school my church ran (Shepherd's School), and God laid it on my heart to start writing down some of the "eureka moments" where He had opened my eyes of wrongdoing that I'd been living in or the bad habits I'd developed and had shown me how to address them biblically in order to heal and move forward. This list of "eureka moments" was the very beginning of what would become this book. By God's grace, a year or so later, we started using it in the counseling ministry that we had back then.

I always say that I wish that I had "before and after" pictures from that time. Though I still have much to learn, it is drastic what God was able to rescue me out of. He rescued me from a demonic dump! Years ago, I saw a movie called *The Exorcism of Emily Rose*. It was based on a true story about a woman who was trying to find deliverance from demonic influences in her past. Unfortunately, she went toward religion and good works to try to be rescued, and she ended up dying without any deliverance. It is a sad story and one that is even more poignant to me because I can relate to her lost state. I am so grateful to God, because while she turned to religion, God showed me how to have a relationship with Him. This study will explore that relationship, and we will see that it isn't about what we're doing for Him or for ourselves. Rather, it's about what He's doing in, around, and through us. This is the true nature of biblical discipleship: growing in a relationship with the Lord Jesus Christ.

Our spiritual growth is like our physical one in that we have to learn the basics in order to grow. Children need supervision, attention, care, and nurturing. A baby cannot feed itself, and a child doesn't know how to tie their shoes unless you sit down with them and practice it with them several times. God uses many physical pictures in His Word to teach us spiritual truths, and just like you were born the first time and began growing, the Lord wants us to be born again spiritually and begin growing the second time. He even says that we have seven stages of spiritual growth! Our spiritual birth is so much more important than our physical birth, and our spiritual mentors help us grow in ways that have eternal impact and value. As we move forward in this study, we are going to look deeper into the biblical pattern of discipleship, as well as what the Bible says about being born again and those seven stages of spiritual growth. We'll see how this thing called discipleship helps us grow through these stages, and how God uses mentors in our life. Discipleship is a decision both to follow Christ and to learn how to grow in our relationship with Him.

Before and even after discipleship, there are sometimes situations that require special attention. Biblical counseling ministry helps individuals and church members address their problems biblically so that they can resolve them and move forward in obedience. In this way, churches and hospitals are quite similar. Back at KCBT, the church that helped lead me to get saved, we had a large counseling ministry. We always said that if the church is like a hospital, then the counseling ministry is the emergency room where people with problems of all kinds can come for help. Back when I was part of the counseling ministry, we would use our first appointment to assign the individual one of three classifications in order to know how to best start helping them.

Classification #1 was "Band-Aid and Merthiolate". This would be someone who had been around spiritual truth most of their lives but never had someone teach them how to have a relationship with God. Our prescription for them would be to pair them with a discipler, and soon they would be on their way to growing in Christ and finding God's purpose for their life.

Classification #2 was "Broken Bones and Appendectomy". This was someone who had one area with which they were really struggling or had a pattern of sin that they couldn't overcome on their own. They would often be assigned a counselor to take them through the basics of discipleship or biblical principles.

Classification #3 was "Heart Transplant and Brain Surgery". This was someone with very serious issues. They would normally have a pastor work with them and they might also have an entire team working on their case.

I remember that when I heard these terms, I went to my pastor and said, "You know, I went through this with you, so I guess you guys must have classified me as a three." He just smiled, shook his head, and said, "No, hon', we classified you as a four. We really didn't think you would make it."

I share this to say that no matter how broken a person is or how hopeless a case may seem, they can get victory if they come to the Bible seeking God and His answers. That's what this book is about: God giving victory over any area in our lives. The Bible has all the answers, and the Lord can heal and bring victory. As long as you are still alive, there is another chance for the Lord to bring healing. Nothing is impossible with God.

The best way to go through this study is not to just read it today and then put it on a shelf. You need to go back through the material over and over. It's the same with discipleship and the basics. The thing that really changed my life was not just going through discipleship with a mentor once, but turning around and taking others through what God had given to me. Going over and over that material is like going over and over the basics. Anyone who has ever mastered anything knows that excellence comes in rehearsing the basics over and over again as a foundation upon which you can build. When I was in elementary school, I sang in a choir, and for the first 30 minutes of each rehearsal, we would just practice scales over and over again, not singing songs! Even football and baseball players practice fundamental skills and drills every day in training and before every game. Repetition is the price of learning.

So, as we go through this study, ask God for "eureka moments" — moments where you are enlightened by His truth and can start applying those principles to your life. Here a little, there a little. As you learn and grow, don't just keep what you have learned to yourself. Teach it to others. Make sure that you are taking others through these same truths often, and that will keep this book and the principles of discipleship from becoming dusty on a shelf.

Ground Rules

Many of you know this, but it has to be emphasized over and over again: the Bible is a supernatural book. When Karen or my pastor would counsel me, they would hold up their Bible and say, "This Book has all the answers. God, the Creator of the Universe, wrote this Book for our instruction. This Book is supernatural. It is unlike any other book you are going to read on the face of the earth. You just have to come to it with a believing heart." It is like a buried treasure, and its own definition of itself is that it is better than rubies, diamonds, jewels, and gold. What's more, the Bible is a treasure trove that we have complete access to at any time. By God's grace, as I began the process of discipleship, I began searching it and looking for answers. Not only that, but I did that believing what it said! And little by little, the Lord opened my eyes to its truth. My prayer for you is that you, too, will begin making God's Word the authority in your life, not only reading its words, but by reading and applying them in faith.

Many churched folk have a saying that goes: "book, chapter, verse." It simply means that we need to filter what we are hearing, feeling, or experiencing through the Bible to find out exactly what God has to say about it. It is the same with our emotions. We need to ask ourselves for the "book, chapter, verse" for the thoughts that are running through our minds. Find the address in your Bible where it talks about that subject. Do a word study. We need to be constantly asking ourselves: "What does God say about this? What advice does He give me on this topic?" We need to be like the Bereans, who were commended for their diligence in studying in God's Word. They received Paul's preaching of the Word with readiness of mind and then would search the Scriptures daily to see if what he was saying was true (Acts 17:11-12).

Our study will include many passages of Scripture, and though it is tempting to skim over these sections, this would be doing yourself a disservice.

Because this book teaches the process of perfecting a call-and-response attitude to God's Word pertaining to our emotions, getting an understanding of the verses is the most important part of this study.

Passages to Consider

> **Hebrews 4:12-13** *For the word of God is quick, and powerful, and sharper than any twoedged sword, piercing even to the <u>dividing asunder of soul</u> and spirit, <u>and of the joints and marrow</u>, and is <u>a discerner of the thoughts and intents of the heart</u>. Neither is there any creature that is not manifest in his sight: but all things are naked and opened unto the eyes of him with whom we have to do.*

The first thing that is powerful about this passage is how the Word of God describes itself. Firstly, it says that it is "quick." The word "quick" in verse 12 means "alive," like the quick of your nail bed which produces the nail. The Bible is alive — it is living, interactive, dynamic, and eternal. And not only that, it is also powerful and sharp. It can divide all defenses, excuses, confusion, and thoughts. Secondly, we see that it is a discerner. It can categorize, organize, and label each and every thought, emotion, and situation. It also says in verse 13 that it is the very eyes of God. The Word of God goes down into the very marrow of our bones and divides between soul and spirit, and there is absolutely nothing hidden from His eyes. When we look down at the Word, God stares right back at us.

> ***Joshua 1:8*** *This book of the law shall not depart out of thy mouth; but thou shalt meditate therein day and night, that thou mayest observe to do according to all that is written therein: for then thou shalt make thy way prosperous, and then thou shalt have good success.*

This is the only time you will ever find the word "success" in the Word of God. Therefore, if we want to learn how to have success, it is only logical that we should consider what God has said about it here in His Word. Contrary to the idea of success that the world gives us, which is found in the right BMI, house, husband, family, and career, the Word of God defines what true success is and how to attain it. According to God, success is to meditate every day and every night on God's Word and to obey it. The reality of walking according to God's Word as we apply it to our lives is the purest and most satisfying success that could ever be achieved.

> ***Romans 12:1-2*** *I beseech you therefore, brethren, by the mercies of God, that ye present your bodies a living sacrifice, holy, acceptable unto God, which is your reasonable service. And be not conformed to this world: but be ye transformed by the renewing of your mind, that ye may prove what is that good, and acceptable, and perfect, will of God.*

This passage tells us that we can renew our minds through His Book! It can transform us from the inside out, like the metamorphosis of a caterpillar to a butterfly. By simply believing His words and allowing them to take root in our hearts, we can be changed into someone unrecognizable to our friends, family, and past, but recognizable to God as the image of His own Son.

> **1 Corinthians 2:16** *For who hath known the mind of the Lord, that he may instruct him? but we have the mind of Christ.*
>
> **John 1:1-2** *In the beginning was the Word, and the Word was with God and the Word was God. The same was in the beginning with God.*
>
> **John 1:14** *And the Word was made flesh, and dwelt among us, (and we beheld his glory, the glory as of the only begotten of the Father,) full of grace and truth.*

We must also realize we have the mind of Christ through the Word of God. There is no reason to wonder what our thoughts should be on any matter or issue in life when we have access to the very mind of God. The limiting factor, of course, is whether we will choose to believe it. The mind of Christ is not of much use to us if we do not approach it in faith and submission.

> **1 Thessalonians 2:13** *For this cause also thank we God without ceasing, because, when ye received the word of God which ye heard of us, ye received it not as the word of men, but as it is in truth, the word of God, which effectually worketh also in you that believe.*
>
> **Hebrews 11:6** *But without faith it is impossible to please him: for he that cometh to God must believe that he is, and that he is a rewarder of them that diligently seek him.*

We must believe the Word of God for it to work in our lives! God has always chosen to limit Himself by allowing us to exercise our own free will. Our approach to the Word is the same. However, "Lord, I believe; help thou mine unbelief" is a great prayer in the Bible for those who desire to grow in their faith and are struggling (Mark 9:24). God also promises that faith even the size of a mustard seed is all that He needs as the catalyst for large changes (Matthew 17:20). We need that "effectual working" in us to cause the spiritual transformation and rebuilding we are looking for, but in order for this to happen, we have to seek after Him in faith. We must ask, "What does God say?" Our faith is the closest we will ever get in this life to seeing Him with our eyes, and it is all in proportion to how seriously we take Him at His Word.

Along those same lines, we see in Matthew 13:58 and Mark 6:5-6 that Jesus, the very Creator of the Universe, the King of kings, couldn't help someone because of their unbelief. Though He has all power, God has allowed Himself to be limited by our free will. He is limited by our desire to believe Him, and God is limited in your life by whether or not you are going to believe Him at His Word.

In Romans 15:31, Paul asks to be delivered from unbelievers. There is a mighty power behind belief in God's Word, and we see here that there is another power that is opposite to it: unbelief, which God calls evil. Though some of God's Word is deep, mysterious, and hard to understand, the majority of it is simple, so much so that even children can read and apply it. Therefore, the problem many of us have is not so much that the Bible is hard to understand. The problem is that it can be hard to believe. Our natural minds cannot understand it and our natural minds desire to live contrary to it in all manner of sin. This is why we fall into so many problems. We either do not have faith in what He says, or we, through sin or ignorance, decide not to learn what He says in His Word.

To add insult to injury, we are often more willing to believe a lie than we are willing to believe the truth. In light of our culture, it makes sense. We see commercials and marketing all the time telling us that if we only buy this, then we'll get that — often tying their products to promises of fleeting things like happiness, sex, and success. The problem is that we believe them and let the Word of God sit on a shelf. Instead of flipping through channels, screens and magazines, we need to realize that it is only by flipping through the Word of God that we can get all the answers and contentment beyond comparison. Only the Word of God can transform us and give us victory, no matter what problems we are facing. Find out what God says about your situation or emotions, apply it, then wait patiently through the proving process as you tear down walls so that God can rebuild you into a more fit temple.

More verses about belief: Hebrews 11:13; Romans 10:17; James 1:21-25; Luke 8:4-15; Romans 15:13; Mark 9:24.

Conclusion

Let us end this introduction by looking at a few key principles that this study will use to delve deeper into the practice of seeing our emotions through the lens of God's Word. The Bible says that God formed Adam out of the ground (Genesis 2:7). Never mind what the theory of evolution says is the origin of mankind. We know the truth: we came from dirt. We can't ever forget that. On the other hand, the Word of God is life. The Bible is what can change us from the inside out and allow God to work in and through us! It is through the Word of God that earthen vessels could be turned into vessels unto honor (1 Thessalonians 4:4; 2 Timothy 2:21).

Another thing to keep in mind as we walk through these principles is that Jesus replaced Himself with three things when He went to sit at the right hand of the Father: the Holy Spirit, the local church, and the Word of God. These are the three things that need to be fully present in our lives in order for us to grow. If even one of these is not fully present or appreciated in your life, there is no way to grow and live in a balanced and healthy way. Spiritual dysfunction will be inevitable.

Though this next principle seems to be unrelated, it is key to our understanding of the purpose and intent of our lives. There are two kingdoms in the Bible: a physical kingdom and a spiritual kingdom. The physical kingdom — the Kingdom of Heaven — is one that God was building through the nation of Israel. This can be traced throughout the majority of the Old Testament in places like Genesis 1:27-28 and Genesis 26:3-4, and it was also provisionally offered during Jesus' earthly ministry (Matthew 4:17). The spiritual kingdom — the Kingdom of God — is one that God is building through the Church. This is best seen in the New Testament in places like Matthew 6:33, 1 Corinthians 15:49-50, and

Romans 14:17. For more details on the Kingdom of God and the Kingdom of Heaven, check out chapter 3 of Mark Trotter's *The Keys of Bible Study*. This spiritual Kingdom of God is the kingdom that we are to seek. This is so important, because if the kingdom we are in is spiritual, then it isn't in the physical that you find the riches given to you by God. This relationship that we're building with the Lord Jesus Christ is a spiritual relationship. This New Testament relationship by grace through faith is spiritual (Ephesians 2:8-9). Therefore, the spiritual should be our only focus as we walk as pilgrims on this earth.

The last principle is that of trichotomy. We see throughout the Bible that God has made us in three parts: spirit, soul, and body.

> *1 Thessalonians 5:23 says, "And the very God of peace sanctify you wholly; and I pray God your whole spirit and soul and body be preserved blameless unto the coming of our Lord Jesus Christ."*

We were made in three parts because we were made in God's image: God the Father, God the Son, and God the Holy Spirit. However, the order that we often quote these three parts is different from what we see in 1 Thessalonians 5:23. While the Bible started with spirit and ended with body, we often say it as body, then soul, and finally spirit. I believe the reason we say it that way is that we usually put emphasis on the body (or physical) and make it our foundation. Think about your life. How much of its foundation is really spiritual, and how does the balance of your concerns and thoughts fall out between body and spirit? It is interesting that we spend so much thought on the portion of ourselves that will go into the ground instead of the part that will continue into eternity.

While the spiritual aspect of the trichotomy is the most important, we need to keep in mind these three "parts" are always working together. They affect each other and are interdependent. However, most of our problems stem from the spiritual and not the physical. Therefore, what we really need to do when we're talking about these three aspects of ourselves is to place them in the order God has given them: spirit, soul, and then body.

> *1 Samuel 16:7* But the LORD said unto Samuel, Look not on his countenance, or on the height of his stature; because I have refused him: for the LORD seeth not as man seeth; for man looketh on the outward appearance, but the LORD looketh on the heart.

In this verse, Samuel is surveying Jesse's sons because God told him that one of them would be the next king of Israel. Initially, Samuel focused on the stature, age, and appearance of his older sons and assumed that their strength would make one of them the right choice. In the end Samuel anoints David, the youngest of the sons and the caretaker of the sheep, to become king. This is because God says man looketh on the outward, but God looketh on the heart. This is the attitude of heart that we need. We tend to focus on the outward, on a physical foundation. However, that spiritual foundation of what is going on internally in our heart is between us and God and is a more sure foundation. The spiritual must become the foundation of our lives. We need to begin asking what God says and how we can connect that to our spiritual circumstances, not looking at the physical first. Start focusing on the spiritual. This needs to become our foundation in everything as we ask what God's Word says and how we can apply that to our lives, acknowledging Him in all things.

Building Blocks of Life

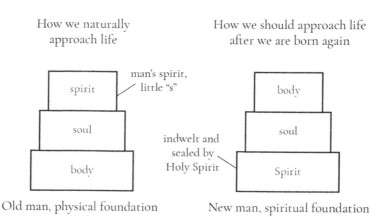

Introduction

Homework Assignment: Read Luke 8:4-15 and consider the four different kinds of hearts mentioned in the passage, remembering that when God speaks about the heart, He's talking about our internal attitude. As you read through these verses, prayerfully determine which heart you have and which heart you want. Why do you have the heart that you currently have? What factors are at play in your life that are keeping you from getting the heart that you want?

Recommended Reading: *The Bible Promise Book*. This is a book where verses are categorized by subject, and it is essential as we begin this spiritual journey of transformation. I used to always keep this little book, along with my Bible, with me. That way when I had a problem, I would have my "first aid kit" on me to find the verses that I needed about that subject. It was a cheat sheet for me that often helped before I grew to know my Bible well.

HEARTS:
1. devil takes away
2. no roots (rocky)   ⎱ I have
3. choked out / distracted by cares (thorn) ⎰ these
4. good soil —— I want this

— immaturity
— Incorrect view of God / what our relationship looks like

how to get good soil to bear Fruit?

Questions to Consider:

1. Do you have a testimony of salvation? If so, what is it? If you're unsure, check out pages 36-37 and see if you've believed on those verses.

2. Consider the things in your life. Write down a list of things or people who are on the throne of your heart or have the potential to be on the throne of your heart.

3. Do you struggle with your emotions? So far, what has been your approach in dealing with your emotions?
   numbing myself

4. What is the biggest area emotionally that you struggle with? (For example: fear, worry, love) *anxiety, sadness*

5. What was your relationship like with your father? How does that affect how you view God? *very distant / non existent. sometimes I feel like God is too busy for me*

6. What have your relationships with men looked like throughout your life? *I've been in a pattern of wanting male attention ever since I can remember*

7. Of the three counseling classifications given, which one most accurately describes where you're at right now?
   #1 & #2

8. What does your relationship with the Bible look like?
   kind of random / inconsistent, sometimes I feel like it will be draining to read

9. Which type of heart are you, as given by the Luke 8 assignment?
   heart w/ rocky soil — No roots
   heart w/ thorns — being tossed by trials

on the throne of my heart:
MY PARENTS
MYSELF
MY SIBLINGS

2

The Real Problem

This lesson is about some of the "eureka moments" God used to help me go from running my life completely by my emotions to running my emotions through the Word of God. As I began this journey, I learned that it is good to start at the beginning of everything: the Garden of Eden.

> ***Genesis 1:27-31*** *So God created man in his own image, in the image of God created he him; male and female created he them. And God blessed them, and God said unto them, Be fruitful, and multiply, and replenish the earth, and subdue it: and have dominion over the fish of the sea, and over the fowl of the air, and over every living thing that moveth upon the earth. And God said, Behold, I have given you every herb bearing seed, which is upon the face of all the earth, and every tree, in the which is the fruit of a tree yielding seed; to you it shall be for meat. And to every beast of the earth, and to every fowl of the air, and to every thing that creepeth upon the earth, wherein there is life, I have given every green herb for meat: and it was so. And God saw every thing that he had made, and, behold, it was very good. And the evening and the morning were the sixth day.*

The Garden of Eden was absolute perfection. It was a utopia made by God for man. Not only was it "good," but God goes so far as to call it "very good." It was flawless. That's because there was something very different about that garden and about Adam and Eve — back then, God walked with them in that garden. <u>They had fellowship with God through a perfect spiritual connection.</u> They were even naked and didn't know it, clothed in the glory of God as they walked with Him in the garden! This is very different from the world's current relationship with God and with each other. The natural state of man today is to be separated from God, not connected to Him spiritually. Why is this perfect Father-child relationship that they had with God so different from what we have today? What happened?

The key to answering these questions is found in John 4:24, which says, "God is a Spirit: and they that worship him must worship him in spirit and in truth." Back in Eden, Adam and Eve could worship God in spirit and in truth. Perfect setting, perfect physical, perfect spiritual, perfect relationship, perfect Father, absolutely perfect and flawless everything. Not only did they have it perfect on their side, but God was completely pleased. Revelation 4:11 tells us that everything God created was created for His pleasure, and that includes Adam and Eve. He had a relationship with them as they walked together in the garden, and He was pleased with this relationship! He created this universe to be filled with beings with whom He could have a loving relationship, and it was the idea of building a loving relationship with us that gave Him ultimate pleasure.

However, even though Adam and Eve were in paradise and had this perfect relationship with God, He still needed to see if they truly loved and believed Him. One of the most amazing characteristics of our God, the Creator of the Universe, is that He does not want to control us. He does not want robots. He wants fellowship — true love — so He offers the choice to know Him and love Him. He created a universe with beings who could choose, by their own free will, to follow and believe Him.

He did this by giving Adam and Eve a choice: an opportunity to exercise their free will to love, believe, and obey Him. In the midst of the garden, He planted the Tree of the Knowledge of Good and Evil, and though He had given them freedom to eat of any other tree in the garden, He gave them one simple command: do not eat of this tree. He gave them access to everything else, but He gave them this test to see if they were going to trust and believe Him, because free will necessitates that a choice be made. He could have easily made Adam and Eve without a free will to obey. He could have had perfectly obedient, loveless beings who obeyed Him out of His own programming, but this infinite and powerful God, who is beyond time and space, chose to limit Himself by our free will. He gave them free will. He let them choose. He lets you choose too. You have a free will, and every day you get to choose whether or not you will trust and obey Him.

I grew up in a world where someone was always trying to control someone else, and I was often the one being controlled. When that wasn't happening, I was on the opposite end of the stick, trying to control others and the situation. From this cycle came anxiety and unsteadiness, and from this came panic attacks. But our God, the Creator of the Universe, the King of kings, and the Lord of lords, is the one being in this universe that actually has the right to control everything in it, including us. But He doesn't. Instead, He allows us to be tested and tempted of our own lusts, and He places a decision before us: will we obey or will we disobey? He waits. He gives us chance after chance time and time again. He patiently waits on us — people that abuse, attack, walk away, and disobey. He chooses longsuffering, in the hope that we would choose to love and follow Him. God often uses chastisement in our lives to open our eyes to the sinful situation we have chosen over Him, but He also often chooses to draw us to Himself by His great goodness. That's God our Father. He and this thing He has chosen to limit Himself by — our free will — simply blow my mind! Take a moment to really think about that.

We know what happened next in Genesis 3: they chose not to believe, trust, or obey. They exercised their free will against what He had commanded. Before we fault them, we should ask ourselves how often we do the same thing. How often do we distrust and disobey?

Unfortunately, we often do not believe God either. Deceived by her own desire, Eve's decision was finalized with the help of the devil. After eating of the Tree of the Knowledge of Good and Evil, she goes to her husband and convinces him to eat, and they both fall. Sin enters the picture, and the Garden of Eden no longer looks so perfect and flawless. No longer could Adam and Eve walk with God in the cool of the day. They could no longer worship Him in spirit and in truth.

But we must remember that God allowed this to happen! Not only that, He created Adam and Eve fully knowing that they would rebel against Him. Through His longsuffering, we are going to see how He had a plan to work it all out in the end.

In that moment of their disobedience, they died spiritually, and a spiritual void now existed in Adam and Eve. This spiritual void was a hole where only the Spirit of God used to reside, but was now absent. They no longer had that glorious spiritual connection with the living God, and they were no longer clothed in God's glory. Where their nakedness had once been a picture of innocence, it became an object of shame, and the spiritual foundation that was supposed to be their reality was gone in a moment. Their perfect relationship with God was replaced with a wall of separation between them and God, and all of this was because sin had entered the picture.

This new hole in their spirits brought a sense of incompleteness in them. Where once it was filled with the Holy Spirit, it was now empty and void. All they had was each other, because they no longer had God. Worse than that, they were also now unfulfilled, because they could no longer fulfill the purpose for which God created them. They could no longer worship Him, and they could no longer bring Him pleasure. They had been created to fellowship with and glorify God, just like all of us. But, as we experience, when something doesn't function the way it was created to work, it becomes unfulfilled! This is the real problem: the problem of a spiritual void that only God can fill, a hole of incompleteness and unfulfillment; the result of broken fellowship. This real problem was passed on to their children, then passed on to their children, and on and on until it was passed on to us.

You could ask a million people what they thought their real issues in life were, and you would get more than a million different answers, but the real problem boils down to this spiritual hole that can only be filled by God. We all need that void filled by a perfect Savior. Ultimately, everyone is looking for that Hero — that one perfect, flawless Person who can fill that void and make us complete and fulfilled. Deep down, we are all trying to get back to the Garden of Eden — back to utopia, back to paradise. Mankind was created in that perfect setting, having fellowship with the flawless, perfect Creator, and deep within us, we all strive to find it again.

So then how do we go about trying to solve this problem? Unfortunately, how we usually try to solve the problem is by putting a square peg into a round hole. We try to meet the need or the problem in the physical realm because we often don't understand this is a spiritual problem. We try to fix a spiritual problem with a physical solution. What we actually need is a spiritual foundation with the living Creator of the Universe. After all, that's why we were made! And yet, we are born without that spiritual connection in check. So what do we do? What can we do if we can only operate in the physical? We treat the symptoms. Those feelings of incompleteness and unfulfillment radiating from our void come out in all kinds of different ways, and we try to address them the best we know how, which isn't very fulfilling in the end.

Just like when we go to the doctor, we must realize that treating the symptoms of the disease of sin is not the same thing as curing the disease of sin which produces those symptoms. The symptoms are not the problem — that void in our heart is. The symptoms are our feelings of incompleteness and unfulfillment, but the problem that these symptoms stem from is that we have a hole in our soul. For example, what is the difference between the fever and the disease? The fever is a symptom created by your body to treat a virus, but the fever is not the problem. We could alleviate the symptom or feeling, but we'll still have the problem if the virus isn't gone, too. Our feelings of incompleteness and unfulfillment are only symptoms, and temporarily soothing them with physical remedies won't fix the real problem.

You know my story. I first tried to fill that void in my soul with my father, and after that I was seeking a man — a husband — to fill that void. I was always trying to find God in another individual, and because I wasn't raised in a Christian home and was unfamiliar with the Bible, these individuals always became my God. They were the square pegs that I tried so hard to make fit in a round hole. I've worked with many girls over the years, and there are countless things that we try to fill that void with, but what I have seen over and over again is that ladies often try filling the void with a physical man. Some may also try to fill it with a career, family, children, food, drugs — the list goes on. There are tons of things that we try to use to fill that spiritual void. But it is just a square peg in a round hole — a physical solution for a spiritual problem.

We could look at Solomon, the wisest man — aside from Christ — who ever lived. Under his rule, Israel reached the apex of civilization, ruling the world as the Kingdom of Heaven. And yet, even with everything he had, his refrain in the book of Ecclesiastes is: "Vanity of vanities! All is vanity. There is no profit under the sun" (Ecclesiastes 1:2, 12:8). Though this sounds so bleak and depressing, it is true! Under the sun, in the physical realm, there is no profit, meaning, or satisfaction. We need the spiritual to find those things! Solomon says that your eye will never be satisfied with seeing, your mouth will never be satisfied with eating, you'll never have enough money, and you'll never labor enough to satisfy yourself. He was in the unique position to be allowed to try it all, and he had it all! In the end, he recognized what actually matters in this life and brings lasting substance is to fear God and to keep His commandments (Ecclesiastes 12:13). Why? It is because we have a spiritual void, and nothing in the physical will ever completely satisfy and fill it.

We might find temporary satisfaction in physical things, but it is only temporary. We say to ourselves that if we had the husband, career, house… then we would be satisfied. We live in the Laodicean church age, which is equally characterized by wealth and by spiritual blindness. We chase money and then throw it at our problems, becoming "me-monsters" in the process. It's just "me, me, me" in the center, with no spiritual connection with God whatsoever. Many women I've worked with have what I call a "Cinderella Complex," which means that they think that marrying "that" guy will solve all of their problems and give them a storybook ending. This thought is instilled in our lives from a very early age, and if we don't have the Bible to offset it, it can really mess with us. Other than Jesus Christ, there is no perfect man, and projecting perfection on any man is simply not fair.

On top of that, we need to remember Genesis 3:16, which says: "Unto the woman [God] said, I will greatly multiply thy sorrow and thy conception; in sorrow thou shalt bring forth children; and thy desire shall be to thy husband, and he shall rule over thee." When Adam and Eve sinned, there were consequences given by God. They had become spiritually dead the moment that they ate from that tree, but they also were given a curse in the flesh. That same curse has been inherited by each one of us, just like our sin nature. We have a whole lesson about this later and will go deeper into the subject, but for now, what I want you to see is that last part of that verse: "and thy desire shall be to thy husband, and he shall rule over thee." Not only do we ladies have a spiritual void inside us, but we also have a desire in our flesh to please a man. That's what that verse says! As we continue, we will see that God put this desire there for our protection, but that does not mean that this isn't a huge source of struggle and sin in women's lives — the spiritual void and the desire in our flesh to please a man, whether a father or a husband. When we do not have a biblical view of these things, they can get all jumbled up in our heart and mind. However, much deeper than this desire to find a man in our lives is the desire to find a solution for that spiritual void in our souls.

When you talk to many married and single ladies with problems in their lives, you will often hear the sentiment that "the grass would be greener on the other side." This is a common attitude for most things in life, especially in relationships. This became obvious to me when I was helping in the counseling ministry at my church. One day, I met with two women, one right after the other, for initial counseling appointments. The first was a single lady. She came in and told me about all her difficulties and problems, and at the end, she said, "If I only had a husband, I wouldn't have these problems." The next appointment was with a married woman. She told me about her life and went over the same problems. At the end, she came to the same conclusion, "You know, if I just had a different husband, then this would be solved!" These two solutions are not uncommon to women. Those who are single desire to be married, and those who are married look back too fondly on the days when they were single or dream about the idea of a new and improved spouse. All of this is because we have a desire in the flesh to please a man, like Genesis 3:16 says, BUT we all also have a deeper spiritual void that aches in our hearts for a spiritual, perfect, flawless Savior. The problem that often arises is that we do not see these as two separate issues, and we do not see them biblically. We fail to realize that we must address the spiritual issue before the physical.

I remember many tear-filled nights going through the Word of God. After I got saved, I wanted my husband to be saved and follow the Lord too, but that never happened and he left me. Then I started thinking that since I was finally seeking God with my whole heart and things were changing in my life that God would finally bring me the right husband. I was so fixated on this idea, and I begged and begged and begged… but He kept closing the door. He showed me that unless I first focused on building a right relationship with Him, I would keep repeating the same, old problem that had plagued me my whole life. So, I gave God six months of my life to wait and to grow in my relationship with Him without chasing a man. By that time I was 27 and had messed up my life so much; I needed to learn what it meant to live according to biblical principles. I had nothing to lose by trying out God's way for six months. As it turned out, it was so needful that those six months turned into a whole year.

Something He kept saying to me was, "Build a relationship with Me." One of the passages He used to do this was Isaiah 40:10-25, which reads:

Isaiah 40:10-25 *Behold, the Lord God will come with strong hand, and his arm shall rule for him: behold, his reward is with him, and his work before him. He shall feed his flock like a shepherd: he shall gather the lambs with his arm, and carry them in his bosom, and shall gently lead those that are with young. Who hath measured the waters in the hollow of his hand, and meted out heaven with the span, and comprehended the dust of the earth in a measure, and weighed the mountains in scales, and the hills in a balance? Who hath directed the Spirit of the Lord, or being his counsellor hath taught him? With whom took he counsel, and who instructed him, and taught him in the path of judgment, and taught him knowledge, and shewed to him the way of understanding? Behold, the nations are as a drop of a bucket, and are counted as the small dust of the balance: behold, he taketh up the isles as a very little thing. And Lebanon is not sufficient to burn, nor the beasts thereof sufficient for a burnt offering. All nations before him are as nothing; and they are counted to him less than nothing, and vanity.* **To whom then will ye liken God?** *or what likeness will ye compare unto him? The workman melteth a graven image, and the goldsmith spreadeth it over with gold, and casteth silver chains. He that is so impoverished that he hath no oblation chooseth a tree that will not rot; he seeketh unto him a cunning workman to prepare a graven image, that shall not be moved. Have ye not known? have ye not heard? hath it not been told you from the beginning? have ye not understood from the foundations of the earth? It is he that sitteth upon the circle of the earth, and the inhabitants thereof are as grasshoppers; that stretcheth out the heavens as a curtain, and spreadeth them out as a tent to dwell in: That bringeth the princes to nothing; he maketh the judges of the earth as vanity. Yea, they shall not be planted; yea, they shall not be sown: yea, their stock shall not take root in the earth: and he shall also blow upon them, and they shall wither, and the whirlwind shall take them away as stubble.* **To whom then will ye liken me, or shall I be equal? saith the Holy One.**

He changed my life forever through these verses! In verses 18 and 25, God shows us the ignorance of trying to make anyone or anything besides Him our God. "To whom then will ye liken me, or shall I be equal? saith the Holy One." When I first began seeing this truth, it cut me to the core. We are talking about the

Creator of the Universe. He measures the oceans in His hands and He weighs the hills in a balance. The nations are as a drop of a bucket to Him. The nations! We attempt to bring Him down and think He's our size, but He's not.

NOTHING CAN TAKE HIS PLACE

Verse 18 is where God first really began convicting me and showing me the fact that I was actually searching for God in a man, trying to fill the spiritual hole with a physical person who didn't even exist. These verses are talking about Israel making little gold idols and bowing down to them, and we look at that and think, "Well, I don't do that." But, ladies, we do! We all can have idols in our lives — things that we worship more than we worship God. These are things we are always running after rather than developing a relationship with the living God, just like the nation of Israel in this passage.

In verses 21-22 we see that, compared to God, we are like grasshoppers! As we read on, we see that God stretched out and created the heavens just as we would hang curtains in our homes! Not only that, but just like we would set up a little tent in our backyard, God spread out the universe! This chapter gives us a glimpse into who He is in all His vastness. I must say again that our Creator is not like us — He is huge, and the heavens and universe He created are enormous and magnificent. And yet, we try to bring God down to our size when He is truly so much bigger and greater! He lives outside of time — in eternity. It is impossible for us to comprehend that, and even when we look up to heavens, we cannot fully understand His size.

The crux of it all for me was in verse 25. In this verse He asks again, "To whom then will you liken me, or shall I be equal?" That was exactly what He was asking me when He asked me to set my heart on Him for a season instead of praying for a man. "Who are you after, Debbie? What do you want in the center of your life? Who are you going to put on the throne and give the crown to? Who or what is number one to you? Stop trying to grasp and hold onto the things I have created and learn to build a relationship with Me! You have access to Me, not just My creation. Do you see how big I am? Why are you chasing after something or someone I have created, when you now have direct access to Me? Wake up! I'm here for you. Learn to walk with Me." He told me that if I continued down that same path, I was just going to keep repeating and falling into the same problems over and over again, albeit in a variety of ways. I could never solve the real problem if I didn't draw near to God and understand that the spiritual void would only stop throbbing if I filled it with God and no one else. No one was equal with God. No one could even come close. We chase after all of the things that surround us, that He created, rather than lifting up our eyes on high and beholding Him, the Creator that formed us. After all, wouldn't our Creator know exactly what is best for us? In the end, whatever we use to try to fill that spiritual void can and often does become our god. And, no matter how much we grow in Christ, we can still get distracted, sidelined, or beelined and begin putting someone or something else on the throne of our hearts.

> ***Isaiah 43:10-12*** *Ye are my witnesses, saith the Lord, and my servant whom I have chosen: that ye may know and believe me, and understand that I am he: before me there was no God formed, neither shall there be after me. I, even I, am the Lord; and beside me there is no saviour. I have declared, and have saved, and I have shewed, when there was no strange god among you: therefore ye are my witnesses, saith the Lord, that I am God.*

Isaiah 43 is another precious passage to show us how to approach our hearts. In it, we see a warning about our purpose and how to fulfill that purpose, and that provokes us to ask what we are worshipping and what we are putting on the throne. Historically and doctrinally, this passage was written to Israel, but it can be inspirationally applied to us as the Church. This passage answers the question of why He chose us — it's so we may know and believe Him! We have to understand that He is God, not all of these other things in our lives that we chase. It is only through acknowledging Him as Creator and the King of kings that this life is going to make sense to us.

An important thing to consider is that God only revealed Himself to them "when there was no strange god among you." It is only in times of surrender to Him that He will reveal Himself to us, and if we run after anything else to fill that spiritual void, He will allow us to chase after it. He respects our free will that He gave us, but He does not reward us in our idolatry. When we are following other gods, idols, or pursuits, He will be awfully silent in our lives. When the discontentment, anxiety, depression, distress, loneliness, and unfulfillment finally reach a peak in our lives, our only option is repentance. Ladies, it is far better to seek after the Lord and walk with Him today than to suffer apart from Him until tomorrow.

Here's a question to ask yourself that may help you understand whether or not you are chasing after idols: "I will be complete, fulfilled, and happy when _____."

When what? How did you fill the blank? We just saw in Isaiah 40 that if you are trying to fill the blank with anything other than the living God, then that thing is standing between you and a fulfilling relationship with the Creator. He will not reveal Himself when there is a strange god on that throne. Be like the believers in 1 Thessalonians 1:9 when they turned from idols unto the living God! This should be a constant, daily process in our lives as temptations and distractions abound. We should be repenting daily of idols that we have picked up in our journey through this life. Remember, there is only one Man who can fill that void in your heart, and His name is Jesus.

> *Revelation 19:11-16 And I saw heaven opened, and behold a white horse; and he that sat upon him was called Faithful and True, and in righteousness he doth judge and make war. His eyes were as a flame of fire, and on his head were many crowns; and he had a name written, that no man knew, but he himself. And he was clothed with a vesture dipped in blood: and his name is called The Word of God. And the armies which were in heaven followed him upon white horses, clothed in fine linen, white and clean. And out of his mouth goeth a sharp sword, that with it he should smite the nations: and he shall rule them with a rod of iron:and he treadeth the winepress of the fierceness and wrath of Almighty God. And he*

hath on his vesture and on his thigh a name written, KING OF KINGS, AND LORD OF LORDS.

This passage in Revelation was another "eureka moment" in my life. Slowly read these verses and let the Holy Spirit illuminate them through your imagination. Picture it in your mind's eye. I remember the first time I read these verses like it was yesterday. I was at work reading my Bible during lunchtime. The Lord had a hold of my heart, and I saw the most amazing picture of this passage in my mind. Later, on that beautiful, sunny day, I walked outside and looked up at the clouds. I imagined them splitting open and the Lord Jesus Christ sitting there on His white horse! It was so glorious, and that moment and picture remain in my heart to this day. Back then, I didn't know my Bible very well, and I didn't know that I would be present with the Lord on the day described in the passage. All I knew was that it reminded me of the recurring dream of my real father coming to rescue me. Now I understand that some very important truths were clarified that day. Yes, the picture I saw in my imagination was a little out of context, but I knew that Jesus would come back some day to "rescue me" and that He was my Knight in Shining Armor! He is perfect, He is our Hero, and He is coming back on a white horse! No fairytale could compare with this truth, and this truth is where we want to start. We need to fill that spiritual void with the Lord Jesus Christ and make Him our foundation by falling in love with Him and building a right relationship with Him.

He pursues me

John 3:16 For God so loved the world, that he gave his only begotten Son, that whosoever believeth in him should not perish, but have everlasting life.

Our real problem was created from not believing and trusting in God. We see this in Adam and Eve who sinned and created that spiritual void that was given to each of their children, including you and me. We are all born in the flesh and are destined to sin. We were all created after the image of Adam after he fell. We have sinned and come short of the glory of God, reserving for ourselves eternal punishment in hell (Romans 3:23, 6:23). Yet the good news is that there is One, the Lord Jesus Christ, who can save us from sin, hell, and God's wrath. He came and died on the cross, taking God's wrath upon Himself, and suffering the punishment for our sins. Through faith in what He did on the cross, we don't have to be eternally separated from the living God. That's why He died — to win back anyone who will choose to accept His sacrifice for us on the cross! He was perfect and sinless, and yet He chose to lay down His life, be buried, and rise again on the third day according to the scriptures (1 Corinthians 15:1-4). Sin, hell, and death could not hold Him! He is that Knight in Shining Armor who was so valiant that He put Himself in harm's way for us, laid down His life for us, and rescued us.

However, no gift is yours unless you take it. It is the same way with the Lord Jesus Christ. You must recognize you are lost and need a Savior because your sin has separated you from the living God. To even begin to chip away at the problems of life and properly fill that spiritual void, you must personally receive the Lord Jesus Christ as your personal Savior! God used the Romans Road to show me how to receive Jesus as my Savior.

Romans Road and Prayer

> **Romans 3:23** *For all have sinned, and come short of the glory of God;*

> **Romans 6:23** *For the wages of sin is death; but the gift of God is eternal life through Jesus Christ our Lord.*

> **Romans 10:9-10** *That if thou shalt confess with thy mouth the Lord Jesus, and shalt believe in thine heart that God hath raised him from the dead, thou shalt be saved. For with the heart man believeth unto righteousness; and with the mouth confession is made unto salvation.*

"Dear Father, I recognize that I'm a sinner, and that my sin separates me from You. I understand that the payment for my sins is hell. Please forgive me and save me from my sin. I recognize Jesus died on the cross for me and receive the Lord Jesus Christ as my personal Savior. Thank you for this gift, and please help me to learn how to grow in Christ and follow You. In Jesus' name, I pray, amen."

This is what Karen gave to me back in the spring of 1984! If you have not started here, please open your heart and receive the Lord Jesus Christ as your personal Lord and Savior. It will be the greatest decision of your life! And, best of all, it is free! There is nothing we need to do or bring to the table to deserve or purchase this salvation (Ephesians 2:8-9). He just calls us to come to the waters, buy, and eat.

> _Inheritance_
>
> (Isaiah 55:1-3) *Ho, every one that thirsteth, come ye to the waters, and he that hath no money; come ye, buy, and eat; yea, come, buy wine and milk without money and without price. Wherefore do ye spend money for that which is not bread? and your labour for that which satisfieth not? hearken diligently unto me, and eat ye that which is good, and let your soul delight itself in fatness. Incline your ear, and come unto me: hear, and your soul shall live; and I will make an everlasting covenant with you, even the sure mercies of David.*

I've worked with many girls who thought they were saved because they had a head knowledge about salvation. They went to church. By their standards, they were "good." They understood what was talked about in John 3:16, but they had never believed that they were a sinner on their way to hell. They had never taken the gift for themselves, though they had an understanding of the message. When Jesus spoke to Nicodemus in John 3, He told him one simple truth: to be in God's Kingdom, you need to be born again through placing your faith on Jesus' substitutionary death on the cross. At that singular moment in time when you confessed your sins before God and accepted that gift of salvation through Jesus' death, the spiritual foundation that was broken in Adam and Eve was restored.

Then, that spiritual foundation is strengthened as you begin growing in the Lord and following the Spirit rather than the flesh! Just like we began physically growing after we were born the first time, we must begin spiritually growing after being born again. We will see in future chapters that we are given all of the Holy Spirit we are going to get at the very moment of salvation. The problem is not that we don't have enough of the Holy Spirit. The problem is that we don't initially give all of ourselves to the Holy Spirit!

We are still following the flesh in many areas of our life when we get saved, especially if our salvation occurs when we are older and have deeper habits and patterns in the flesh. It is possible to stop following the flesh, but only if we learn how to follow the Spirit. There are seven stages of spiritual growth which we will talk about later, but the bottom line is that you need help. We need the three things that Jesus replaced Himself with when He ascended back on high to the Father: the church, the Word, and the Holy Spirit. A mentor in the faith (or even mentors) through the local church will help you fall in love with and truly see the Lord Jesus Christ as He really is. As we plug into these resources, we also learn to die to self and to the flesh and live unto God as we follow the Spirit. This is a journey we begin once we are born again! With God all things are possible, including the huge changes He wrought in my life after I was saved. No matter where you come from or what you're trying to overcome, all things are possible with God. It may be hard, but anything can be overcome if brought to the Bible. This Book can change our lives if we let it! And it is through this Book that we will look more and more like the Lord Jesus Christ as we begin growing and maturing.

Colossians 2:10 *And ye are complete in him, which is the head of all principality and power:*

This next point blows me away. We are only complete in Christ — not in a spouse, children, career, or anything else. You are complete in Him and not in any other person! In our natural state, we are incomplete and unfulfilled, which can be revealed in a variety of symptoms that we call problems. All of those feelings of incompleteness and unfulfillment that lead to us chasing so many different things are just the aching of that spiritual void that is present without Christ. When we are born again in Christ, we become complete in Him. He has filled the hole in our soul. You are a new creature in Christ at the moment of salvation, but it's important to realize that we now have two different natures: the flesh and the Spirit. This is something that we need to understand and act upon so that we can seek Him and follow the Spirit instead of the vain things of the world that our flesh loves. As children of God, we can still chase after many things but will only find dissatisfaction because our satisfaction can only be found in Christ. Some of these things are actually good and God-ordained for us. Marriage is a good thing, and children are a good thing. But we can't let them become the sole or primary source of contentment and meaning in our lives. We can't let them try to fill the spiritual void that only God can fill. There are only two things that have sinless perfection and are flawless and absolute: God and the Bible. In order to make our lives full of joy and contentment, these two things must be on the thrones of our hearts. We were made by God for God. All of these other pursuits are things that He may very well want in your life, but they are never to replace Him and your relationship with Him. He and He alone must be on the throne and stay on the throne.

> **Psalm 73:25-26** *Whom have I in heaven but thee? and there is none upon earth that I desire beside thee. My flesh and my heart faileth: but God is the strength of my heart, and my portion for ever.*

These verses showed me that Jesus is my all, and I needed to love Him with my all. Even if I had a husband or children, God would still be the only One that I should desire upon the earth. He is the only One that we have in heaven. He is the only One for us, and He deserves all of our heart, soul, mind, and strength (Mark 12:30). If you understand these verses and live them out in your heart attitude, then — whether you are single, married, barren, or abounding with children — you will be fulfilled. Who is on the throne of your heart?

> **Matthew 6:33** *But seek ye first the kingdom of God, and his righteousness; and all these things shall be added unto you.*

This verse is the cap to a passage in which Jesus tells the disciples not to worry about food or clothing. Instead of focusing on the physical things that they wanted or needed, He tells them that they need to seek the Kingdom of God — the spiritual connection with God — first in their lives before any physical desires. After that, He promised to provide everything that they actually needed. So don't worry! Don't worry about tomorrow or about the things that you think that you need, whether they are relationships, physical necessities, or wants. Paul said in 1 Corinthians 15:31 that he chose to die daily. He chose to seek God and the things of God first and then trust God to take care of the rest. Your life will not "begin" once you have that thing that you want: that man, relationship, career, or dream life. Your life began when you placed your faith in Christ! Start living that life for the Lord with Him as Number One. He is a good God, and we are His children. He loves us so much, and He gives good gifts! He doesn't give a snake or a scorpion when we ask for something good (Luke 11:11-13). Trust that if He withholds something from you, it is actually far better than if He had given it to you. Seek Him first in surrender and faith.

In summary, Adam and Eve were created without flaw. Sinless, they lived in the Garden of Eden, a paradise made by God for them. They were created by God to fellowship with Him, and this pleased God. At that time, they were complete, fulfilled, and happy. Additionally, out of the love in God's heart and desire for true, chosen fellowship with His created beings, God gave us a free will. He wanted to see if they would trust and believe Him, and He gave them a choice: eat of the tree and die, or obey and live. They chose to disobey, and this is the source of all our problems today. They were made spiritually dead in that moment, and they were clothed in shame instead of the glory of God. No longer could they walk with God in the cool of the garden, and no longer could they have that spiritual connection with God. Instead of a spiritual connection they had a spiritual void, and we are all born with that same spiritual void in our souls.

We try to fill this spiritual void with physical things and always come up empty, incomplete, and unfulfilled because this hole can only be filled by one man: the Lord Jesus Christ. This filling can only happen at salvation, and from that point on, any choice we make either honors Christ on the throne or seeks to replace Him, which would lead to dissatisfaction, anxiety, and depression. Our relationship with Him is strengthened through our relationship with the Word, the church, and the Holy Spirit as we learn to seek God's Kingdom first in our lives and submit all other desires and pursuits to Him. Don't let anyone take the place of God on the throne! There will be many distractions, but we already have victory in Christ — He won the battle two thousand years ago on the cross, and we need to live in light of that reality.

Before we go on, let's revisit and add to the foundational Building Blocks of Life. I think this visual may help you as we move forward.

Building Blocks of Life

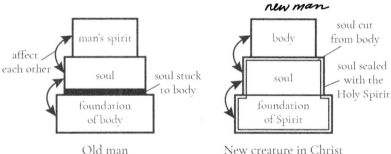

Old man   New creature in Christ

Here are a few more principles to begin adding to this illustration. Unfortunately, we initially put most of our emphasis on the body (physical things) and begin with that as our foundation. What we need to understand about our makeup before we get saved is that our body and soul are stuck together and we do not have the Spirit of God inside us. What we do have access to, as far as the spiritual connection goes, is either access to man's spirit (little "s") or the devil's spirit. We have access to both these as an unsaved person, but the Holy Spirit is on the outside, always wooing us and working all around us, trying to lead us to receive the gift of Jesus Christ as our personal Savior. However, here's what happened the day we get saved:

> **Colossians 2:10-13** *And ye are complete in him, which is the head of all principality and power. In whom also ye are circumcised with the circumcision made without hands, in putting off the body of the sins of the flesh by the circumcision of Christ: buried with him in baptism, wherein also ye are risen with him through the faith of the operation of God, who hath raised him from the dead. And you, being dead in your sins and the uncircumcision of your flesh, hath he quickened together with him, having forgiven you all trespasses.*

Before salvation our body and soul were stuck together, and that means that no matter how hard we tried, our flesh was going to sin and our soul had no choice but to sin. "For all have sinned and come short of the glory of God" (Romans 3:23). Now, according to Colossians 2, a couple things happened when we got saved. Firstly, at the moment of salvation, there was a spiritual operation where our soul and body actually got "unstuck." The best illustration I can give you of this is an ice cube tray: when the water freezes to the tray, you have to jiggle the tray in order for the ice cubes to get unstuck. God performed a similar operation when he cut the flesh from your soul at the moment of salvation. Another way to think about it is like circumcision, as mentioned earlier in Colossians 2. Your soul is now not stuck to your flesh! So now you have a choice about sin. God not only unstuck your soul and your body, but He also made you a new creature in Christ Jesus and He literally sealed your soul with His Holy Spirit!

> **2 Corinthians 5:17** *Therefore if any man be in Christ, he is a new creature: old things are passed away; behold, all things are become new.*

> **Ephesians 1:13** *In whom ye also trusted, after that ye heard the word of truth, the gospel of your salvation: in whom also after that ye believed, ye were sealed with that holy Spirit of promise.*

At the time of salvation we're filled and sealed with the Holy Spirit! When we were sinners (this is the old man — the flesh, so to speak), we always followed the flesh, and we were going to follow the flesh no matter what because it was stuck to our soul. But now we have a choice and need to begin learning how to be led by the Spirit so that we can make THIS spiritual block our new foundation. This is what discipleship is all about: edifying believers to help them grow through those seven stages of spiritual growth so this spiritual block is our new foundation. Now, depending upon how old you are when you get saved and because we are creatures of habit, this can be a very difficult process, because we have only known the flesh/body as our foundation. For me, since I didn't know anything about biblical principles and had formed many bad habits in the flesh, learning how to follow the Spirit instead of the flesh was very hard. Yes, while it can be a hard process for all of us, the longer we build patterns in our physical flesh, the more difficult the process may be. Remember though, God can still change it, you just have to really work at it and want it. What we're doing is we're learning to die to the flesh as we follow the Spirit. It is going to be a tug-of-war the whole time.

Also, be aware that most of our problems are spiritual problems. Remember that 2 Timothy 1:7 says that God has not given us the spirit of fear! It's a "spirit" of fear— we will see that many of our problems, such as depression, anger, fear, and more, are initiated by spiritual problems. Unless we've grown up in a biblical church, we've just not been equipped to know how to build on that spiritual foundation. But that's what this study is all about, and it can be done. These issues MUST be fixed in the Spirit. We're not going to fix them in the flesh — we're supposed to be dying to the flesh. We have to believe in God and what He says (book, chapter, verse) about each and every difficulty. We must believe HIM. One prayer that I always pray is, "Lord I believe, but help my unbelief," based on Mark 9:24. Along with that, I pray for that good heart described in Luke 8. That's David's request in Psalm 51:10: "Create in me a clean heart, O God; and renew a right spirit within me."

In addition to praying, please meditate on all the verses and review your notes before moving on to the next chapter. Begin letting God speak directly to you through His Word.

Happy journey with your Lord.

Questions to Consider:

1. Why did God create you? **By Him & For Him**

2. Have you ever experienced the spiritual hole described in this chapter? What have you tried to fill it with in the past? What about right now?
   my dad, family, attention from guys & friends

3. Complete this sentence: I will be complete, fulfilled, and happy when _____.

4. Who or what makes us complete? **only the one that created me**

5. We aren't supposed to run our life by our emotions. Instead, we are to run our emotions through what? **The truths of the Bible**

6. How do you handle not feeling in control?
   very anxious & try to control other things

7. Do you often feel like grass would be greener on the other side as it pertains to your marital status?
   yes

8. Do you have a mentor in the faith to build you up in Christ? Who is it?
   Evangelyn & BJ

3

Developing Confidence and Security

One of the areas that women often struggle with is that of confidence and security. The issue is not whether or not we have these qualities, but where we find them.

Jeremiah 9:23-24 Thus saith the LORD, Let not the wise man glory in his wisdom, neither let the mighty man glory in his might, let not the rich man glory in his riches: but let him that glorieth glory in this, that he understandeth and knoweth me, that I am the LORD which exercise lovingkindness, judgment, and righteousness, in the earth: for in these things I delight, saith the LORD.

Jeremiah 9:23-24 gives us so much insight into how to develop confidence and security, but it gives it from a unique perspective. It tells us where not to find it! It cannot be found in man's wisdom, might, or riches. These things will only let us down. We need real confidence and security, and they can only come from understanding and knowing God through His Word. Since God's preserved Word is as perfect as He is, we can get real confidence and security through knowing Him and knowing what He says. Just like with any other relationship, to really know God, we need to spend time with Him and understand the boundaries that He has given us.

Growing up, I was very close to my mom. Out of everyone in my life, she was who I was closest to, so much so that people used to call me her shadow. Now, I could sit down with you and tell you all about my mom, and I could share so much that you might begin to feel like you know her too, but in reality, you wouldn't know her until you met her face to face. Until you actually met her and spent time with her, everything I would tell you about her would just be head knowledge — not an actual relationship. This is what happens in our relationship with the Lord. We learn so much about God from church or from those around us, but if we are not actually spending time with Him in the Word and in prayer, then we don't really know Him. Our confidence will come as we begin to really know the Lord. In the rest of this chapter, we will be looking at the foundational principles of how to begin developing this confidence and security.

Step 1: Eternal security. If we don't start with eternal security, then the foundation will be missing and the building will easily fall. When eternal security is in question, you'll find yourself asking "Am I on my way to heaven?" Every sin will be a chance to tear down and start over, and this flies in the face of progress in your walk with God. God won't be able to use you to your full potential if you're always questioning Him about whether you're on your way to heaven. That's a huge insecurity, so eternal security must be grounded at the base of your relationship with Him. This is the first hurdle that needs to be overcome, otherwise it will be a roadblock to growing in Christ. Complete forgiveness of sin and full assurance of salvation are promised to us when we place our faith in Christ. But if eternal security is not understood, every sin will be a crisis of faith, leading to a tumultuous and insecure relationship with Christ.

> **Ephesians 1:13-14** *In whom ye also trusted, after that ye heard the word of truth, the gospel of your salvation: in whom also after that ye believed, ye were*

> *sealed with that holy Spirit of promise, which is the earnest of our inheritance until the redemption of the purchased possession, unto the praise of his glory.*

Grab hold of these verses! We often feel like complete failures when we sin, especially in areas of stronghold, but remember to ask yourself, "What does God say?" and not "What do I feel?" or "What do I think?" In verse 13, we see we were sealed to God by the Holy Spirit at the moment of salvation. Your flesh and soul were unstuck from each other, and your soul was sealed with God's Spirit. You became a new creature in Christ Jesus! Verse 14 says that His Spirit is the earnest of your salvation. When you buy a house, you put down earnest money: the down payment. It is proof that it belongs to you. God says that He put His Spirit inside of us as a down payment the moment we got saved. No ifs, ands, or buts about it! Ephesians 1 clearly says He sealed us at the moment of salvation. If you do not see that, you will struggle with insecurity every second of every day. Do you remember when you heard the word of truth, the gospel? You trusted and believed it, and you didn't have to do anything else. You didn't have to go get in water and be baptized to be saved and sealed, and you didn't have to go to church to be saved. It says right in these verses that at that moment of salvation you were sealed! Period. Nothing added to it.

> ***Ephesians 4:30*** *And grieve not the holy Spirit of God, whereby ye are sealed unto the day of redemption.*

On the day that you trusted and believed the gospel, you were sealed until the day of redemption. He put that down payment inside of you and said, "She is Mine." You are a purchased possession; you are His, and He is coming back to get you. We must see that we do not have to question our security after receiving salvation through Jesus Christ as our personal Savior. Anytime you have doubts, go to God's Word in faith. Claim those verses as yours. Memorize them. It doesn't matter if your emotions are telling you that you couldn't possibly be saved — we have to learn to live by the facts of the Word of God and stop trusting our feelings.

> *1 John 5:12-13 He that hath the Son hath life; and he that hath not the Son of God hath not life. These things have I written unto you that believe on the name of the Son of God; that ye may know that ye have eternal life, and that ye may believe on the name of the Son of God.*

This passage anchors our firm foundation of assurance of salvation. After you get this verse down, teach it to those in your life. This verse explicitly says, "that ye may know that you have eternal life." When I'm discipling someone, I always take them through these verses in 1 John 5. I draw their attention to the fact that they can know that they have eternal life. How? Not because they believed the gospel or feel a certain way. Rather, they can know that they have eternal life because God has said it. We have the Son and we have believed in His name. Therefore we have life, and He wants us to KNOW that we are eternally secure! And here is the kicker: now that you've seen what God says, if you ever decide in the future that your salvation is not eternally secured, you're actually calling God a liar. The Bible says, "Let God be true, but every man a liar" (Romans 3:4). Jeremiah 17:9 tells us that our hearts are "deceitful above all things." Therefore, why would we trust the emotions of our deceitful heart instead of believing God, who cannot lie (Number 23:19)?

We must understand that God is not like us at all. We are petty and often place stipulations on our love. Our love is conditional, but He gives us an unconditional gift of love. He's not waiting for us to mess up so that He can pull the rug out from underneath us. This is why it is called "eternal" life and not "eternal until you sin and lose it" life. He loves us so much that He doesn't want us cowering around in uncertainty thinking we're going to lose our salvation. Uncertainty is not what He wants, and He is not a God of confusion! He wants us to know. I'm a child of the King, and I'm on my way to heaven, and I know it. I know it because I'm believing what God says in His Word. This is the source of our confidence and security. This is what we call running our emotions through the Word of God: relying on the boundaries and facts of the Bible instead of our feelings. Even if we do not fully understand this gift, we can still simply choose to believe what God has said about it.

A good example is my age. I am 63 years old, and though some days I feel younger or older, my feelings don't change the fact that I am 63 years old. It is the same with how we apply the Word of God. We need to take the facts and believe them and stop trusting our feelings. My feelings change a million times a day and have nothing to do with the facts. We must learn to recognize when we are believing and trusting in our feelings and replace that habit with believing and trusting in the words of the living God.

Step 2: Find perfect peace by developing a prayer life. As much as the ladies in beauty pageants always say that they would like world peace, the Bible clearly teaches that there will be no world peace until the Lord Jesus Christ comes back. But until that happens, we can have peace with God and we can also have the peace of God. These little words in our Bible — "with" and "of" — are very important. We want to learn how to have both kinds of peace.

> ***Romans 5:1*** *Therefore being justified by faith, we have peace with God through our Lord Jesus Christ.*

Let's start at peace with God. Before salvation, we are God's enemies, separated from Him because of our sin. But according to Romans 5:1, through salvation in Jesus Christ we have peace with God! It's like we signed a peace treaty with Him. At the very moment we got saved, we were born again, became His children, and received peace with Him. People try to make peace with God through various means, such doing good works or being part of the right church, but the Bible says the only way we can have true peace with God is if we have signed that "peace treaty" of salvation that is sealed with the blood of Christ.

After salvation, there is another type of peace that we can access. I was desperate for this peace and was filled with insecurity because I did not have it. I was saved and knew it, but my insides were still tied up in knots. The thing I was missing was "the peace of God, which passeth all understanding" (Philippians 4:7). This peace isn't equivalent to the peace with God that we receive at salvation. It was something I heard people talk about, but it was something that I didn't have, so I began searching my Bible for this peace to see what God said about it. I had started out desperately seeking the perfect man, and I found him in the Lord Jesus Christ. Next, I went on a desperate search for the perfect peace of God. However, before we go over this peace of God, let's look at some biblical facts about peace and fear.

> ***2 Timothy 1:7*** *For God hath not given us the spirit of fear; but of power, and of love, and of a sound mind.*

We've all experienced fear. As I've mentioned before, this has always been something that I've struggled with. This verse says that fear is a spirit and that it is not a spirit that comes from God. God has given us the "Spirit of power, and of love, and of a sound mind." So if we're struggling with fear, it's either from the world, the flesh, or the devil. It's not of God, and it's not something that He wants His child to be experiencing.

> ***1 John 4:18*** *There is no fear in love; but perfect love casteth out fear: because fear hath torment. He that feareth is not made perfect in love.*

This verse is one of the greatest verses about getting rid of fear. Before I got saved, I was plagued with fear, had frequent panic attacks, was filled with phobias — I was afraid of everything! Fear and anxiety are the opposite of peace, and all fears result in torment. The only way to cast these things out is through perfect love, and that perfect love can only come from God.

> ***Hebrews 2:14-15*** *Forasmuch then as the children are partakers of flesh and blood, he also himself likewise took part of the same; that through death he might destroy him that had the power of death, that is, the devil; and deliver them who through fear of death were all their lifetime subject to bondage.*

To understand this perfect love, we must first understand the origin of our fear. The Bible says that the first fear is the fear of death. Adam and Eve were told in the garden that if they ate of the Tree of the Knowledge of Good and

Evil, they would die. Though they'd always been walking with God in the garden, they were suddenly afraid of His presence after eating of the tree. That's because they knew that they were going to die. And, just like Adam and Eve, we are all afraid of death, so we hide from God in our sin. For all of our life, through fear of death, we are subject to bondage. Yes, we may experience many different fears in many different shapes and sizes, but all of this started with the fear of death. Not only that, but fear is a byproduct of that spiritual death that happened in Adam and Eve on that day in the garden. Fear begins the moment we sin and naturally run and hide. Then different fears take off and spread out from there as we hide in the darkness and sin more and more. In the end, we're hiding because we know that what we did was wrong, just as God told Adam and Eve that "the day ye eat thereof, ye shall die" (Genesis 2:17). Fear and death are inseparable.

John 8:32 *And ye shall know the truth, and the truth shall make you free.*

However, the good news is that God has freed us from this fear! This is that perfect love that casts out fear. Notice that the Bible doesn't say that He "set" you free. It says that He *made* you free. He's not setting the body free, the old man of sinful flesh. Instead, He sealed us and made us a new creature in Christ Jesus. He made us free. Ultimately, the key to having the peace of God is a matter of letting go of the flesh and following the Spirit, realizing that our new creature in Christ Jesus has been made free. Death has no hold over this new man, and as we walk in the Spirit, we will not fulfill the sinful lusts of the flesh.

Some additional passages about being made free from death: 1 Corinthians 15:54; 1 Thessalonians 4:13-18.

Even though we are all our life subject to bondage through fear of death, we don't have to be afraid of death anymore now that we are born again. The new creature in Christ has been sealed with His Spirit and is eternally secure. And He's coming back to get us!

> **John 14:27** *Peace I leave with you, my peace I give unto you: not as the world giveth, give I unto you. Let not your heart be troubled, neither let it be afraid.*

Another fact about peace is that it is a choice. The verse says, "Let not your heart be troubled," so we have a choice to let our hearts be troubled and also a choice to not let our hearts be troubled. We might have developed a stronghold or habitual pattern to let our hearts be troubled, but we don't have to fear. We have to decide to fear God and not man or our circumstances. We have to decide if we are going to believe God or our feelings. As I sought the peace of God, one of my prayers became, "Lord, help me to fear You and not man. Help me to believe what You say, and not man or my feelings."

More passages about peace: Romans 14:17; John 14; Matthew 6:25-34.

> **Isaiah 26:3** *Thou wilt keep him in perfect peace, whose mind is stayed on thee: because he trusteth in thee.*

This verse was key for me. Do you realize that you cannot think of two things at the same time? In the same way, if your mind is fixed (stayed) on God, then your mind cannot be fixed on the troubles and fears of your life. As you start thinking about God and His Word instead of those things, you will start seeing that things are changing in your life. Think on the Word of God. Commit His Word to memory and choose to meditate on it instead of on those fears or insecurities that want to steal your peace.

> **Philippians 4:6-7** *Be careful for nothing; but in every thing by prayer and supplication with thanksgiving let your requests be made known unto God. And the peace of God, which passeth all understanding, shall keep your hearts and minds through Christ Jesus.*

I really began to grow in my relationship with God when I finally began to understand this verse. I was used to going to see a psychiatrist back when I was in my abusive marriage. After I began growing in a personal relationship with Jesus, it occurred to me that I should pour out my heart in a "counseling session" with Him before I paid to see a counselor. I began to schedule meetings with the Lord at least once a week — sometimes more than that — and I began to see Him grow and heal me. As I've mentioned earlier, I was plagued by panic attacks at that time, and He began showing me in these verses how to have peace in the gut of my soul. Through that peace He began transforming my life, and my panic attacks stopped! I came to realize that the way to find peace that passed all understanding was in His Book this whole time.

Back then, I was a computer programmer, and it made sense to me to approach these verses in a step-by-step fashion. Logically, this passage made sense to me in this way: you do verse 6 to get verse 7. In that way, this peace is a conditional peace, meaning that the Lord says, "Do this, and you will get the promised result." At salvation, we get peace with God, but we do not get the peace of God, because the peace of God is a conditional peace. These verses show us that this peace of God which passes all understanding can only be developed through a proper prayer life. The key is to break down verse 6 into three components and do them in sequential order to get this peace!

The first thing He says to do is to be careful for nothing. He is telling us not to be full of cares, so we obviously have to give our cares to the Lord! You have to be careful for nothing by casting all your cares on Him.

> *1 Peter 5:7* *Casting all your care upon him; for he careth for you.*

I remember reading *The Pilgrim's Progress* by John Bunyan, an allegory about our Christian walk. In it, the main character, Christian, was going through life with this HUGE bag on his shoulders filled with tons of stuff. It was so big that it caused him to labor in carrying it, and he always had to hunch down as he walked under the weight of it. That's what many of us women do — we carry this invisible bag on our shoulders in which we accumulate all our cares, worries, and responsibilities. That bag gets fuller and fuller throughout our life and continues to weigh us down. I had lived 27 years of my life trying to figure things out how to make life work, and I was terribly loaded down with hundreds of cares and burdens. But God says, "I don't want you to do that! You're Mine now. You don't have to carry them anymore. Give them to Me." They're His cares now because we're His kids now. In short, He says that the first thing to apply here is to be careful for nothing and learn to start giving our cares to Him.

Next, He says to let your requests be made known unto Him with prayer and supplication. What's the difference between prayer and supplication? Prayer is just communicating and spending time with God, and supplication is a specific request. It's important to note that this doesn't mean that He's going to say yes to every request! I used to make a lot of plans for my life without consulting God at all, and I used to ask Him for these things without seeing any results. What He's actually saying is, "No, bring all your requests to Me first!" Big and small, bring them to Him and see what His Word has to say about them. He is our Creator. He knows what's ahead and He knows the plan for your life. Therefore, it's essential that we take all our needs and wants to Him.

The third thing He says to do in order to learn how to have this peace is seen in how we are to make these requests to God: "with thanksgiving." As we bring our requests to God, we need to do so in a spirit of thanksgiving. Sometimes this is the hard part, because we often make the most requests when we are in the most need.

> **1 Thessalonians 5:18** *In every thing give thanks: for this is the will of God in Christ Jesus concerning you.*

> **Ephesians 5:20** *Giving thanks always for all things unto God and the Father in the name of our Lord Jesus Christ;*

We need to learn to give thanks "in" everything and "for" everything, because this is God's will for our lives. The question, then, is why we can give thanks in all things. The answer to this is found in Romans 8:28-29, which says "all things work together for good to them that love God." Therefore, even if the situation is really difficult, we know that God is working it for good. It is better to go through that trial and time of need so that we can benefit more from it than if it had never happened. We must learn to give thanks even for what may not seem good to us, because that verse says that if we love God, He can work every difficult thing for our good.

As I saw this laid out, I decided that it was time that I put this into practice. It was like I had been hiding in a cave all my life, and when I decided to meet with God in prayer and address my burdens, I finally came out of that cave and into the light. I needed to stop hiding from God and begin telling Him everything. I told Him that I desperately wanted peace that passes all understanding, and so I was going to talk to Him as if He were actually physically present, because I had faith that He was there and was listening to me. This is what led me to set up those weekly meetings with God.

For some reason it was easier for me to talk to Him in the dark, and it might have been because I was so scared and insecure. As you begin to meet with God just like I did, you don't need to do it in a dark room, but be sure to do it in a place where you are not conscientious about what you're going to say. You have to be totally alone, with no fear of someone coming in or overhearing. If you haven't done this on a regular basis already, and if you're loaded down with cares or requests, then I would suggest setting aside at least an hour. The first time I did this it took two hours and a roll of toilet paper (I didn't have a box of Kleenexes). So, get yourself a box of Kleenexes and get with the Lord, verbally applying those steps laid out in Philippians 4:6-7.

The Prayer Exercise

First, give Him all of your cares. I had been living with all of these cares and burdens for years and had developed a way to stuff everything inside, rarely crying at anything. However, once I started pouring my heart out to the Lord, tears started flowing and they wouldn't stop. God gave us tear ducts for a reason, and Jesus wept in the garden. He wants us to be completely open and transparent with Him. I was pouring out all of these things that I had been carrying for years, the things that had loaded me down with an incredible weight. I remember so much about that night, and it was a moment of turning in my life.

Second, after pouring out all of your cares and burdens to the Lord, talk about what you think you need. Lay all of these requests before God, both big and small. I had many, many needs during that time, and the thing that I needed most of all was for God to heal all of the abuse that I had received throughout the years.

I poured out my requests, and then I turned around and, **third**, I gave thanks. I had to be thankful and give thanks in the midst of need and pain, and it was hard! If you have something that you're having trouble giving thanks for, all you have to do is ask Him for the grace to do it. I would look back at my life and think, "I don't see how I can give thanks for my ex-husband who beat me up!" Now, realize that that relationship was never God's perfect will for my life. It was the penalty of sin. But you know what? I asked for grace to give thanks for that, too. I didn't want it to be a roadblock between me and the Lord. As I learned to give thanks, He began showing me that the abuse was actually what led me to God in the first place. I was way out of God's will at the time of the abuse, and I was suffering the consequences of my choices. But I can give thanks for the fact that it brought me to Jesus. He even used my own mistakes and sins to bring me to Christ. It's amazing how the Lord can turn things around when we will just be thankful and accepting.

So, give Him all your cares, give Him all your requests, and give Him all your thanks. It's a process of turning it all over to the Lord, and He says that when we do that, we can experience the peace that passeth understanding! It's amazing! However, it is a continual process that needs daily obedience. Shortly after my prayer meeting with the Lord, I began to take back pieces that I had given to the Lord. I hadn't yet developed a habit or pattern of giving it to the Lord and letting Him keep it. We need to keep going to Him and applying these steps and learning to leave everything at His feet. It may take some time if you've developed a stronghold, but keep at it. The stronghold or habit can be overcome, and a new habit of always taking it to God can be strengthened instead.

I would talk to other people too, but I always wanted to talk to God first. Many times in the following week, He had already begun answering prayers before I had even had a chance to talk to anyone else about it. This is what helps to build our relationship with the Lord — seeing Him come through with these things and answering our prayers. But you've got to talk to Him first! We often forget that He can't answer if we're not talking to Him and spending time with Him.

Sheep are a good illustration of this. A typical sheep usually has a fleece coat that weighs about ten pounds that the shepherd cuts off once a year, but sheep that run away or get lost have no one to take care of the weight of their fleece. Once, a sheep was lost for 5-6 years and they found that his fleece was nearly one hundred pounds. For years he had been walking around with a burden that was ever-growing and never being addressed by the shepherd. That's just like what we do! God says, "Come to Me! Don't be careful for anything! You've got Me." But we don't listen — we hide, carry the burden ourselves, and try to figure it out and fix it. Instead of this, we just need to go straight to our Shepherd and allow Him to trim off that heavy fleece. Just go and talk to Him about it, and you will find that you will walk away lighter than you came.

Here's another illustration. Let's say you're returning home on an airplane and it's a stormy, snowy day. You arrive at the airport, and you sure don't want to have to drive home in such bad weather. There is one problem. The person who planned to pick you up can't, but there's a guy that you knew 20 years ago who happened to be on the plane with you. You don't know him that well, but he offers to take you home because he lives in the same direction. You don't have any other options, so you decide to go ahead and do it. The whole way home, you're scared. You've got your eyes open on the road and you're watching him, ready to jump out in case something happens.

Now let's tweak that scenario. Instead of it being this guy that you met 20 years ago, it's your dad who's on the plane with you, and the two of you have an amazing relationship. The same thing happens — you fly into your hometown and when you land, there's a terrible blizzard. Fortunately you have your dad there with you, and he's the one who drives you home. Instead of being scared and keeping one eye open, you settle in your seat and actually fall asleep on the way home. You have complete peace!

Unfortunately, Jesus is often like that stranger to some of us. We don't talk to Him or spend time with Him, and as a result, we just don't know if we can really trust Him. That's how I was! I didn't know that He was always going to come through for me. I was skeptical, just as if I were riding with a stranger. Are we skeptical of the Lord due to a lack of familiarity, or are we building that relationship, spending quality time with Him, and really getting to know Him as our awesome Father? Prayer is two-way communication: we must listen to Him and talk to Him. We must spend time with Him. How much time this past week did you spend with your Heavenly Father? Have you made any appointments with Him lately? Is He more like a stranger or a good Father to you? You and you alone have the choice to know Him as a great Father.

Step 3: Focus on God and not yourself. This book is not a self-help study. It's not about teaching you how to have better self-esteem, better self-awareness, or better self-sufficiency. Instead, this book is meant to teach and encourage you how to have a high God-esteem. This is a high God-esteem study. He and His Word are the only things in this universe that will never let us down. He and His Word are the only places where we can find flawless and absolute truth, the only real foundation upon which we can rest our naked souls.

Romans 3:4 says, "Let God be true and every man a liar." Despite our best efforts or the best efforts of those around us, everything in this life will, at some point, let us down, and it's simply because nothing and no one else is perfect, complete, infallible, and absolutely flawless. Therefore, knowing God

Developing Confidence and Security

and His Word are the only sources of true confidence. We don't need high self-esteem, we need high God-esteem!

Low self-esteem is the result of focusing on the old man, the flesh. And it's interesting that, if we drop the "h," flesh spelled backward is the same as "self." Our flesh is carnal. It cannot please God, and, in fact, is "enmity against God" (Romans 8:7-8). So, instead of focusing on our corrupt flesh, we must learn to focus on who our Heavenly Father is and who He's made us to be in Christ: the new man.

> ***Isaiah 41:8-14*** *But thou, Israel, art my servant, Jacob whom I have chosen, the seed of Abraham my friend. Thou whom I have taken from the ends of the earth, and called thee from the chief men thereof, and said unto thee, Thou art my servant; <u>I have chosen thee</u>, and not cast thee away. Fear thou not; for I am with thee: be not dismayed; for I am thy God: I will strengthen thee; yea, I will help thee; yea, I will uphold thee with the right hand of my righteousness. Behold, all they that were incensed against thee shall be ashamed and confounded: they shall be as nothing; and they that strive with thee shall perish. Thou shalt seek them, and shalt not find them, even them that contended with thee: they that war against thee shall be as nothing, and as a thing of nought. For I the LORD thy God will hold thy right hand, saying unto thee, Fear not; I will help thee. Fear not,* **thou worm** *Jacob, and ye men of Israel; I will help thee, saith the LORD, and thy redeemer, the Holy One of Israel.*

Though this passage is doctrinally written to Israel, it is also written to us inspirationally to see New Testament principles. God goes on and on about how much He loves His servant, His chosen! He talks about how He will protect and take care of him. There are so many spectacular promises in this set of verses, but notice how He refers to His chosen in verse 14 — He calls him "thou worm." He tells us so much about how He's going to watch out for and take care of His chosen, but then says His chosen is a worm. This is something you would not find taught in a self-help or psychology course, but it's the truth, and it contains the right formula for how to think. The Lord wants us to remember that we are like worms compared to Him. Remember how He formed Adam? <u>Adam was made out of dirt</u>. We can't forget that our flesh was made from the dirt of the ground, and we cannot forget that we are <u>born in sinful, weak flesh</u>.

However, now that we are saved, our true identity is that we're children of the King! We are new creatures in Christ Jesus. Instead of finding "our own truth" or our own identity, this is the truth now, and our identity now needs to be found in Christ alone. We are made free, and we are "made perfect, throughly furnished [inside] unto all good works" in Christ as we learn to follow the Spirit through God's Word (2 Timothy 3:17). We are internally matured, equipped and perfected for the work God has for us. In the end, it is not about what we can do for ourselves. We need to step back and let Christ have control over our lives, because He is the One who will do all of it! We have to realize that this is about focusing on Him and letting Him do it through us, and this can only happen when we die to self and follow the Spirit.

Where do you find your identity? It shouldn't be in the flesh because your flesh will only let you down. You can be a wife or a mother, have a career, or even be the head of a ministry. There are just so many things that we can say make up our identity, but what God wants us to see is that our true identity is only found in the person of Christ. Who or what defines you? Instead of your strengths, weaknesses, culture, education, or skin color, let yourself be defined by the words of the living God. That is where true confidence and security will come from.

> ***Job 42:1-6*** *Then Job answered the LORD, and said, I know that thou canst do every thing, and that no thought can be withholden from thee. Who is he that hideth counsel without knowledge? therefore have I uttered that I understood not; things too wonderful for me, which I knew not. Hear, I beseech thee, and I will speak: I will demand of thee, and declare thou unto me. I have heard of thee by the hearing of the ear: but now mine eye seeth thee. Wherefore I abhor myself, and repent in dust and ashes.*

Job was the most righteous man of his time, but when he finally gets a real glimpse of God, he says, "You're awesome God, and I'm just dirt!" We must begin getting a real glimpse of our living God and cast away any confidence in the flesh.

If we decide to look at ourselves and at each other, we will begin to compare amongst ourselves and will always find someone a little better or a little worse. But God says, "Don't look to yourself or others. Look up! Look at Me!" We need to get our focus off of our flesh, off of ourselves, and put the focus on God Almighty. We live in a Laodicean culture — we think we are rich, increased with goods, and have need of nothing (Revelation 3:14-22). It's always about our flesh, our rights, and what we want in the physical realm. We need to fight against this culture by setting our flesh aside and embracing the new creature in Jesus which sets its affections on things above. Don't compare yourself to others. Compare yourself to the standard of the Word of God. When you do this, you will find that you fall short of what God is calling you to in the Word, but you will also find the hope that God offers us through the Holy Spirit. Finding our identity in Christ and seeing Him and not our flesh is a lifelong process as we grow in Christ and walk after the new creature, as described in 2 Corinthians 5:17.

Step 4: Maintain a good conscience toward God and others.

> *2 Corinthians 10:12 For we dare not make ourselves of the number, or compare ourselves with some that commend themselves: but they measuring themselves by themselves, and comparing themselves among themselves, are not wise.*

This important passage says not to compare ourselves to each other! In the end, we are all the body of Christ, and each and every part of His body is important to Him. There is no need for competition amongst Christians because God called you to a specific job that He wants to do through you. In 1 Corinthians 12 Paul paints the picture of the church being like a body. Your body is built up of all different parts, but they're all necessary parts that work together as one. That's how the Lord wants us to operate in His church — He doesn't want us to operate against each other, comparing ourselves amongst ourselves. Unfortunately, until we learn this important principle, we often do compare ourselves to others.

It's not about what somebody else is doing — it's about finding the living God in the Word of God, seeking Him, and growing in a relationship with Him! As you grow closer to Him, you will see more of who He is and you will get a proper perspective on just how much your flesh stinks. We have to get to the place where we say, "I don't want to follow the flesh anymore; I want to follow the Spirit." The more that we see Him for who He is, the more we're going to ask Him to help us to follow the Spirit and not the flesh.

The spiritual trajectory of growth is seen in the seven stages of spiritual growth: baby, little child, child, youth, father, elder, and ancient. We start out as babies, and babies are little "me-monsters" — in those early stages of our walk with the Lord, we are only focused on ourselves. The more that we see God and let Him work through us, the more we learn to focus on the Lord and others. All of creation and time are about Him and His Kingdom.

Even the disciples went through this growth process, and even though they walked with Jesus, they still struggled. They asked Jesus which one of them would be greater, and James and John even had their mom go to Him and ask who would sit on His right hand. At the end of the book of John, Peter asked Jesus what He was going to have John do. He was concerned about what Jesus had in store for another disciple. In our flesh, we have the same tendency! Comparing and competing are not going to be healthy for us. We're trying to die to our flesh and let God live His life through us. When we do that, we don't have eyes to compare ourselves to others around us. We will only have eyes for God.

What needs to begin happening is that we have to learn to have a work **of Him** instead of a work *for* **Him**. And sometimes the only way you can really learn how to have a work of Him is to try to do it yourself by doing the work for Him. I know that sounds confusing, but let me explain. Abraham, who believed that God could work through him, immediately tried to do this work himself instead of allowing God to do it through him. He hearkened unto Sarah instead of waiting on God and ended up having a baby with Hagar! After he realized that this wasn't the right plan, he fell before the Lord, surrendered, and died to himself, and God was then able to do it through him. God provided a son through Abraham and Sarah, just as He had promised. When we focus on God (God-esteem) instead of on ourselves (self-esteem), we'll see that God is always faithful to work through us to fulfill His promises.

> **Acts 4:13** *Now when they saw the boldness of Peter and John, and perceived that they were unlearned and ignorant men, they marvelled; and they took knowledge of them, that they had been with Jesus.*

This verse is key. If you're spending time with Jesus, it will show. Spending time with God can't be something that you do once a year or whenever you are going through a trial. You have to spend time with Him to become like Him and to be used by Him. Our relationship with the Lord is like an iceberg. You can see the very tip of someone's relationship with God on the outside, but the most important part is the foundation built by all the time they've spent with God, and that is the part that is private and invisible. This is why each one of us needs to be spending quality time with God. We need that strong base and foundation of all the time we spend with Him. God is the only one who can solve our problems and help us make sense out of what is going on with our life, but we usually try everything else before we finally understand that and rest in Him and His Word.

The question we have to ask ourselves is: "Have I been with Jesus?" We must let go and let God (Romans 8:31; Acts 5:38-39). As we learn to do it God's way, we grow in confidence and security, and He begins establishing a track record with us.

Our motive also has to be right, and we can't take things personally. We must learn how to have a right heart with God. When difficult things happen, we often throw ourselves a pity party. Don't get me wrong, you may have to have your pity party sometimes. But instead of throwing your pity party alone, get with the Lord and have your pity party. You may have many! However, remember to then listen to Him and let Him pick you up and move you forward. His is the best shoulder to cry on. Go and cry to Jesus, but don't let the downer stop you. What we're upset about may not even be real! Realize that no matter what it is, He's there for you, and He loves you.

As we focus on pleasing Him, seeking Him, and seeing Him, that's when life begins making sense. Remember, we are here to glorify God. That's what we were made for, and since that is our true purpose, we cannot focus on pleasing others or ourselves. My life was so messed up because I was such a people-pleaser and wanted people to like me. But after meeting the one, true, living God, life became about wanting to please Him. An "audience of One" is a good phrase to apply to the thoughts and actions of your life. Who are you trying to please? Please the Lord with your life.

> **Galatians 1:10** *For do I now persuade men, or God? or do I seek to please men? for if I yet pleased men, I should not be the servant of Christ.*

We need to be conscious of whom we are trying to please. We need to pray, "Lord, help me fear You and not man!" I was fearing everyone else and was so scared of what they would think of me instead of focusing on the One who offers full grace, peace, and love.

> **Ephesians 1:6** *To the praise of the glory of his grace, wherein he hath made us accepted in the beloved.*

Being rejected is another place where we often get hit and have our pity parties. No one likes to feel rejected. And though it can be real rejection by others, it can also be rejection that is perceived. Either way, whether real or perceived, it hurts. Jesus often hit rejection. After all, John 1:11 says that "He came unto his own, and his own received him not." Therefore, if He faced rejection, we will too! But if you are saved, He says you are accepted in the Beloved. In the end, that is all that matters!

If your Creator has put His stamp of approval on you, who cares what anyone else thinks? This is the foundation you must lay, turning away from feelings and focusing on the facts. The fact is that you are accepted in the Beloved! You are accepted, and in this acceptance there is no room to fear the rejection of men. The whole book of Romans was written so that you would know that you are justified in Christ. He made it "just as if you'd never sinned." You belong here. You have a place here. You're justified and accepted by God, the Creator of the Universe, the King of kings, and Lord of lords. It's His universe, and He has placed His stamp of approval on you. Our validation comes from God alone. Who cares if somebody else rejects you if God accepts you? He says you're supposed to be here. He has a reason for you. You've got to hold onto that, and the only place you will clearly see that is in His Word.

Step 5: Find Bible characters to whom you can relate. This is so important! When I was growing up in Christ, I had four or five close friends. We went to Shepherd's School together, did ministry together, and went on all the mission trips together. We were single, and we fellowshipped a lot! However, when I was alone, I would sometimes have a pity party because I felt like a thorn amongst the roses. I had been divorced twice (divorce was a major taboo 35 years ago). None of them had even been married, they were virgins, and they had been raised in church. Here I was — two divorces, all screwed up — and the pity parties would come because I was comparing myself to them.

This is what I am talking about: sometimes we experience perceived rejection. They certainly didn't reject me, but I just felt like I wasn't good enough. They didn't think that. I mean, we were great friends! I would think, "How could God ever use me with my background?" I remember having one of my times of self-pity, and as I was asking God for help, I happened upon Mary Magdalene in John 20. I can get chills thinking about this passage and what God showed me. It said that the Lord had cast out seven spirits from her (Luke 8:2), and I could relate to that because I had come from such an occultish background. The disciples and ladies all came to the tomb, looking for Jesus. Then they all left and went to their own homes — all of them except Mary. Mary didn't leave. She stayed, desperately seeking God. And whom did she see? She saw Jesus.

It blew me away that He stopped to comfort her. Here was Mary, of whom He had cast out seven devils, and she was the only one at the tomb. Jesus stops on His way to the Father to comfort her. Remember, He had been separated from God the Father, had gone down into the center of the earth to preach to those in hell, and was then on His way up to present the perfect, sinless sacrifice to the Father in the third heaven. But on His way He saw Mary, the only one at His tomb, weeping and looking for Him. And He stops to comfort her. She's the first one to see the risen Christ! Jesus gave Mary the privilege of seeing Him and being comforted by the risen Savior! He not only stops to comfort her, but He also gives her a task. He tells her to go tell the disciples that He's back! This girl, out of whom Jesus had cast out seven devils, was the first one to preach the gospel — she was the first one to tell people about Jesus, the risen Savior!

During my pity party, I saw that and it blew me away. Ever since then, I've loved reading her story and realizing that that is how the Lord is with us. If we're seeking Him, we'll find Him. It doesn't matter what our background is. He wants a relationship with us — that's why He created us. If we just set time aside and get with Him, He will meet us there. No matter your background or situation, there is always a Bible character (woman or man) to whom you can relate. We are going to learn things in this study about some of the prophets. We are the bride of Christ, spiritually speaking, but the Bible also says that we are the sons of God! We can learn spiritually from both the women and the men. Find the characters to whom you can relate. Seeing how the Lord related to them can greatly build our confidence in Him. When you go through those tough times, you can remember that God can use all kinds of people.

So, as we reflect on developing confidence and security, we must begin by being born again (Chapter 1), then we build on that foundation eternal security through Christ (Step 1). After that, we begin to build a proper prayer life as we grow in our relationship with Him and we find the peace which passeth all understanding (Step 2). As we grow, we start that lifelong process of learning to have a work of God, not a work for Him. We have a job out there that He wants to accomplish through us, and as we focus on Him and not on trying to better ourselves (our flesh), we find our identity in Christ (Steps 3 & 4). That's the key, and as we continue to grow, we begin relating to Bible characters, learning from how God helped to show them His plan for their lives (Step 5). We are here to glorify God. The only way that will happen is if we spend time with Him in His Word. That's the only way we will begin developing confidence and security. Have you been with Jesus?

Homework: Get alone sometime in the next week and verbally talk to the Lord, giving Him all the cares, burdens, and worries you're carrying. Tell Him ALL your needs and requests and give thanks for all the good and bad. Do this once a week, taking no less than thirty minutes. This helps develop a good prayer life and results in you attaining the peace that passeth all understanding by faith in God's promise through prayer.

Recommended Reading: *Fact, Faith, Feeling*. This author talks about the facts of the Word of God and how to mix them with faith. Though we often feel emotions tied to God's Word, these emotions cannot be the foundation, root, or engine of our relationship with Him. They must be the caboose, never the engine. As we build upon the facts of the Bible, the Lord builds our sense of confidence and security!

Questions to Consider:

1. Have you ever been afraid that you would lose your salvation? Do you see in the Bible that you can know that you have eternal life after you've been born again?

2. Why do you think that understanding eternal security will cause you to be more confident and secure in your relationship with God and others?

3. Do you have peace with God? How?

4. Do you often struggle with fear? What does that mean about your relationship with God?

5. Can we decide whether we have peace or fear in our hearts? Check out John 14:27. "Let not our hearts be troubled"

6. Do the Prayer Exercise assignment. What happened, and how did it go? Was it difficult? How did you feel afterward?

7. Do you ever feel like a sheep that has heavy wool on it that needs to be sheared off? How do you free yourself from these burdens?

8. When you have trials, do you often find yourself focusing on yourself or on God?

9. Do you compare yourself to others? If so, what should you do instead?

10. What does your devotional time look like each day? Can people tell that you are spending time with Jesus?

11. Whom are you trying to please in life? Do you find that you are a people-pleaser? Who is your true audience?

4

Making God the Center

We are learning to let God sit on the throne of our heart and will, and as we practice setting aside old habits and giving the Lord the crown, there are two key phrases we need to start saying in our relationship with Him. These phrases are usually very hard for our old man, the flesh, to say. The first one is, "I'm wrong." God's right, I'm wrong — even in our relationships with others we need to learn how to begin saying that. The next phrase is, "I surrender," which is another phrase we often have trouble with. We will be talking a lot about these two phrases in many of our lessons as we move forward. You see, what keeps us from easily saying these terms is our pride and our self-righteousness. These qualities are hidden in our old man and will often get in the way of our relationship with God if we're not careful.

Our key verses for this section are Matthew 6:33 and Luke 9:23. These two verses are prime, foundational verses, meaning that you can return to them time and time again because they can solve so much in your life. Keep going back and spiritually exercising these verses in your life.

> **Matthew 6:33** *But seek ye first the kingdom of God, and his righteousness; and all these things shall be added unto you.*

> **Luke 9:23** *And he said to them all, If any man will come after me, let him deny himself, and take up his cross daily, and follow me.*

These verses tell us that we need to deny ourselves and focus on the spiritual things that belong to God's Kingdom. Unfortunately, what we often do in Laodicea Land is the exact opposite. We seek after these physical "things" mentioned in Matthew 6 as if they could provide all our needs and satisfaction, but in the process, we end up placing these things on the throne instead of God. However, God says if you can manage to seek first the Kingdom of God (the spiritual kingdom) and make that and His righteousness the goal, then everything else is going to fall into place. It's really amazing, and it really works. Then, if we add following Jesus by denying ourselves and taking up our cross, spiritual growth happens! So <u>set God as your number one priority</u>, just like Daniel did.

> **Daniel 1:8** *But Daniel purposed in his heart that he would not defile himself with the portion of the king's meat, nor with the wine which he drank: therefore he requested of the prince of the eunuchs that he might not defile himself.*

Daniel purposed in his heart not to defile himself with the sins of the land where he had been carried away into captivity. He knew that he had to <u>set himself apart for God alone</u>, and that God was better than the king's food or favor. We have to purpose to make God the center. This isn't just a one-time deal, this is a daily decision. If we decide to make God number one in our lives, we won't have issues in singleness with always trying to find a husband, repeating the same mistakes over and over again. If you desire to be married, then purpose to focus on your relationship with God first. It's the same with jobs, education, and lifestyle. Instead of chasing these things, chase God first and see what things He has in store for you. We have a Heavenly Father who is so much better than anything we could chase on this earth, and He deserves all of our attention and pursuit.

This lesson, and many lessons after it, will focus on submission. This word has a very negative connotation, especially in our culture. However, what we will see is that it is one of the most powerful tools we have in our relationship with God. It gives us incredible access to Him that we could not get otherwise. If we can learn how to truly submit it is life-changing, because when we can get out of the way of God, He can truly work out His perfect will in our lives.

That being said, I want to touch on some key definitions before we begin.

1. **Free Will:** God has given each of us a free will. In other words, the Creator of the Universe chooses to limit Himself by our choices. God, the One who has the right to control everything, chooses not to. Free will is something that we must exercise as we walk toward God. It is not something that we give to others.

2. **Control:** This is the opposite of free will, and this is what the world tries to force upon us. Everyone is after control. That's why we have wars — everyone wants to be in control, including ourselves.

3. **Submission:** Submission is not an action, it is an internal attitude. It is a willing surrender of our free will. We need to surrender our free will to God's control because we have faith that He knows best. Submission is a conscious decision to give Him control, and it is the key to all relationships, for we are told to submit one to another.

4. **Obedience:** What we're going to see in this lesson is that true obedience is not just the outward action of a submitted heart. True obedience is true worship springing from our submitted hearts. It is faith in action.

I heard this example when I was a young Christian, and it stuck with me. Imagine you have a four-year-old child who does not want to sit in his car seat. Try as you might, you cannot get him to obey, regardless of your words or discipline. You tell yourself, "I'm going to get a lock and put a lock on that car seat so he can't get out of it." So you do, and you think as you're driving down the road, "Ah, he's finally obeying me. Yes, I've finally got him to understand obedience!" However, if we could see the internal heart of that strong-willed child, we would see that though he is sitting on the outside, he is standing inside his heart. What should really matter is the internal attitude. This is why parents often say that they want their child to want to do right, not just to do right. We must remember that God is always looking at the heart, not at the outside of a person.

> *1 Samuel 16:7* But the LORD said unto Samuel, Look not on his countenance, or on the height of his stature; because I have refused him: for the LORD seeth not as man seeth; for man looketh on the outward appearance, but the LORD looketh on the heart.

The thing that God looks at is the attitude of our heart. As we grow in Christ, it is our goal to align this attitude of the heart with what we see in the Word of God — making sure we have the right heart, and then bringing what's right on the inside to the outside in our actions. This is exactly what Philippians 2:12 is talking about when Paul says to "work out your own salvation with fear and trembling." You are given everything that you need at salvation to have a right heart attitude before God. You are given the church body, the Holy Spirit, and the Word of God. However, submission is an internal decision, the surrender of your free will. This heart attitude will then produce an external expression of obedience.

Any obedience without a right heart attitude is not pleasing to God, but God is also able to create that right heart attitude if we ask Him for it (Philippians 2:13). It's important to remember that we can fake outward obedience. God is the only One who can see inside the heart and the motivations and desires of mankind, and so there must always be a proving out process. Just like others can "fake it," we can fake it too and even go so far as to deceive ourselves. We need to get into contact with what our heart is thinking. We need to be completely honest before God about the contents of our heart and take off all the masks we have placed upon it to deceive or hide. There is no better place to start this process than in prayer.

> ***Ephesians 5:22*** *Wives, submit yourselves unto your own husbands, as unto the Lord.*

This is one of the most commonly quoted verses about submission. Unfortunately, the ultimate clue or instruction about how to submit in this verse is often overlooked, especially when we're talking about submission to earthly figures. When we prayerfully dissect this verse, we can see that it is written to "wives," however we know that all women, whether single or married, are the bride of Christ. We often focus on the physical relationship here between the wife and her own husband, and we neglect to realize that the focus of this verse is not to tell us to submit. The focus is to show us how to submit: as unto the Lord.

So first, we have to learn to submit to God. It's hard to submit, but it is easier to learn submission with a perfect, sinless Savior than it is to submit to a man who is a sinner just like us. That's why He's saying that the way you learn to submit to your husband is by placing it into the frame of reference of how you submit to the Lord. Learning how to submit to the Lord is key for any relationship, and it also applies to actions outside of submission, like love and forgiveness. We must learn to first apply them in our relationship with the Lord, and then we can turn around and give them to somebody else. So whether married or single, we must first learn to submit to the Lord. In fact, it is far easier to learn this principle when single, because single women are forced to learn submission to Christ first, as they have no earthly husband. Then, if and when the right man comes along, you already have the foundation needed to submit to him as well.

Now, it's also very interesting that Ephesians 5:21 says, "Submitting yourselves one to another in the fear of God." Submission is instrumental in all of our relationships. The solution to any relationship issue is so simple: lay down and let God! Until we learn this important lesson, we so often get in the way of God fighting our battles and try to fight the battles for ourselves. This is such a simple concept, but it is an incredibly hard lesson. Submit yourself to one another, and let God sort out all the rest.

Let's look at some examples! We're going to see the first unsubmitted heart in biblical history, and then we're going to see the perfect, submitted heart. With these two examples we can evaluate our own hearts and see which path we would like to take, knowing that the submission of our heart affects the reality of our life.

Here's where we find a picture of the first unsubmitted heart: Satan's fall from heaven.

> ***Isaiah 14:12-14*** *How art thou fallen from heaven, O Lucifer, son of the morning! how art thou cut down to the ground, which didst weaken the nations! For thou hast said in thine heart,* ***I will*** *ascend into heaven,* ***I will*** *exalt my throne above the stars of God:* ***I will*** *sit also upon the mount of the congregation, in the sides of the north:* ***I will*** *ascend above the heights of the clouds;* ***I will*** *be like the most High.*

Read through that illustration slowly and ask yourself what Satan is rebelling against. He is rebelling against the will of God and choosing instead to follow his own will. He exercises his free will in unsubmission and disobedience. Remember, everyone has a free will, including Lucifer, who later became Satan. Lucifer was the covering cherub. He was fourth in control back then — first God the Father, then God the Son, then God the Spirit, and then Lucifer. Five times in this passage he says "I will." I will override God's will. I will be as God. The attitude of his heart is so plain here, and it is clearly in unsubmission. His heart says that he knows better than God, so he will do it his way. His will is to be just like God, worshipped as Him and ruling as Him. His will is to override God's will. He's decided not to trust and obey God because he thinks he knows better and he covets control.

I'll never forget the first time I read 1 Samuel 15:22-23, which says that rebellion is like witchcraft. Even back then, when I was still coming out of the world, witchcraft seemed like a terrible thing. Even before I was a believer, I never wanted to do that, though I was deceived into thinking that astrology and witchcraft were different entities! Now, on the other hand, being self-reliant, strong, and even a little rebellious is actually promoted in our culture, especially in the work world. They can be looked upon as good characteristics in Laodicea Land! That's what I thought until I saw this verse.

Saul was told to destroy a whole tribe of people because they were evil — they were practicing witchcraft, bestiality, and other wicked things. Though God told Saul to wipe them off the earth, Saul decided to keep some of their animals. When confronted by Samuel the prophet about his disobedience, Saul had a good excuse. "True, I didn't exactly obey God, but I got this stuff for Him, and now I can sacrifice it to Him!" Rationalizing and excusing sin are exactly what we do, and we end up behaving the same way that Lucifer did. We think that we know best and that we are the exception to every rule. We think that God doesn't know what He's talking about. We think that we know better than He does.

And here is what Samuel says to Saul about that:

> *1 Samuel 15:22-23 And Samuel said, Hath the LORD as great delight in burnt offerings and sacrifices, as in obeying the voice of the LORD?* **Behold, to obey is better than sacrifice**, *and to hearken than the fat of rams.* **For rebellion is as the sin of witchcraft**, *and stubbornness is as iniquity and idolatry. Because thou hast rejected the word of the LORD, he hath also rejected thee from being king.*

Samuel corrects Saul's thinking, pointing out the wickedness of Saul's heart attitude. A lack of submission is just like witchcraft. It is that bad. And then he goes on to say stubbornness is like worshipping ourselves instead of worshipping God. How often are we stubborn? To God, obedience is better than sacrifice. Saul said he disobeyed and kept those animals because he wanted to sacrifice them to God, but God says that what He wanted was plain and simple obedience. Obedience is what we are first after if we are seeking after the Lord with all our heart, mind, and soul, not what we can do for Him or sacrifice to Him. Parents often tell their children to do something because "I told you to," but God is such a good Father in that He wants us to understand His commands as His friends. We just need to obey without question or excuse.

Another thing we need to realize is that we all have elements of rebellion and "I will" in our flesh. Job says that the devil cannot submit because of pride. We have elements of that same pride in our flesh, and that's why we struggle so hard with submission. Our pride gets in the way, just like the devil's does. Lucifer came up against God, thinking that he knew better and could do better. And though we feel that Satan is so much worse than us, we actually do the same thing in our flesh. We think that we know better than God. That is the wrong way, and it is trusting in the example of the devil for our desired outcome. We are either following the devil or we're following Jesus. We are either saying "I will do it my way" or we are going to follow the Lord and do it His way. There's no in between. To choose our own way is to choose Satan's way and throw away God's way.

Peter and Job, both men of God, also had the same issues with pride and self-righteousness in the flesh. It's there in our flesh. We all have to let the Lord work it out of us, and none of us are exempt from these same temptations.

Now that we have looked at the first unsubmitted heart, let's look at the biblical example of the perfectly submitted heart:

> *Matthew 26:36-46 Then cometh Jesus with them unto a place called Gethsemane, and saith unto the disciples, Sit ye here, while I go and pray yonder. And he took with him Peter and the two sons of Zebedee, and began to be sorrowful and very heavy. Then saith he unto them, My soul is exceeding sorrowful, even unto death: tarry ye here, and watch with me. And he went a little further, and fell on his face, and prayed, saying, O my Father, if it be possible, let this cup pass from me: **nevertheless not as I will, but as thou wilt**. And he cometh unto the disciples, and findeth them asleep, and saith unto Peter, What, could ye not watch with me one hour? Watch and pray,*

that ye enter not into temptation: the spirit indeed is willing, but the flesh is weak. He went away again the second time, and prayed, saying, O my Father, if this cup may not pass away from me, except I drink it, **thy will be done***. And he came and found them asleep again: for their eyes were heavy. And he left them, and went away again, and prayed the third time, saying the same words. Then cometh he to his disciples, and saith unto them, Sleep on now, and take your rest: behold, the hour is at hand, and the Son of man is betrayed into the hands of sinners. Rise, let us be going: behold, he is at hand that doth betray me.*

This submitted heart belongs to our Hero. This is how our Creator showed us and taught us how to submit. This is the greatest example we could ever find on submission, and to grow in Christlikeness means to grow in displaying this same heart of submission.

Three times Jesus goes to the Father to ask Him to remove the cup of suffering and wrath. When we compare this same example to Paul's crossroads decision in 2 Corinthians 12, we see that Paul had a thorn that he carried just as Jesus carried the cross. Both Paul and Jesus asked for their burdens to be removed three times, but it was the Father's will that they bear their burdens, and so they continued forward in submission. What is the burden that you are bearing that God has not yet removed? <u>Bear it in submission.</u>

As we examine this crossroads, we see that the Lord did not want to go to the cross! Jesus was going to be totally separated from God the Father for the first time. He was going to die to pay the price for sin, and the wrath of God was going to be poured out upon His sinless body. Here's the example we must learn from and follow: Jesus was honest with God. He didn't just say, "I'll do whatever!" He wasn't a robot. He didn't say, "Oh, You choose." He told Him, "Father, I would rather not do it this way." Then, He says the most important conclusion we must all face if we want to truly follow the Lord and learn to submit and biblically obey: **"Nevertheless, not my will but thine."** He died to self-will.

This is the difference between Him and Lucifer. Jesus submits His will to God's, knowing that God's will is perfect and supreme. He's acknowledging that God knows what's best, and that His emotions and desires need to be submitted to Him. Many times in life you're going to come to a crossroads, and it's going to be very hard. You're going to be in the same place that Jesus was in the sense that you must be honest and pour out your heart to God, but you also must submit your will to God's. These are the steps to true submission. First, be totally honest with God. Second, acknowledge God is God and that He knows best. Finally, choose to die to self-will.

A key phrase in the book *Hinds' Feet on High Places* is "acceptance with joy." It is a willingness to accept whatever God brings into our path because He knows best. This acceptance with joy should be exactly what we are looking for. But for us to attain this, we need to understand that joy is not found in having all of our desires fulfilled as we walk through blessed seasons of life. Instead, joy is found as we walk through hard trials in life and learn to submit our will to God's. Following the things of God is the only way to have true, unspeakable joy, and coming to crossroads and learning to accept His will for our lives over our own is the only way to exercise "acceptance with joy." Jesus is our example in this too. We see that He chose acceptance with joy in Hebrews 12:2-4.

> **Hebrews 12:2-4** *Looking unto Jesus the author and finisher of our faith; who for the joy that was set before him endured the cross, despising the shame, and is set down at the right hand of the throne of God. For consider him that endured such contradiction of sinners against himself, lest ye be wearied and faint in your minds. Ye have not yet resisted unto blood, striving against sin.*

Though Jesus was in such agony before the cross, He did it for the "joy that was set before him." I have heard many preachers say that His joy was the reality of bringing us into God's Kingdom, but I do not think that it is as simple as that. I think that this joy was based on knowing that His obedience as God's Son would bring the Father ultimate glory. His obedience in submitting His will to the Father's brought Him such joy, and He trusted that God's will was the best will there was.

We don't always know why we're going through what we're going through, but we have to acknowledge that God is God, and we are not. This is easier if we can accept it with joy. It's an attitude of submission, accepting whatever it is that God has brought into our path, because we know that we can trust Him. This is a great mystery about suffering, and we will cover it much more in later chapters.

> ***Hebrews 5:7-9*** *Who in the days of his flesh, when he had offered up prayers and supplications with strong crying and tears unto him that was able to save him from death, and was heard in that he feared;* ***though he were a Son, yet learned he obedience by the things which he suffered;*** *and being made perfect, he became the author of eternal salvation unto all them that obey him;*

This is the key passage that shows us what true, biblical obedience is: an outward action from a submitted heart. In this passage, we can see the internal heart attitude of Christ on the verge of the cross. We see, too, that it says He feared! He did not fear the suffering of the cross, but He did fear the One who called Him to it. He feared God. He knew God's principles and feared the consequences of not doing it God the Father's way. God the Father always knows what's best for you and me, right? Even when I don't want to do it His way, He knows what's best because He is God. Jesus is giving us this example so that we can seek after this same obedience in our own lives. He learned obedience through His suffering, not just the suffering on the cross, but the suffering of laying down His own will. Just as Jesus died to Himself, we also need to die to our own will and dedicate ourselves to God's. This is the cross we bear, and it is obedience.

The Bible says that we all have a burden, and as we live out our Christian walk, we are learning how to bear that burden. It is the cross we bear.

Coming to Crossroads

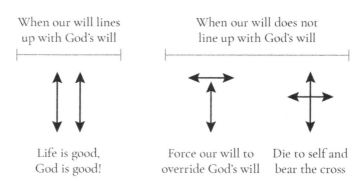

When my will and God's will are parallel, things are awesome. Things are beautiful. However, often there are times when our lives are a collision between going our way and going God's way. We all have a choice we need to make every second of every day: will we try to override God's will with our will (like Lucifer) or will we bear the cross (like Jesus)? Knowing God's will for our lives might seem like an expansive subject, but it is actually quite simple. God's will for our lives is for us to become more like Jesus, and the only way that transformation will happen in our lives is if we keep our eyes on God and see all things in our lives as opportunities to grow spiritually. Yes, sometimes the hard things are consequences of our wrong choices, but at the same time, He's allowing that to teach us and grow us up. All things truly do work for our good!

> **1 Corinthians 15:31** *I protest by your rejoicing which I have in Christ Jesus our Lord, I die daily.*

> **Romans 12:1** *I beseech you therefore, brethren, by the mercies of God, that ye present your bodies a living sacrifice, holy, acceptable unto God, which is your reasonable service.* ← 'dying

We see in these passages that this process of obedience is a daily death to self, choosing to allow Christ to live in and through us instead. Every day, we must present our bodies a living sacrifice to God. It is only reasonable — it isn't asking too much — that we do that, especially compared to what Christ did for us.

> **Matthew 16:24-27** *Then said Jesus unto his disciples, If any man will come after me, let him deny himself, and take up his cross, and follow me. For whosoever will save his life shall lose it: and whosoever will lose his life for my sake shall find it. For what is a man profited, if he shall gain the whole world, and lose his own soul? or what shall a man give in exchange for his soul? For the Son of man shall come in the glory of his Father with his angels; and then he shall reward every man according to his works.*

Deny self, pick up your cross, and follow Him. We all want to hear: "Well done, thou good and faithful servant." If we choose to follow the things that we desire in this world and in our own will, then we will end up with nothing. In fact, we will suffer loss at the Judgment Seat of Christ. We'll have less than nothing. But, if we deny ourselves and seek to let God's will reign in our lives, then we have much reward waiting for us in heaven and our joy will be full.

I remember the first time I came to a hard crossroads. It was right after salvation, and there was a night when my husband and I were in bed, getting ready to sleep. Something was said, and we started to argue. At that point, he kicked me out of the bed, so I went and laid on the sofa. I was crying my eyes out to the Lord, feeling sorry for myself and wondering what the Lord was doing. As I was laying there crying, Matthew 16:24-27 came to my mind. Convicted, I decided to surrender, deny myself, and pick up the cross of staying with my husband until God told me differently. I had asked God to change the situation, but He hadn't, so I trusted that He would use me to share the gospel with my husband through my words and through my testimony. Though I was willing to stay, it wasn't God's will, and the church leadership soon advised me to move out of the abusive relationship and stay with my mom. If I had tried to fight my way out, all I would have done was get in the way of God. Instead, He made a way out for me, and He changed my heart in the process, teaching me how to submit to Him.

I approached another crossroads when my mom was diagnosed with Alzheimer's ten years ago. I had prayed so many times for her to be healed from this horrible disease, and watching her slowly die from Alzheimer's was one of the most difficult trials of my life. It resulted in many different crossroads in my relationship with the Lord. I knew God could heal her, but He chose not to. She was a believer in Christ, so I know she is now with the Lord since her physical death. I couldn't fight her battles, even though I sometimes tried. Instead, I had to learn to give it to God and let Him do it His way. It's amazing how He has used this suffering and difficulty to teach me as He has provided for me and directed me in how to care for her each step of the way. It also brought me and my brother so much closer as we took care of her together. God used such a difficult thing for good in my life and in my brother's.

Now, these are examples of major crossroads in my life where God taught me to die self, to deny how my flesh wanted to react, and to respond His way instead. But as we read in 1 Corinthians 15:31 and Romans 12:1, we are to die daily. So it's not just in the big issues of life we need to choose to mortify our flesh, but in the less obvious moments, too. The following poem captures what these subtle opportunities to die daily could look like for us.

When you are forgotten, neglected, or purposely set aside — and you sting from the insult, but are happy at being counted worthy to suffer for Christ...
THAT IS DYING TO SELF.

When your good is evil spoken of, your wishes are crossed, your advice disregarded, and your opinions ridiculed — yet you refuse to let anger rise in your heart, but take it all in patient, loving silence...
THAT IS DYING TO SELF.

When you lovingly and patiently bear any disorder, irregularity, annoyance — and you endure waste, folly, extravagance, and spiritual insensibility as Jesus did...
THAT IS DYING TO SELF.

When you are content with any circumstance, food, offering, clothing, climate, society, solicitude, and interruption by the will of God...
THAT IS DYING TO SELF.

When you never care to refer to yourself in conversation, record your own good works, seek after commendation from others, and are content with being unknown...
THAT IS DYING TO SELF.

When you see your brother prosper and you can honestly rejoice with him in spirit without feeling envy or questioning God — even though you have greater needs or more desperate circumstances...
THAT IS DYING TO SELF.

When you can receive correction and reproof from one of less stature than yourself and can humbly submit inwardly as well as outwardly without rebellion or resentment rising up in your heart...
THAT IS DYING TO SELF.
—Anonymous

Each one of us is going to come to difficult crossroads. As soon as you get through one of them and learn to exercise complete biblical obedience in victory, you will come to another. Each crossroads is an opportunity for another surrender to the Lord. Yes, things will eventually change for us as we pass through these crossroads, but only when we come to the end of self. The place of surrender, of letting the Lord do it rather than ourselves, is the end goal of every crossroads. We may never know what He's trying to accomplish through the fiery trial, but we have the faith to believe that His Word is true — He truly will work all things for our good (Romans 8:28). I've met God at this intersection of the unknown and God's known promises many times in my life, and He has never let me down.

> *1 Corinthians 10:13* There hath no temptation taken you but such as is common to man: but God is faithful, who will not suffer you to be tempted above that ye are able; but will with the temptation also make a way to escape, that ye may be able to bear it.

God has promised that there will always be a way to escape in every trial. Watching someone you love suffer may be one of the hardest things we endure, yet even in that we learn that God's grace is sufficient. Now, my mom's suffering is over. She's home with Jesus, and she's whole and in her right mind. I may never know on this side of heaven all the reasons for everything that happened, but I do know God's sufficiency and grace provided for us every step of the way and got us through it all. He says that we're not going through anything that others haven't gone through, and that Jesus was tempted in every way that we will ever be tempted. So, we have to remember that God's grace is sufficient. He's going to give us the verse that will sustain us, and He's going to direct us. We have to deny ourselves, pick up that cross, and follow Him. He may take the cross and give you a different one, but we have to be willing to face whatever He has given us. We have to surrender our will.

> *Jeremiah 3:12-15* Go and proclaim these words toward the north, and say, Return, thou backsliding Israel, saith the LORD; and I will not cause mine

> *anger to fall upon you: for I am merciful, saith the LORD, and I will not keep anger for ever. Only acknowledge thine iniquity, that thou hast transgressed against the LORD thy God, and hast scattered thy ways to the strangers under every green tree, and ye have not obeyed my voice, saith the LORD. Turn, O backsliding children, saith the LORD; <u>for I am married unto you</u>; and I will take you one of a city, and two of a family, and I will bring you to Zion: and I will give you pastors according to mine heart, which shall feed you with knowledge and understanding.*

God is also in charge of our leadership. I've worked with so many women who say, "You just don't know how bad I've had it. You don't know my leadership. How can this work? How can these principles apply to me? I've got it so much worse than others." Whether it be a husband, pastor, or ministry leader, God is in control and He can even work through ungodly leaders. God gave me Jeremiah 3:12-15 at a time when I felt hopeless due to the poor spiritual leadership in my life. This principle is so powerful! When we are not content with our leadership, God tells us to get our hearts right. It is only when we have a content, submitted, and thankful heart that God will see it fit to change or grow our leadership. Israel wasn't backslidden because they had poor leadership. They had poor leadership because they were backslidden. When you find that you have poor leadership, maybe you should start by looking at yourself for the reason rather than at them. Get your heart right, trust God, and let Him take care of the rest.

This principle is actually similar to what I was praying back when I was in my abusive relationship when I first got saved. This principle was working behind the scenes, even through my marriage, because He gives the same principle to wives in 1 Peter 3:1-4.

> **1 Peter 3:1-4** *Likewise, ye wives, be in subjection to your own husbands; that, if any obey not the word, they also may without the word be won by the conversation of the wives; while they behold your chaste conversation coupled with fear. Whose adorning let it not be that outward adorning of plaiting the hair,*

> and of wearing of gold, or of putting on of apparel; but let it be the hidden man of the heart, in that which is not corruptible, even the ornament of a meek and quiet spirit, which is in the sight of God of great price.

Do you have poor leadership? God says to check your heart, get right with Him, and let that leader see you growing in submission and trust. Don't fight your own battles. Let God fight them for you. God will always take care of us when we do what is right. Even in my abusive marital relationship, God took care of me, and He brought me out. I know the Lord could have changed my husband's life like He did mine, but my husband chose not to let that happen. He exercised his free will to walk away from the Lord, and in His right timing, the Lord took care of the situation too. We have to learn to lay down and let God. Just follow Jesus' example of submission instead of Lucifer's.

> **2 Corinthians 8:12** For if there be first a willing mind, it is accepted according to that a man hath, and not according to that he hath not.

> **2 Corinthians 9:8** And God is able to make all grace abound toward you; that ye, always having all sufficiency in all things, may abound to every good work.

Two verses you want to get down through this principle are 2 Corinthians 8:12 and 9:8. If you're willing to do whatever God asks of you, God accepts it as if you did it. He's always checking your will. Are you willing? Where we get in trouble in our relationship with the Lord is when we say, "Well, I'll do everything but _____." We need to keep a soft and pliable heart where we can say, "Yes, Lord. I'm willing." There are times that He will ask us things just to see if you're willing, like Abraham and Isaac in Genesis 22.

One time, I thought He was calling me to Texas, and I went back and forth on the idea. Finally, I stopped thinking about what I wanted and decided to follow the Lord's example and confess to God that I was willing to go. I was completely surrendering my will to His, asking just that He show me His direction. After laying down my will, He showed me that that was not where He was calling me. He directs us as we pass through the crossroads, dying to our self-will, laying it at His feet. 2 Corinthians 9:8 says that if you are willing, God is able. We don't have to be able. We just have to be willing! There is so much that comes out of our will, and all God is seeking is a willing heart and mind.

So, where do we start with all of this? How do we develop a submitted and obedient heart? Obviously, we have to start with salvation, for we had to say, "Not my will, but thine," when we accepted the Lord as our Savior. Then we start going to a local church, we get baptized, we get discipled, we begin growing and submitting to our authorities, and we start tithing. We learn to surrender to God first and give that submission to our leaders. We learn to keep a willing heart and mind toward the Lord as we see what He says in His Word and faithfully apply it to our lives. We will all face many crossroads, and every time we come to an intersection, we must make that decision to follow the right example: Christ's.

Questions to Consider:

1. What are the definitions of free will, control, submission, and obedience?

2. According to 1 Samuel 16:7, God doesn't look at the outward appearance. What does He look at instead?
   THE HEART

3. All women, whether married or single, are to submit to whom as His bride? **God first**

4. All people — men and women alike — are to submit to whom? Why?

5. Why did Satan fall? **He wanted his will**

6. The Bible says a lack of submission is as the sin of what?
   witchcraft & idolatry

7. To whom did Christ submit?
   THE FATHER

8. Obedience is the outward action of what kind of heart?
   submitted heart

9. What does it mean that Jesus learned obedience?

10. Who is ultimately in charge of our leadership? What should you do if your leadership isn't right or righteous?
    check my heart

5

Running Your Emotions Through the Word of God

Emotions are a God-given part of life, and though they can certainly be a negative influence in your life, they can also be good! They can be negative when we give them a place that they do not deserve, whether that is "stuffing" them in or letting them control our lives. However, the psalmist is very emotional in his pursuit of God's heart, and these emotions can be as wonderful as yearning for God's Word or having your heart break for the things that break God's heart.

This is the pendulum that we must learn to balance, and the right balance can only be found as we run our emotions through the boundaries of the Word of God. Swinging this pendulum from side to side is found in those who have no control over their spirits, and they are like cities with broken down walls — anything can come in and plunder them (Proverbs 25:28). In other words, an unbalanced emotional life can lead to disaster through insobriety. To prevent this, we need to learn to check our emotions against the Word of God. Remember "book, chapter, verse" — what does God say about this struggle I'm facing? It all boils down to knowing His Word and learning to apply it to every circumstance we find ourselves in throughout our relationship with Him.

This lesson is the hub of biblical counseling. Biblical counseling seeks to apply "Thus saith the LORD" into our lives, which means letting God be true and every man a liar — this includes your pastor, parents, spouse, and even yourself. You want to learn about real counseling? It's all found in these simple words: "Thus saith the LORD." When you really think about it, this is the only form of true counseling there is. God is the author of life, the answer for sin, the creator of marriage and relationships, and the shelter for every difficulty. He left us the Book of "how to's," the instruction manual for all of life, and all we have to do is learn to apply His truth! We need to be concerned with His facts, not ours, for His words contain everything pertaining to life and godliness, and through His Word we can be throughly furnished unto all good works (2 Peter 1:3; 2 Timothy 3:16-17). His Word is the water that washes us and makes us clean.

Psychology is held in high regard in our culture today, but this subject can only be true as far as it aligns with God's Word. Unfortunately, much of psychology is conjecture, and much of it goes against what God's Word says, seeking to better man through man instead of through a renewing relationship with God. God's Book lays out the truth — He says we've all got a sin problem and that the issues of our lives usually arise from this sin problem. Psychology, on the other hand, often teaches a way around sin by teaching how to rationalize, justify, or cover it up. Most of the time, it tells us that we aren't responsible for our sin. Freud, a great frontiersman in psychology, hated God and publicly declared that his goal was to set out to destroy and take the place of the pastoral priesthood. He wanted this so badly that he actually hung his psychology sign on his office door to say he was open for business on Easter Sunday! Not all of psychology is bad or unuseful, but students of God's Word must always be using the Bible as our anchor for truth.

Like I mentioned before, we're not learning how to have self-esteem, we're learning how to have God-esteem. This is not a self-help study; this is a "God-help" study. It's about putting God on that pedestal and asking what God has to say about the subject — book, chapter, and verse. This is the only true counsel in our life because it's the only counsel that can transform our very core in comparison to the opinions or counsel of others. Some elements of psychology might be helpful, but in the end they are only the best that man can come up with. Only biblical counseling will transform us!

> **Proverbs 3:5-6** *Trust in the Lord with all thine heart; and lean not unto thine own understanding. In all thy ways acknowledge him, and he shall direct thy paths.*

Psychology is not the true foundation. Unfortunately, in our Laodicean times, psychology can make some sense and often seem easier than just going to the Word of God, especially when psychology is a non-convicting substitute for the realization of sin. However, God tells us not to lean on our own understanding but to acknowledge Him.

> **Proverbs 25:28** *He that hath no rule over his own spirit is like a city that is broken down, and without walls.*

This verse is a great foundation for this subject of running our emotions through the Word of God. I just returned from a trip to Israel, and what I saw was that the city of Jerusalem is surrounded by a wall. In ancient times, all cities had walls around them as a defense against enemies. This verse is saying that you're like a city without a wall around it if you don't have a rule over your own spirit — you are defenseless. We need to build walls, but walls also have doors and windows, ways in and out. We need to learn how to allow for them and guard them, too. God's showing us we can't let our own spirit be in control. When you let your emotions be in control, you allow yourself to be vulnerable to whomever or whatever you're around. You make yourself totally defenseless.

We also need to learn how to respond and not react. Reacting is often our emotions or feelings controlling our words and actions. We have to learn to put a buffer in there, and the Word of God and its principles must become our insulation and filter. It must be our authority to give us the boundaries for our emotions and for everything else. For instance, I love dogs and I have a fence around my yard. When I went house shopping, a yard with a fence was a priority because I love my dogs. It's a boundary to keep them from getting into trouble, and my desire for a fence is based on my love and care for them. It's for their protection. It's the same for those of you who have kids — you want to protect them, so you give them boundaries. You start with a crib and then move on to a playpen, and the boundaries grow as the child grows. It's the same with our Father — our boundaries grow as we learn to follow Him. God uses them to transform us as we surrender to Him. We often think God gives us boundaries because He's mean or because He doesn't want us to "have fun", but this is not the case! He loves us, and because He loves us, He gives us boundaries. We must learn to trust Him and run our emotions through His boundaries even when, and especially if, we don't understand them.

The transformation that we are after is to be transformed into the image of the Lord Jesus Christ. Romans 8:29 clearly shows us that from the moment you were born again, God predestined you to become conformed to the image of the Lord Jesus Christ. That's His absolute perfect will for your life, and it's the same for each and every one of us Christians. He wants to transform us step by step to become more like Jesus. I know a lot of people that call themselves Christians who never pick up the Word of God, yet they claim to know God. Unfortunately, if they aren't learning and reading their Bibles, how do they know what a Christian truly is or should look like? A Christian is supposed to be Christ-like, and the only way to be transformed into the image of Christ is through the Word of God. There is no other way!

Now, that transformation doesn't come from just reading your Bible, although I do believe there is profit in reading your Bible even if you don't apply it. I also believe that there is profit in having biblical principles around your life. I've seen so many girls who didn't have a relationship with God but were protected in many ways just because they grew up in a home that was governed by some biblical principles. I'm not going to say there is no profit in just reading the Book, but I will say that you can't be transformed by only reading it.

> **Revelation 1:3** *Blessed is he that readeth, and they that hear the words of this prophecy, and keep those things which are written therein: for the time is at hand.*

There are three things that we have to do with the Bible according to Revelation 1:3. Read it. Hear it. Keep it. You have to go through all of those stages if it's going to transform you from the inside out. So, as you read God's Word, hear what God's saying, and begin asking Him to help you apply it to your personal life, you will begin growing in your relationship with the Lord! God will start to conform you into the image of His Son, and you will see your emotions fall into line.

Romans 12:1-2 says that we are transformed by the renewing of our <u>minds</u>. This all depends on establishing boundaries in the Word of God and allowing it to renew and wash our minds so that we can have the mind of Christ. And that's why I say that this lesson is the hub of counseling. Everything that you need to change your behavior and emotions is going to take you through this process, and all of the lessons in this book will go through this same process. We just saw this example in this last lesson: attitude versus action. You may have to think through this a little, but we're trying to change the attitude, not the action. The world focuses on the outside, but that's not how the transformation will happen! The transformation happens internally as we change our thoughts to line up with God's thoughts. We have the mind of Christ in the Word of God, so we can read His mind and let Him teach us how to change our thoughts to His.

$$\underset{\text{thoughts}}{1} \longrightarrow \underset{\text{attitudes}}{2} \longrightarrow \underset{\text{actions}}{3}$$

The foundation for all of this isn't rocket science. You don't need to pay a lot of money for it. It is found in our relationship with our thought life, and the Bible promises that we can rebuild those broken down walls by addressing these first. Recently, I had a lady in one of my classes tell me after we finished this lesson that she wished she'd heard it a year ago before had she paid a counselor hundreds of dollars to explain how to solve her problems. He, too, told her that the real battle was with her thoughts, but she never had success, because his approach didn't address this foundation correctly with the Word of God.

Proverbs 23:7 For as he thinketh in his heart, so is he:

Our thoughts create our attitudes, and our attitudes create our actions. Therefore, changing our actions on the outside doesn't cause a transformation that lasts. This is why a lot of people always resort back to an old habit in time, or their old bad habit turns into a new bad habit. In other words, our outward flesh doesn't have the ability to transform our internal heart. We have to learn to let God help us change our thoughts, which in turn will change our attitude of heart, and only then will we have a true, biblical, outward action that's not faked or forced by our own will.

Proverbs 4:23 Keep thy heart with all diligence; for out of it are the issues of life.

Our actions are a manifestation of the state of our heart. Remember that when we talk about our attitude, we're referring to the attitude of our heart. The guardian of our heart is our mind. Our mind must guard our heart in order to guard our attitudes. So, because our thoughts will cause the development of our attitudes, we have to keep and guard our attitudes by applying the boundaries of God's Word to our mind. We keep and guard our attitudes by the thoughts we take in and accept as reality or truth.

That's why the battle truly is in your mind. As we grow up physically, our character is established by the foundation of thoughts that we build as we experience and interpret the world around us. It is the same way with our Christian character. The thoughts that we have and apply as truth, whether biblical or unbiblical, will shape our character. They become habitual. Now, if you were raised around the Bible and took in biblical thoughts, you may have biblical attitudes of heart that result in actions that line up with the Bible, whether you meant them to or not. And those actions have become so quick and so reactive that we don't even realize how that attitude or action developed in the first place. Unfortunately, this also applies to the attitudes we have built upon unbiblical thoughts.

Let me give you an example that might help make these principles clearer. This is an uncomfortable example, but its ability to cause discomfort will help us to understand our principle. Let's talk about rape. Rape is horrible — it's hard to imagine anything worse for someone to do to another individual. And yet, what we need to understand about the action of rape is that when a man goes and rapes someone else, that sick thought didn't just start that day! Those thoughts started in his mind years and years before. Some time along the way, he didn't take in the right thoughts about women, or maybe he never had right thoughts about women to begin with. Somehow, he saw and heard wrong or unbiblical things about women and as he took in and believed these wrong thoughts, he began building his foundation and developing wrong attitudes about women, and those wrong attitudes led to his act of violence against another person. Though this is a morbid example, it does show that sin becomes a stronghold that we call a pattern or habit. All our sinful actions begin that same way — as thoughts and attitudes that develop into actions. Our internal thoughts produce an internal attitude of heart that eventually produces an external action. Understanding this process is the key to letting God teach us how to have victory over our sin.

When I started learning this, I was working as a computer programmer. We used to have the phrase "garbage in, garbage out." You put the wrong thing in a computer, and the wrong thing is going to come out. It is the same way with us! We begin our "programming" in childhood by what we're taking in and what is invested into us. If we're not around biblical principles, we are often taking in the wrong things. The only thing that is going to stand and produce right actions is biblical thoughts that have produced biblical heart attitudes. That's why it's good for kids to be around the Bible — they don't have to rebuild and change the foundation of attitudes they started out with in life. But realize, too, that no matter how bad or wrong our foundation begins, it can be changed or transformed through the Word of God and a relationship with the Lord! It may be hard, but it's always doable. All things are possible with God.

Again, this is the hub of counseling. As I was being discipled as a young Christian, I remember thinking, "I've got these really big problems! How are these simple lessons and biblical principles going to change my life?" However, through time, repetition, and obedience, God was faithful to use these simple things to transform my life. Start with these simple biblical principles. Sooner or later, as you "seek ye first the kingdom of God," all the things will fall into place! If you can replace your foundation with a biblical foundation and put this process in place by thinking the right thoughts, the right heart attitude will follow with the right biblical actions, no matter the stronghold.

Sin starts in the heart, within the thoughts. That's why Jesus said to the Pharisees that if you lust on a woman in your heart, you've already done it: you've committed adultery (Matthew 5:28). Sin starts in your heart, long before the actions of your body. So, to change the sin pattern, we have to begin by changing the thought patterns of our mind. We have to reprogram our thoughts. That's what biblical discipleship is all about, and that's what we'll be doing throughout this study. When trying to change a sinful action in our lives, we must go back to the Bible and build our thoughts on what it says! That is why it is so important to know how to find key verses in the Bible about any subject, either through cataloging them yourself or through a tool like *The Bible Promise Book*. That way our thoughts can begin guarding and redeveloping our attitude of heart, and as God changes our heart, our actions can change and become correct. This is also why scripture memorization can be so helpful in our walk with the Lord, especially when we are dealing with a stronghold.

> ***2 Corinthians 10:3-5*** *For though we walk in the flesh, we do not war after the flesh: (for the weapons of our warfare are not carnal, but mighty through God to the pulling down of strong holds;) casting down imaginations, and every*

> *high thing that exalteth itself against the knowledge of God, and bringing into captivity every thought to the obedience of Christ;*

If this chapter talks about the hub of biblical counseling, then this set of verses is the centerpiece of such. This passage is the key to changing your thoughts and transforming your attitudes, ultimately leading to a change in your actions. First, it says that we must cast down our imaginations. God gave us our imagination to be able to see what His Book says through our mind's eye. Our imagination can be — and was meant to be — used for good, but our imagination can also be used to host wrong and sinful things. Our imaginations can take us places that we would never take our body, and that's why He says we have to cast them down! We think we're getting away with it because it's only happening internally and no one else sees it, but God, who looks at the heart, sees all of it. These imaginations are where many of our problems begin, so we must learn to cast down the harmful imaginations and every high thing that exalteth itself against the knowledge of God: anything that is contrary to the Word of God. The Word of God is the mind of God, so cast down anything that goes against it!

Second, this passage tells us to bring captive every thought to the obedience of Christ. We just learned about what true obedience is and that it is an internal attitude of the heart. We can get to this place of true obedience by casting down thoughts that are contrary to the Bible and focusing on bringing every thought into captivity to the obedience of Christ by lining up our thoughts with His Book. However, our flesh — that distraction that we always carry with us — is constantly trying to keep us from seeking first the Kingdom of God, starting first with our imaginations. God gives us many warnings about not using our imaginations for evil, however, there is one place in the Scriptures where they are said to be used for good:

> *1 Chronicles 29:16-18 O LORD our God, all this store that we have prepared to build thee an house for thine holy name cometh of thine hand, and is all thine own. I know also, my God, that thou triest the heart, and hast pleasure in uprightness.*

> *As for me, in the uprightness of mine heart I have willingly offered all these things: and now have I seen with joy thy people, which are present here, to offer willingly unto thee. O LORD God of Abraham, Isaac, and of Israel, our fathers, <u>keep this for ever in the imagination of the thoughts of the heart of thy people</u>, and prepare their heart unto thee:*

King David was a man after God's heart and fulfilled all of God's will (Acts 13:22). Here in 1 Chronicles 29, at the end of his life, he's asking the nation to willingly consecrate themselves before the presence of the Lord to the service of building the temple. David's last recorded public prayer to God for Israel is that they would keep this forever in the imagination of their thoughts. As we examine his prayer, it's clear that David knew that the imagination could help the people enter into God's presence, just like music. His prayer is power-packed for them. He wants them to keep one thing forever in the imagination of the thoughts of their hearts: coming into God's presence, willingly giving of themselves to build God's temple. This was to be in their thoughts every day and every hour of every day forever. We are to do the same according to Romans 12:1-2.

We can use our imagination for good as a tool to come before God's throne in boldness just as Hebrews 4:14-16 says. <u>2 Corinthians 8:12 tells</u> us, "For if there first be a willing mind, it is accepted according to that a man hath, and not according to that he hath not." It all goes back to our will. Willingness is the key. God sees the willingness of our hearts, which is why actions without the right heart do not please God. If you're willing, God is able. David's key to fulfilling God's will was setting his imaginations on God and God's purpose, allowing his thoughts to take him before the throne so that he could willingly offer his service to the will of God.

> **2 Corinthians 7:1** *Having therefore these promises, dearly beloved, let us cleanse ourselves from all filthiness of the flesh and spirit, perfecting holiness in the fear of God.*

This passage says that having these promises gives us the ability to be cleansed! We can be clean from our sin. We think of brainwashing as having a bad connotation, yet my brain oftentimes does need to be washed — I take it places and think things that I shouldn't! The promises in this book will motivate us to turn to the Book for the washing of our brains so that our thoughts can change. The Bible is unlike any other book on the face of the earth because when we go to it and we believe it, it changes and transforms us from the inside out. It's the words of the living God, the Creator of the Universe, the One who created life and knows how to make it work as He intended. We take in His words and receive them. We keep them and obey them, and all the while they are constantly changing us. They're washing our brain. This same thing is what He's talking about in Ephesians 5:26 when He says that He may sanctify our minds with the washing of the water by the Word. This Word washes our mind, and when we allow that to happen, we create the right attitudes and make the right adjustments that result in right actions.

The remainder of this lesson contains some simple illustrations of how this principle of running our emotions through the boundaries of God's Word can work in our lives through love, overcoming fear, and forgiveness. We could look at many different struggles that we could face emotionally, but this study will focus on the one thing we need to face any difficulty: running our emotions through the Word of God. There are so many great, simple principles that can immediately help govern our lives. While before we were stumbling along in our walk and falling into pits and running into barbed wire, taking in just a little bit of light through obedience to God's Word can change everything. So, that's what our goal is to be: abandoning ourselves and our thoughts to obey the promises of God.

Before we can focus on the principles, we need to have the right heart attitude toward God's Word. "Where your treasure is, there will your heart be also" (Matthew 6:19-21). Where is your treasure? The Bible needs to be your treasure. This Book says that it is better than silver or gold. Do you believe that? Do you treat it like that? It's like a buried treasure. We would immediately search for buried treasure if we knew where it was hidden, but the Bible describes itself as even better than silver and gold. If you really thought that was true, you would be looking for it! This is where you can find the answer for any area of life.

The first principle that we need to understand is that we are to follow God's Word regardless of our emotions. A good example of letting God's Word reign over our emotions is seen in dating relationships. When it comes to physical attraction for a man, we can sometimes lose focus on what God's Word says. This can lead to what I call "missionary dating," which is when a saved woman seeks to date an unsaved man with the assumption that God will "work it out" or save him through her influence. We have a whole lesson on marriage, divorce, and remarriage later, but just realize now that falling in love with an unsaved person is not of God! There are clear guidelines against that, like 2 Corinthians 6:14-18. Dating an unsaved man goes against everything that God has planned for marriage.

Another principle is that we must prove all things. 1 Thessalonians 5:21 says: "Prove all things; hold fast that which is good." Oftentimes, when I start discipling someone and this person starts plugging into discipleship and connecting with the Lord, an old boyfriend or a job offer in another state or country will come along. All these kinds of things begin pulling them away from discipleship and learning how to grow and follow the Lord. But God says to prove it out! Just because some guy says he's a good Christian doesn't mean it's true. Don't just accept and believe him without checking it out — you don't have to immediately take someone at their word! Prove it out. Put it to the test. Just because the job sounds awesome doesn't mean it is. You don't have to just accept it.

Instead, look at the fruit that could come out of a man's life (Matthew 7:15-20). There are certain guidelines as well as a proving process. God has placed mentors in the body of Christ who can help you to seek what would please the Lord. People can mask their intentions, but everything is made clear when given enough time. Not everything that looks good is of God — remember that the devil can do miracles too, just like in Revelation 13:14. We have got to learn to wait on God. <u>Our emotions tell us to hurry, but God tells us to slow down and seek His will.</u> However, if you find yourself in the position where you have made the wrong decision, do not give up hope. God will allow even that to conform us into the image of Christ. If you made the right decision but are suffering for it, remember that God can send us difficult things in life to also conform us to the image of the Lord and learn to help others.

This leads to our next principle: God wants us to focus on the spiritual, not the physical, when we face trials. I have go-to chapters when I'm going through hard times, and 2 Corinthians 4 is one of them. It explains so much! The end of the chapter is a great place to rest when the circumstances of the world get rough.

> ***2 Corinthians 4:16-18*** *For which cause we faint not; but though our outward man perish, yet the inward man is renewed day by day. For our light affliction, which is but for a moment, worketh for us a far more exceeding and eternal weight of glory; while we look not at the things which are seen, but at the things which are not seen: for the things which are seen are temporal; but the things which are not seen are eternal.* **it's worth it**

We will go through hard times as we follow the Spirit. We're going to come up against hard things that distract us and try to get our focus off the spiritual and onto the physical. But 2 Corinthians 4 holds so many keys to get us through any trial. Remember, God says that each trial is only for a moment, but it will bring an exceeding glory in the eternal because of what we're going through in the physical. We have to learn to look beyond the temporal and physical. God loves us more than we can ever imagine, and He knows exactly what He is doing when He leads into difficult times. What is being produced through that difficulty? Instead of focusing on the physical side of it — how you are feeling or what you are facing — focus on what God is doing through it spiritually. We must walk by faith and not by sight (2 Corinthians 5:7). We can see this perfectly through the example of Moses walking by faith and seeing the eternal rather than the physical in Hebrews 11:23-29.

Whenever there is an outbreak of disease, doctors and nurses wear bodysuits to try to protect themselves from infection, but even those bodysuits aren't failsafe. But Ephesians 6:10-18 talks about the full armor of God and the shield of faith that we can use against the enemy. It's a bodysuit — a filter or armor of faith — that is failproof! We're building a boundary through the principles of the Word of God through which we are filtering everything that comes at us. We're building a wall of faith based on God's Word, for faith cometh by hearing, and hearing by the Word of God (Romans 10:17). Through His Word, God absorbs the problems of life for you.

Remember, too, that it's not your fight — it's God's, and the best part of it is that He's already won the battle (Job 41:8; Job 40:19)! Take a moment and read 2 Chronicles 20:1-30. The story is about how three huge armies are coming to fight the nation of Israel. But you can see the Lord tells them that the battle isn't theirs in verses 15 and 17. He says, "Ye shall not need to fight in this battle." All He wanted the tiny army to do was to approach the enemy while praising Him. Now, that took some big faith, and as we read on in the chapter, we see that the very moment that they obey and start singing and praising the Lord, the enemy's armies begin to fight amongst themselves. By the time Israel gets there, they are all dead, and Israel is given all of their spoil. They did nothing except walk toward the battle and praise the Lord, but God blessed them with a great victory. So, when you feel overwhelmed by the trials in your life, choose to mount up your shield of faith and understand that God has already won the battle. All He wants you to do is to praise Him and walk forward in faith.

Another great principle is learning how to be content, recognizing the difference between needs and wants. Paul says in Philippians 4:11 that we have to learn to be content. Contentment doesn't just come naturally; we have to learn it, and Paul describes how to do that in verses 12-13. He says that God takes us through hard things, and when we go through difficult circumstances, God is constantly stretching us from the deepest valleys to the highest mountaintops in order to teach us how to maintain a constant balance in our relationship with the Lord. When we learn this balance, we also learn that we can do all things through Christ. It's not about whether we're going through a great time or difficult time, it's all about maintaining a connection with Him.

> *Hebrews 13:5 Let your conversation be without covetousness; and be content with such things as ye have: for he hath said, I will never leave thee, nor forsake thee.*

This verse is the key to contentment. It says that knowing that God will never leave you nor forsake you is the answer to not being covetous. If you have God and believe that He is really God, what more could you want? Really think about that for a moment! If you have the Creator of the Universe, the King of kings and the Lord of lords, and He's with you everywhere you go, then you are overwhelmed with blessing. We can learn to be content because we have God, and He is far more than enough. The focus has to be on enjoying and developing your relationship with God. When you find yourself discontent over something, go back and remember that you have access to the Creator of the Universe! Remember to set your affection on things above (2 Timothy 2:4; Colossians 3:2; 2 Chronicles 31:21). He's always there with you and for you, and that is the means to help you learn contentment. In any trial or temptation, He always makes a way out (1 Corinthians 10:13).

Another principle is to focus on trusting God. We all are always trusting in something, and that something is often not the Word of God. We trust in our manipulation of a situation. We trust in our looks or beauty. We trust in our physical relationships. We trust in our career or our education. All these things will let us down. The key is to always trust in the Lord. Instead of leaning on other things, lean on God (John 7:24; 1 Timothy 6:5-9; Jude 16; 1 Peter 3:17; Proverbs 31:30; Psalm 118:8; Proverbs 3:5-6). If we are not focusing on God, then we are walking in instability, and instability is the result of being double-minded (James 1:8). Anytime you find instability in your life, it means that you are riding the fence or being double-minded in some way between your relationship with God and your relationship with the world. We must stay single-minded and keep God first on the pedestal of our hearts, like Matthew 6:22-34 says. Who's on your throne? Return to your First Love. Delight in Him.

You have probably heard it said: "Birds of a feather flock together." We need to be careful with whom we spend time, because these are the people we are most likely to become. The key here is to spend time with God so that we can become like Him. However, don't just spend time with Him. Delight yourself with Him! Don't come to the Word of God with dread or begrudgingly. Approach it like it's awesome, because it is (1 Corinthians 15:33; Proverbs 13:20; Proverbs 22:24-25; Psalm 37:4; Psalm 1:1-4; Joshua 1:8)! Ask yourself: Where am I finding delight? Is it in God? Is your time with Him in His Word sweet to you? Is it something you look forward to? God wants our fellowship with Him.

Jesus is your First Love, and if you have ever been in love, you know that love produces an attitude, and that attitude produces an action. This attitude of love is what Jesus wants from us, and that is why He told the church of Ephesus in Revelation 2:4 that there was something wrong: they had left their First Love. And then He told them what to do in verse 5. He told them to remember, repent, and do the first works. Remember that time when you first met Him and were walking in love with Him? Just like in marriages, if you focus on that first love, your whole attitude changes. We get so focused on ministry and the busyness of our lives that we get our eyes off the Lord. Then we'll find that, all of a sudden, we are not walking in love with Him. So, you must first remember. After you begin remembering, repent of your loss of love and do what you did when you were first in love with Him.

Another principle to remember is that conviction and guilt are not the same thing. I have often felt guilty about past sins that had already been dealt with biblically. I had already repented, yet I felt like I was still haunted with feelings of guilt. When that happens, the problem is merely that we've chosen to believe our feelings rather than the Word of God. 1 John 1:9 is the promise to claim when struggling with guilt, as it says: "If we confess our sins, [God] is faithful and just to forgive us our sins, and to cleanse us from all unrighteousness." It's a one and done deal. When sin has been dealt with, conviction of the Holy Spirit has gone away, because it has done its work in our hearts to bring us to repentance. Therefore, guilt is not a biblical or constructive emotion — guilt is from the devil! Revelation 12:10 says he is the accuser of the brethren. Guilt comes through our feelings as the enemy seeks to condemn us. Conviction is from God as He calls us to repentance and walking rightly before Him. If guilt has become a stronghold, you must erase the habit of giving heed to your emotions of shame and condemnation and build your emotions instead upon God's Word. Here is a chart that might help:

Distinguishing Between the Sources of Conviction vs. Guilt

Holy Spirit	Devil
Convicts in love	Accuses in hatred
Uses facts of Word as foundation	Uses feelings as foundation
Draws us closer to God with faith	Draws us away from God with doubt
Has hope	Uses failure
Looks back to see what God did	Looks back & sees what God didn't do
Looks forward with promise	Looks forward in fear and despair

These are some basic Bible principles that can help us as we continue to grow in our walk with the Lord. The Bible says David was a man after God's own heart, and that's what we want to be. It says that he fulfilled all of God's will, and that is the joy that we are searching for. We want to live a life that is pleasing the Lord, doing all things God's way.

We need to take the facts of the Bible and mix them with faith as we seek to apply them to our lives. As we do this, there may be an emotional response, but it will not be our foundation. The facts of the Word of God are our foundation, and they stand true regardless of how we feel. The two key things we've been learning in the last two chapters are to surrender to God's will and to have a foundation of the right thoughts. Both of these things are spiritual and internal, and they will produce the right outward expressions of inward attitudes.

Questions to Consider:

1. Are emotions always bad? Why? When are they bad?
   when they are bigger than God
2. What should we be running our emotions through? What does that look like? *The WORD - I need to know it*
3. What does "book, chapter, verse" mean in the context of emotions?
   see how it lines up w/ the truth
4. What should we have instead of "self-esteem"?
   God-esteem (putting God on the throne of my heart)
5. What does it mean to be a city without walls in Proverbs 25:28?
   boundaries
6. What does it mean to respond instead of react?
   its filtered
7. What are the three things we have to do with the Bible (Revelation 1:3)?
   read, hear & keep the commands
8. What does Proverbs 23:7 mean about our actions?
   they start in the thoughts
9. What should we do if we want the right attitudes and actions to come out of us?
   renew our minds
10. Where does sin start: with the actions or with the heart?
    our thoughts
11. What does it mean to take every thought captive in 2 Corinthians 10:3-5? How can we use our imaginations for good?

12. What is our shield when we run against obstacles (Ephesians 6)?
    the word
13. What is the difference between needs and wants, and how does this play into contentment?

14. What are the differences between conviction and guilt?
    ↳ hope   ↳ no hope

6

Grace - Life's Most Important Commodity

Grace is life's most important commodity, and learning to both receive and exercise this unspeakable gift is key to walking in victory. If you feel overwhelmed, if you have a hurt that won't heal, if you're facing an obstacle that you think is too big, or if you're hitting up against something that you think you can't find victory in, this is where you want to go. You must tap into the grace of God.

Though the world often sees no difference in "mercy" and "grace," they mean very different things. Mercy is exercised when you do not get the negative consequences that you deserve. We are shown mercy by God when we do not go to hell, though we deserve hell for our sins. Grace is found when you are given something that you don't deserve. It is God's mercy that saved us from hell, but it is His grace that gave us eternal life.

Here is an illustration that might help you to better understand these two definitions. If you were speeding down the highway at 20 mph over the speed limit and you were stopped by a police officer, mercy would be shown if he decided to not give you a ticket. That's what God gave to us at salvation. We deserved hell, but He chose not to send us there. Now, if the police officer took out his wallet and decided to hand you a one hundred dollar bill, that would be grace. You see how totally remarkable, amazing, and unbelievable that is? That's what God has done for us! Not only does the Lord spare us from the hell we deserve by His mercy, but He also gives us things like eternal life and the Holy Spirit by His grace! Grace is totally awesome, and tapping into God's grace is something we must learn how to do.

Now that we understand what grace is, it is important to speak about what grace is not. Grace is not something that is earned — when we try to do things for God, we fall from His grace. Rather, to walk in grace is to let God do all through us instead of us doing all for God. This is why grace comes as we walk by faith — it is faith that God will do the work as long as we are willing. Grace is free, undeserved favor and love of God, just like what we saw at salvation (Ephesians 2:8-9). It is unmerited by us, but merited, solely and completely, by the Lord Jesus Christ. Because we placed our faith in Christ, God's grace acted in our lives.

As we delve into this subject, let's first walk through some biblical facts on grace. Grace is mentioned 159 times in your Bible: 37 times in the Old Testament and 122 in the New Testament. The first mention is in Genesis 6:8, and it says that "Noah found grace in the eyes of the Lord." Pay attention to the words here: he *found* grace. Hebrews 4 says that we can come boldly to God's throne of grace. Grace is something that we must seek out; it must be found. This is what brought me to ask God, "Lord, how do I access Your grace?"

In 2 Peter 2:5-9, God compares Noah and Lot's relationships with grace. In fact, Noah is the first time we see grace in the Bible and Lot is the second. As we compare the two men, we learn that Noah did something with God's grace — God gave him grace, and he decided to submit himself to God. God brought all of the animals and gave Noah the blueprints to the ark, and Noah let God work through him. Lot, on the other hand, is a picture of a carnal Christian. In Genesis 19:19, Lot talks about grace as though he deserves it. Instead of a willing heart to obey and submit, Lot was stubborn and acted out of necessity. Grace is totally undeserved by us, but God is so good that He gives it to us. All we have to do is ask Him to teach us how to exercise it!

John 1:17 says, "For the law was given by Moses, but grace and truth came by Jesus Christ." If we want grace in our life, we need to realize that grace and truth come by Jesus! John 17:17 and John 1:14 tell us that God's Word is truth and the Word became flesh and dwelt among us as Jesus Christ. While the Old Testament contained the law — a series of dos and don'ts — the New Testament gives grace through Jesus Christ. Grace is not about our strictness or self-discipline. It is about our relationship with Jesus.

In this chapter, we are going to learn three things about exercising grace: it takes grace to be saved, grace to grow, and grace to serve. If we don't have grace to be saved, then we are going to end up in hell. If we don't have it to grow, we will end up being legalistic and performance-based Christians. If we don't learn how to use grace to serve God, we will be full of pride and self-righteousness. Do you see the opposites there? Learning the foundation of how to let God work through us by His grace is key to our entire walk.

> **Romans 3:21-28** *But now the righteousness of God without the law is manifested, being witnessed by the law and the prophets; even the righteousness of God which is by* **faith of Jesus Christ** *unto all and upon all them that believe: for there is no difference: for all have sinned, and come short of the glory of God;* **being justified freely by his grace** *through the redemption that is in Christ Jesus: whom God hath set forth to be a propitiation through faith in his blood, to declare his righteousness for the remission of sins that are past, through the forbearance of God; to declare, I say, at this time his righteousness: that he might be just, and the justifier of him which believeth in Jesus. Where is boasting then? It is excluded. By what law? of works? Nay: but by the law of faith. Therefore we conclude that a man is justified by faith without the deeds of the law.*

Pay close attention to a few things in these verses. In verse 22, realize that the faith of Jesus Christ lives inside of you. Once saved, we have the faith of Jesus

Christ inside of us. It also says in verse 24 that we are justified freely by His grace. It's free — we all have access. He is the just one, and He is the justifier.

Realize that salvation has to be personal. In other words, how did this free gift become yours? You had to take it! To have this free gift, we have to personally receive it. Some people think that they are saved, but they actually aren't. They believe in their minds that Jesus died for the sins of the world, but they never personally recognized that they're a sinner going to hell, that Jesus Christ died for them, and that they have to personally receive that gift. We have thoroughly explained how to be saved in previous chapters, but understand you were exercising God's grace the day you were saved. All you did was make the choice through your free will to receive this unspeakable gift of salvation. It's all about His grace, and none of it depended on our own works or righteousness (Romans 4:4-5; Ephesians 2:8-9)!

We were saved by grace, and grace is also what we need to grow. Physical growth is a process, and it is the same when we grow in God's grace. It's not just going to happen overnight because it takes grace to overcome obstacles in life as we grow and become conformed to the image of Jesus Christ. Otherwise, we're going to live by a set of rules and become legalistic in thinking those rules define our relationship with the Lord. Or we're going to become performance-driven in thinking we can earn our relationship or growth process with the Lord. We must remember that we are building a relationship with God through the new creature, the new man. It's not religion, it's relationship, and that means that our relationship with God is based on who He has made us to be in Christ, not on our works. It isn't about striving hard — grace is found in submitting to God and allowing Him to work through us as we walk by faith. Galatians 2:20 is a great memory verse as we learn to exercise the Spirit, not the flesh.

> ***Galatians 2:20*** *I am crucified with Christ: nevertheless I live; yet not I, but Christ liveth in me: and the life which I now live in the flesh I live by the faith of the Son of God, who loved me, and gave himself for me.*

This verse talks about the faith of Jesus Christ that lives inside of us, and when we hit up against something hard, it is about dying to self and flesh and letting God — who lives inside you — do it through you. You live by the faith of the Son of God which is inside you once you're saved. Dying to self and living for Christ sounds easy, but in actuality it's one of the hardest things in the world to do. For some reason, it seems easy to accept God's grace at salvation, acknowledging that He did all for us. Dying to self and living for Him requires that same grace, but it is harder for us to accept. All of a sudden we think that we need to help God out, and our flesh starts getting involved.

When we look at the Old Testament saints, we see them hearing from God and believing God, but then trying to help God out. Look at Abram. He believed and trusted God, but eventually he tried to help God out and ended up having Ishmael. Our flesh is subtle, and we often don't even realize that we are trying to help God out in our actions. It took Abraham 25 years to learn to quit trying and to let God do his work. Moses took 40, Joseph took 17, and the disciples took three and a half. There are so many examples throughout the Word of God that show that growing is a process of learning to let go and let God and exercising grace instead of works. Learning to rest in Christ is a part of that process.

How do we rest in the Lord? How do we die to self? If you look at the Old Testament individuals, they had to do it the wrong way first. They had to start by trying to do it in the flesh and then realize what they were doing and repent! I notice the same thing in my own life — I try to help the Lord out even though I know that my flesh can't do it. I hear from God. I believe God. I know He can do it. But somehow my flesh gets in there and tries to help Him out.

It is only logical that the next thing that happens to us when we start doing things in the will of the flesh is that we get burned out. Being burned out is one of the best ways to tell if you are operating in the flesh. Letting God do all is different, because when we walk in the Spirit and rest in the Lord, our burden is light. When we do it in the flesh, we become performance-based and we start living by rules and carrying His burden instead of Him carrying it through us. It is a heavy burden to bear.

Matthew 16:24 says to deny self, pick up our cross, and follow Christ, and this is what we have to do as we're growing in grace. We are going to look at a step-by-step process of how to die to self, and then some examples of how to exercise Jesus' promise of "I will give you rest." This promise of being able to rest is given to all of us.

Even when we are in busy seasons, we can be resting in Christ. If we aren't resting, we will get burned out and start complaining. Being overwhelmed and complaining are some of the first signs of doing it in the flesh and not in the Spirit. Anytime I start noticing those signs, I immediately go back to this exercise to get back to the feet of Jesus and under His yoke, which He says is easy.

> *Hebrews 4:9-11* *There remaineth therefore a rest to the people of God. For he that is entered into his rest, he also hath ceased from his own works, as God did from his. Let us labour therefore to enter into that rest, lest any man fall after the same example of unbelief.*

Doctrinally, these verses are talking about the millennial reign of Christ, but inspirationally, we can learn how to find rest in our walk with Christ. If we can enter into His rest, we've ceased from our own works as God did. On the seventh day, God rested, and we can enter into that rest with Him. Let's carefully examine and break down these verses. In verse 11, it says we labor to rest. This sounds like a contradiction, but it isn't. It is natural for us to labor in the flesh and do things ourselves, so we have to labor to stop our flesh getting its own way. Instead, we need to let God work through us. This is the only way to rest in Him. We need to continue the struggle that Paul talks about in Romans 7 of dying to self over and over so that the new man can walk as the Holy Spirit leads.

There are clear ways we can tell when we are starting to live by rules. So what do we do at those times? Here is what Paul said about this very topic: "I die daily." There are two other passages that I like to focus on whenever I find that I am walking in the power of my own flesh, instead of exercising grace and letting God work through me.

> *Matthew 16:24-27* Then said Jesus unto his disciples, If any man will come after me, let him deny himself, and take up his cross, and follow me. For whosoever will save his life shall lose it: and whosoever will lose his life for my sake shall find it. For what is a man profited, if he shall gain the whole world, and lose his own soul? or what shall a man give in exchange for his soul? For the Son of man shall come in the glory of his Father with his angels; and then he shall reward every man according to his works.

> *Matthew 11:28-30* Come unto me, all ye that labour and are heavy laden, and I will give you rest. Take my yoke upon you, and learn of me; for I am meek and lowly in heart: and ye shall find rest unto your souls. For my yoke is easy, and my burden is light.

Paul talks about this grace in 1 Corinthians 15:10. He says that he labored more abundantly, but it wasn't really him who was at work — it was God's grace! This is exactly what we need to do. We need to come to the end of self and remember that Jesus said, "It is finished!" He doesn't need our help. Instead, He wants to use our bodies as a living sacrifice.

> *1 Corinthians 15:10* But by the grace of God I am what I am: and his grace which was bestowed upon me was not in vain; but I laboured more abundantly than they all: yet not I, but the grace of God which was with me.

I used to be a computer programmer, and I worked as a contractor for Marion Labs, which was one of the greatest places in Kansas City to work thirty years ago. They told me that they liked my work and said that in a few months when they were looking to hire again and had an opening, they would hire me. I was so excited! I loved my job. We had a Bible study at Marion. My job was close to church, it was close to my home, and I could see God really using me there, so I just assumed that He would give me a permanent job. However, just as they were ready to hire me, my contracting company was bought out by another company, and the new company decided that they were not going to let their programmers be hired out. It seemed that I wasn't going to get the job that I wanted.

I was on my knees! I just knew that God was going to give me that job — I just felt that God was in this and wanted me to work there! I prayed for it for weeks, but the job never came. Finally, I got real with the Lord and surrendered. I told God that it was okay if He didn't want to give me the job, but I also asked to have the opportunity to witness to whomever would get the job instead of me.

I didn't get the job, and it was a devastating experience for me at the time. However, I soon met the girl who was given the job. Marion was big, and this lady originally sat in another part of the building. But now our office cubes were right next to each other; we started getting lunch together and slowly became friends, and she started coming to our small group Bible study at work. She lived way up north and felt it was too far to come to our church, but she asked to be discipled. I got permission to take her through my church's discipleship lessons; we went through all of them and she was very faithful. She got saved (on lesson two!), then her husband got saved, and then her kids! Eventually, they became missionaries to Africa!

After spending several years in Africa, they came home and her husband became an associate pastor at a sister church. She is one of the greatest blessings of my life. I love telling that story because it shows us that we never know what God is going to do. He wanted her to have that job, He wanted us to become friends, and He wanted to use me in her life. And because of all of this, He didn't care about me getting the job at Marion — His plan was way more important than mine. I could have gotten mad and walked away from

Him when I didn't get that job, but the job itself did not matter, and Marion Labs doesn't even exist today. This is why it is so important to surrender our will to God's will. He knows what's best. I could have tried to force that job situation, but I chose instead to abandon my will to the Lord's. Through the biblical principles we just went through about dying to self as we labor to rest, God was able to do His work through me! My acceptance of God's will brought eternal joy into my life. This is what I call "acceptance with joy," a key phrase we will talk about more in the coming chapters.

Helen Keller once said, "When one door of happiness closes, another opens, but often we look so long at the closed door that we do not see the one that has been opened for us." Or, as I like to say, "When God closes one door, He often opens another; but we so often focus on the closed door that we miss the one He's opening." This is so true! Sometimes He is going to say no to us, and we are not going to understand why, but that's when we have to trust Him, let go, and die to self. We must learn to give up on our flesh but not give up on God. It sounds easy and logical, but it's often hard to do. Remember, when God says no, there's a reason: He's often trying to protect you or wants to bless you another way.

Paul was probably the greatest Christian that ever lived, but we see that God also denied his requests. We see in 2 Corinthians 12:6-10 how he responded to God telling him no.

> ***2 Corinthians 12:6-10*** *For though I would desire to glory, I shall not be a fool; for I will say the truth: but now I forbear, lest any man should think of me above that which he seeth me to be, or that he heareth of me. And lest I should be exalted above measure through the abundance of the revelations, there was given to me a thorn in the flesh, the messenger of Satan to buffet me, lest I should be exalted above measure. For this thing I besought the Lord thrice, that it might depart from me. And he said unto me, My grace is sufficient for thee: for my strength is made perfect in weakness. Most gladly therefore will I rather glory in my infirmities, that the power of Christ may*

> *rest upon me. Therefore I take pleasure in infirmities, in reproaches, in necessities, in persecutions, in distresses for Christ's sake: for when I am weak, then am I strong.*

Paul wasn't healed; whatever was wrong wasn't taken away. God says sometimes all we have to lean on is His grace, and He doesn't change the circumstance or problem. So, here is what we have to remember: God's grace is sufficient. Trusting in God's grace results in humility, whereas trusting in self results in pride. Whatever we're facing, and with anything that may seem impossible, grace is always the answer.

Now, it also takes God's grace to serve the Lord and be used by Him. Otherwise, if we are doing it ourselves, we develop pride and self-righteousness. Learning to serve through God's grace and growing in God's grace often envelop and overlap with each other. We learn them at the same time through some of the same biblical principles.

As Christians, we often face difficulties when we understand that God has saved us unto good works, but we don't understand how to approach these works correctly. Paul says in 1 Corinthians 8:1-3 that the key to everything is our love for God. As we invest in our relationship with Him, we will desire to serve Him. There is a big difference between having to serve Him because He commanded it and wanting to serve Him because we love Him. We usually start off focused on our love for Him, and then our expectations aren't met or something goes wrong, and all of a sudden our desire to serve Him turns into a feeling of obligation. We must find a way to get back to desiring to serve Him by rekindling our love for Him. A wife and a housemaid often do the same work in the house, but only one receives a paycheck. Hopefully the wife is operating out of an abundance of love. Similarly, because of our love for God, we should naturally want to get involved with Him. We love Him and want to be with Him, and as we are with Him and resting in Him, His grace brings about the right works in our life. Letting God work through us as we serve Him must be based off of our love for Him.

Mary and Martha in Luke 10 is another great illustration of this. Martha had put together a huge meal. She had an agenda and was busy fulfilling it. Then Jesus walked in, and right away He wanted to share a word with everyone. Mary got right at His feet to listen and put aside her tasks to listen to what Jesus had to say. Martha, on the other hand, was still thinking about the meal and plans to feed everyone. She started out with the right heart because she wanted to serve the Lord, but then she started focusing more on the service to the Lord than on the person of the Lord. This led to complaining as she began focusing on what her sister was doing and expecting her to help with the plans. She thought her plans of serving were more important than what Jesus had to say — her plans had taken center stage instead of Jesus.

Jesus' words to Martha are so important. He said, "Martha, Martha, thou art careful and troubled about many things: but one thing is needful: and Mary hath chosen that good part, which shall not be taken away from her" (Luke 10:41-42). He rebuked Martha, stopping her in her tracks, because she was serving Him out of her flesh. Just like Martha, we need to watch and examine ourselves to make sure that we are letting the love of the Lord do His service through us and that we are following His agenda and not ours. I've learned to watch myself, and the minute I start complaining or caring about what my sister or brother in Christ is doing, I've learned that my relationship with the Lord might be getting out of whack. In that moment I know that I am operating from the flesh, just like Martha did. I've got to listen to what Jesus said to her and take a time-out, repent, and get back to following the Spirit, putting Jesus on the throne and sitting at His feet.

We know that grace is accessed by our faith and that we must rest from our work by letting that same faith rule in our lives. This can be seen in Hebrews 4 and 11. When I am striving in my flesh, there is no faith, grace, or rest. Instead, I need to surrender myself to Him completely in faith and allow Him to use me through the powerful working of His grace. That is the only way to rest like Mary did. Trusting in God's grace results in flexibility and humility in our lives and keeps us from getting mixed up in performance-based Christianity.

> **Proverbs 13:10** *Only by pride cometh contention: but with the well advised is wisdom.*

We must also keep in mind that pride is the number one killer of relationships. Corrie ten Boom was a great woman of God, and if you don't know about her, you need to read some of her books (I highly recommend *The Hiding Place* and *Tramp for the Lord*). One phrase that Corrie always used when people would ask her how she stayed so humble, despite how mightily God had used her, was this: "Be like the donkey!" She was talking about the donkey upon which Jesus rode in the triumphant entry into Jerusalem. All the people were singing and praising, laying palm fronds on the road, and proclaiming His greatness. Well, do you think for one single second that the donkey ever thought that all the rejoicing and celebrating had anything to do with him? Of course not! He knew it was all about the One who was riding on his back. It was all for Jesus! When the Lord happens to use us, we, too, need to remember that we are just the donkey. The glory is all to and for Him — it has nothing to do with us! When we are used of God, we just are along for the ride, a co-laborer with Him. Our labor has to do with letting Him do the work through us, and we just have to die to self and surrender ourselves to Him in faith. Remember, be like the donkey!

> **Romans 3:26** *To declare, I say, at this time his righteousness: that he might be just, and the justifier of him which believeth in Jesus. To declare, I say, at this time his righteousness: that he might be just, and the justifier of him which believeth in Jesus.*

> **Romans 4:5** *But to him that worketh not, but believeth on him that justifieth the ungodly, his faith is counted for righteousness.*

> **Romans 4:17-20** *(As it is written, I have made thee a father of many nations,) before him whom he believed, even God, who quickeneth the dead, and calleth those things which be not as though they were. Who against hope believed in hope, that he might become the father of many nations, according to that which*

was spoken, So shall thy seed be. And being not weak in faith, he considered not his own body now dead, when he was about an hundred years old, neither yet the deadness of Sarah's womb: he staggered not at the promise of God through unbelief; but was strong in faith, giving glory to God;

As New Testament believers, the emphasis is on who we are in Christ, not on us or our works. It's His works. As we learn to let Him do it instead of ourselves, we just have to learn how to obtain this glorious grace. The first step in this pursuit is to humble yourself.

> ***1 Peter 5:5*** *Likewise, ye younger, submit yourselves unto the elder. Yea, all of you be subject one to another, and be clothed with humility: for God resisteth the proud, and giveth grace to the humble.*

First, we are to surrender and submit. Step two is to ask God for His help and His grace by coming to His throne for the help that we need.

> ***Hebrews 4:14-16*** *Seeing then that we have a great high priest, that is passed into the heavens, Jesus the Son of God, let us hold fast our profession. For we have not an high priest which cannot be touched with the feeling of our infirmities; but was in all points tempted like as we are, yet without sin. Let us therefore come boldly unto the throne of grace, that we may obtain mercy, and find grace to help in time of need.*

Just ask God. The Bible says that ye have not because ye ask not (James 4:2). It is so easy to try to fix things on our own, but when we get overwhelmed, we need to go to the Lord! Tell Him you surrender and ask Him to help. After all, He's the only One who can truly help. Verse 15 in Hebrews 4 has a double negative, and a double negative equals a positive: we have a high priest that can be touched by our feelings. When no one else wants to hear about our feelings, Jesus says He does! Our infirmities are our weaknesses, and this passage says that Jesus can be touched by what we're going through. What an encouragement for us to reach out to Him when we need help! When you think no one else cares and you're having a pity party, go to Jesus! We need to get used to going to the Lord, spending time with Him, and pouring out our heart to Him. The passage says He was in all points tempted as we are but was still without sin. He has been there and He can help us. It says to come boldly to the throne of grace to obtain mercy and find grace to help in our time of need. What is stopping you from grabbing hold of this powerful promise?

> **Matthew 6:34** *Take therefore no thought for the morrow: for the morrow shall take thought for the things of itself. Sufficient unto the day is the evil thereof.*

The funny thing about this grace is that it is time-sensitive. When you're asking for grace, realize that He's only going to give you grace for today, not grace for tomorrow or for next year. He promises us grace for today. This doesn't mean that when we ask for grace tomorrow that He won't give it. What it means is that we need to be focused on how God can give grace for the things immediately before us and walk in faith for everything else.

The greatest promise that is given to us is that of salvation through faith in Jesus Christ, but after we claim that promise, this next promise is one of the greatest promises for those of us who are believers. This promise is like a blank check!

> **2 Corinthians 9:6-8** *But this I say, He which soweth sparingly shall reap also sparingly; and he which soweth bountifully shall reap also bountifully. Every man according as he purposeth in his heart, so let him give; not grudgingly, or of necessity: for God loveth a cheerful giver. And God is able to make all grace abound toward you; that ye, always having all sufficiency in all things, may abound to every good work:*

Verse 8 is the key verse, but it is dependent on what is said in verses 6-7. The promise in verse 8 is tied to your attitude of giving, and giving isn't just about money. Giving is about your life and your heart. It's your time, talent, and treasure. Your attitude about giving is directly tied to what God promises us in verse 8. Here's what He says we have access to through this promise: "God is able to make all grace abound toward you; that ye, always having all sufficiency in all things, may abound to every good work." What a positive and overflowing grace! So, if God has called you to that work you're doing, this is a promise that you need to cling to in faith. Anytime you get overwhelmed, this is where you need to go. You need to bow before the Lord, go to the throne of grace, ask for help in your time of need, and pray this verse. Try it out — it works!

The Bible has a lot to say about grace, and it is the gas that both starts the engine and keeps the car moving. Grace isn't deserved; it is accessed by faith and bestowed upon us by God that we might both be saved and grow. Grace does not end at salvation, and it's needful to keep us operating in the Spirit and not the flesh, lest we labor hard in our flesh and get burned out instead of laboring to put away the flesh and surrender to God's Word through us. Grace is very generously given to the believer, but it must first be asked for in faith! So ask yourself: Are you allowing grace to cover your life and your ministry, or are you self-sufficient and burned out? Come to the throne of grace and abound in every good work. Cling to grace.

Questions to Consider:

1. What is the definition of grace? How does it differ from mercy?

2. Do you have a hard time receiving God's grace or giving grace to others?

3. Do you ever struggle with trying to do things on your own first before surrendering to Him to allow Him to do it?

4. Do you often live by a set of rules, or do you do the exact opposite by allowing sin in your life?

5. What does it mean to "die to self"? Do you die to yourself daily?

6. Do you have any circumstances in your life right now that you have prayed over but still haven't seen deliverance in? Why do you think God hasn't "solved" the problem yet?

7. What were the differences between Mary and Martha's approaches to Jesus? Which one do you tend to be?

8. How is grace accessed?

9. What did Corrie ten Boom mean when she said to "be like the donkey"?

10. What does it mean that we are only offered grace for today?

7

Dealing with Anger
(or Any Emotion that Becomes Sin)

We will begin this chapter by learning some practical steps in dealing with sin. Learning to deal with our sin nature is one of the most important hurdles we all must learn as we grow in our relationship with the Lord. When we first get saved, we often think we will never sin again! We just met Jesus, and we are head over heels in love. This First Love focus and beautiful God-consciousness often makes us completely forget about the old nature that we still carry in our flesh. However, the old man is still there. He didn't leave. Just pinch yourself and you will see that he is alive and well. This old man is as sinful as he was before you were saved, and it would be so easy for us to walk in that same old sin nature.

Before we talk about anger, let's first go over some important principles about dealing with sin. Having a good foundation to deal with our sin will also help us with our anger issues. Note, too, that these simple biblical principles will work for any emotion that becomes sin. Yes, emotions can be good, and they are God-given. However, they can easily turn into sin when they are out of control, when they are controlling us, or when we stuff them inside or ignore them. Remember when we went over Proverbs 25:28 in Chapter 5? We talked about how when our own spirit is out of control, we become defenseless. Our walls are broken down. We should also note here that when we become defenseless, we can easily cross the boundary lines of sin. Any emotion that carries us off so that we are not in control over our own spirit is an emotion that will allow us to wander into sin.

> *1 John 1:7* But if we walk in the light, as he is in the light, we have fellowship one with another, and the blood of Jesus Christ his Son cleanseth us from all sin.

The first thing we need to discuss is learning to be honest with God about how we are walking. We need to memorize 1 John 1:7 and remember that we can only have fellowship with Him and with one another if we are walking in the light and not in sin. This verse is a foundational verse for so many difficulties and attacks.

What happened after Adam and Eve sinned in the garden? What was the first thing they did when they heard God walking in the garden in the cool of the day? They hid! Think about that. Before, they peacefully walked with God in the garden. They enjoyed awesome fellowship with the living God. But after they sinned, all they were left with was fear. They had never experienced fear before this, but suddenly they were afraid of God. That fear drove them to hide from the light in the darkness. If you watch any child, you'll see that when they do wrong things, they hide their guilt as best as they know how. They may try to cover it up, but you can usually tell. The younger they are, the more obvious they are with what just happened. Soon they gradually learn how to hide their sin. We were all there at one point in our lives — doing something wrong for the first time, fearing authority, and trying to hide. Then, over time, we gradually learn how to hide it, and we eventually are able to hide it so well that we often deceive even ourselves. We learn to mask our own heart, and it becomes so automatic and habitual that we don't even realize that we're hiding.

This is why it is so important to start meeting with the Lord in prayer. We must learn to take the masks off with Him and be totally honest. The more we spend time telling Him everything and seeing Him come through for us, the more we learn to take the masks off. You might think that you're doing this already, but a lot of times our pattern to hide has been so ingrained in our habits that hiding has become a stronghold.

We have to learn to come out into the light and stop hiding. It sounds easy, but depending on how late in life you were born again and the level of fear you absorbed, this could be very difficult. When I first started doing the Prayer Exercise (Chapter 3), I always did it at night. I'm sure that I chose this time because I was afraid and felt comforted in meeting with the Lord in darkness and quietness. I was afraid of being totally honest — afraid to come out of the darkness and go to the light. I think that because I was so used to covering up my sin, I was terrified of everything. It was difficult to let go of this fear. Slowly, the Lord began opening my eyes to the fact that walking in the light means being totally honest with Him. I had to bring everything — every thought — out into the open.

Step one in dealing with any sin is to bring it out into the open. He tells us in 1 John 1:7 that if we just learn to bring it out into the open, then the Lord can fix it, "and the blood of Jesus Christ His Son cleanseth us from all sin." That's totally amazing. We don't have to clean ourselves up because He does it! All we have to do is to start learning to acknowledge our sins and confess them to Him by being honest with God. 1 John 1:7 also says we have fellowship with one another once we start walking in the light — He not only takes care of our sin, He also takes care of all our relationships! Relational problems are another thing that we sometimes hide. When we're upset or mad, we often don't tell anybody; we stuff it deep inside. Instead, we need to start telling the Lord. Learn to consistently take things to the Lord in prayer. Another great set of verses that goes along with this is John 3:19-21:

> ***John 3:19-21*** *And this is the condemnation, that light is come into the world, and men loved darkness rather than light, because their deeds were evil. For every one that doeth evil hateth the light, neither cometh to the light, lest his*

> *deeds should be reproved. But he that doeth truth cometh to the light, that his deeds may be made manifest, that they are wrought in God.*

This passage says that there are only two kinds of people in the world: those that go to the light and those that go to the darkness. Our flesh — our human nature — always initially runs to the darkness, just like Adam and Eve did. Fortunately, God has given us all a free will, and we can choose to turn to the light instead! John 1 says Jesus is the light that lighteth every man that comes into the world (John 1:9). This is why with anger, just as with any other sin, we need to choose to go to the light. We need to choose to be honest with God.

The next step is a little bit deeper because the next thing we must do in dealing with our sin is to take responsibility for it. What did Adam and Eve do after they sinned? First they hid, then they blamed someone or something else for their sin. Remember, you can't change what you don't acknowledge. We have to acknowledge our sin in order to change it. We all have a sin nature, and we are all going to sin. In order to get out of the mess we get ourselves into, we must take responsibility. Yes, life is unfair. Yes, you might have been dealt a rough deck, and in your flesh or old man you may have excuses for your sin that seem reasonable. But the day you were born again everything changed because from that moment on you became a new creature in Christ Jesus and have the power and faith of the Lord Jesus Christ living inside of you! He can change everything, so that means that there are no more excuses. This step is exactly why psychology doesn't work when it comes to dealing with our sin. Why? Because psychology and philosophy often place the blame on something or someone else, using an external locus of blame instead of an internal one. We all have a free will, and we all use that free will to sin. The only way to overcome that sin nature is to choose Jesus, acknowledge our sin, and take responsibility for it. We must keep learning to say, "I did it. I'm wrong. I surrender."

The last step is repentance, and that means a 180 degree turn in how we think and act. Before we were saved, we were walking towards the darkness. Then God called us to the light and we turned around from the way we were going and went the other way. Repentance means being honest and open with God and revealing our sins to the light so that we can leave behind the darkness. The closer we get to the glorious light, the more we see how rotten our flesh really is and the more we want to turn away from walking in the darkness.

> *2 Corinthians 7:8-10* *For though I made you sorry with a letter, I do not repent, though I did repent: for I perceive that the same epistle hath made you sorry, though it were but for a season. Now I rejoice, not that ye were made sorry, but that ye sorrowed to repentance: for ye were made sorry after a godly manner, that ye might receive damage by us in nothing. For godly sorrow worketh repentance to salvation not to be repented of: but the sorrow of the world worketh death.*

These verses give us more information on what it looks like to get to a place of repentance. It says there are two sorrows we can experience — godly sorrow and worldly sorrow — but only one of them leads us to repentance. Godly sorrow is when you know what God says about something and it convicts you in your heart, which in turn leads to repentance. The best examples of the two sorrows I can think to give you would be the examples of Peter and Judas Iscariot. In Mark 14:72, after the cock crowed twice, Peter went out and wept bitterly because he had denied the Lord three times. He was sorry in his heart because he didn't live up to God's words. Peter wanted to change his will to line up with God's. That's godly sorrow.

Worldly sorrow, however, is a completely different thing. In Matthew 27:3, Judas would be a picture of worldly sorrow. He was only sorry he got caught, but he wasn't sorry to God. He was sorry what he did didn't work. The verse says that he repented to himself, but he didn't repent to God. He was only sorry that he didn't do it a different way so that the result would turn out the way he wanted. That's worldly sorrow. We need to examine ourselves to always make sure that we're experiencing godly sorrow, not worldly sorrow, because godly sorrow is what will lead us to repentance, and repentance to God will allow Him to change us from the inside out. In the end, what we want is an inward change, not an outward redirection.

> ***Ephesians 4:26-27*** *Be ye angry, and sin not: let not the sun go down upon your wrath: neither give place to the devil.*

Now that we have laid a biblical foundation on dealing with sin, we can finally talk about anger. There isn't a lot more to add to this foundation, but God gives us some very important information about how to run our anger through the words of the living God. Realize first that anger is an emotion God gave us and that being angry, in and of itself, isn't sinful. Even God was angry (Psalm 7:11) and Jesus got angry (Mark 3:5). The problem is when we allow our anger to lead us into sin. God warns us about this in Ephesians 4.

For some reason, growing up, I thought getting angry or mad was related to "being a bad girl." I didn't know that anger could be okay, so I would always deny it and stuff it down inside, pretending it wasn't there. Then I would go out drinking and all the things that were stuffed down inside would often explode after a few drinks. Ladies, if it gets inside, it is going to come out one way or the other, either through physical ailment or a verbal explosion (Luke 6:45; Proverbs 4:23). It festers in there and eventually works its way out. Many of our physical problems often come from not dealing with our emotions biblically. Remember that we are a trichotomy and our spirit, soul, and body all work together and can actually ripple into each other. Much of what puts us in the hospital can be simply overcome by dealing with our sin correctly. Our emotions become sin when we let them get out of control so that they are controlling us, or when we stuff them inside and deny their existence.

The key to not sinning in your anger is found in not letting your anger become wrath. If we do not deal with our sin right away it will fester, and the molehill will become a mountain. Over time it grows so that in a moment, it becomes wrath. These verses in Ephesians 4 say that we must deal with our anger before the sun goes down — this means immediately! Go to your brother or sister as soon as possible and deal with it. Or, if possible, put it under the blood of Jesus and forbear. Forbearing means "covering over with silence." Forgive and forget (Proverbs 17:9). But always be sure that when you're forbearing, you're really forgiving and not just keeping a scorecard of offenses.

These verses in Ephesians 4 go on to say that we should not give place to the devil (Ephesians 4:27). There are only two times in the New Testament that Paul warns us about the tricks that the devil plays on us, and this is one of those places. Here, he says to deal with anger immediately so that the devil does not have a place at our table. If we don't deal with it diligently, the anger will become wrath, and Satan can use it. You're opening the door wide open for him to come in and fellowship with you, and that will cut off your fellowship with the Lord.

> **Hebrews 12:15** *Looking diligently lest any man fail of the grace of God; lest any root of bitterness springing up trouble you, and thereby many be defiled;*

Once anger becomes wrath and starts to control you, it easily turns into bitterness. Hebrews 12:15 says it can take root and destroy many! When anger gets out of control, that's when it becomes sin, and that's when it hurts those around you. When you get angry, deal with it right away — don't let it take root. The other way anger becomes sin is when we deny that we are angry. When we stuff it inside, we are lying to ourselves and ultimately to God. Just like David in Psalm 51, we're all going to sin because we've still got the flesh, but when we do sin, we need to approach the Lord in full surrender.

When I first got saved, I had such a bad habit of stuffing my anger that it took a long time for me to recognize this about myself. But the more I grew in my relationship with the Lord, and the more I did the Prayer Exercise and learned to take all the masks off of my heart, the more I learned how to recognize my anger and deal with it biblically. Sometimes, a biblical mentor or discipler can help with this process and help you learn to be accountable.

Achan in Joshua 7 is another great example of the wrong way to deal with emotions. He stole a lot of things he was not supposed to have and buried them in his tent. That is exactly what we do — we sometimes bury our anger and pretend it's not there. And that's dangerous, because just like with Achan, there are consequences for our sins. Achan's initial sin was in stealing, but burying those objects only intensified the matter. Similarly, hiding or suppressing our feelings will only make matters worse for us and for those around us. When God sees us, He can easily see the things that we are hiding, and we suffer greatly from it. Additionally, our sin not only hurts us, it hurts those closest to us, too. Achan's whole family was affected by his disobedience. We must learn to deal with things and not bury them, or else we are no better than Achan, and his demise will be our demise, too.

Even though these verses in Ephesians are short, they are power-packed. Deal with anger immediately, and learn to respond, not react. Often, if we don't stuff our anger, we jump to conclusions instead. To deal with it biblically, we must first acknowledge our anger, then step back for a moment and ask the Lord to help us see it the right way. This means removing ourselves from the situation for a moment and allowing each other the benefit of the doubt. Sometimes anger can be initiated by a totally wrong perception or misunderstanding. The bottom line in dealing with anger is that we must confront the problem and focus on the solution. Don't focus on the anger, and don't focus on the person. Instead, take a step back to focus on a solution. What was the trigger here? Was it real and not just perceived? How can it be solved? Sometimes this is hard, and it often means that we need to ask our offending brother or sister questions to clarify the situation! In the end, sometimes we just need to forbear and put it under the blood. But God also says that working out our anger is what we need to do. Don't run and hide, and don't pretend it's not there. Deal with it, and ask God to help you! Take a moment to leave the situation, pray for God's help, and then work it out in a way that is pleasing to God and promotes unity.

When I was learning these principles, it was so hard that I would literally shake. I had been stuffing emotions for so long that it had become such an ingrained habit. Then when I began trying to deal with my anger immediately instead of stuffing it, I was somewhat fearful and would become shaky. Regardless of my fear, I decided to trust the Lord and figure out a way to let Him work this out in me. Instead of trying to hide my shakiness, I would just tell people that I was trying to learn to deal with anger and ask them to be patient with me. And they were!

However you have become accustomed to dealing with your anger —whether by denying it, stuffing it, or just exploding — you need to start putting it under the blood of Christ instead. Walk in the light, confess your sin, and repent. Rightly deal with it by focusing on the problem and the solution, not the other person. Go in a spirit of meekness and ask for help.

Sometimes there are things that trigger a past memory of some anger that you have not dealt with rightly, and when that trigger is hit, you will explode all over a person when you're actually angry with someone or something else. This has been the case in my own life and for many ladies I've worked with, and the key to defusing triggers is to get to the root of the issue. Ask the Lord to help you clearly see the true source of the anger or hurt. Once this is identified, deal with that root cause through the biblical steps outlined in this chapter. Since triggers can be activated unexpectedly, it is important to stay consciously aware of your anger triggers and choose to respond according to God's Word instead of reacting. This is a process, and if this is a deep-rooted problem that you struggle with often, seek a mentor to hold you accountable and guide you in applying these principles.

Also, sometimes anger turned inward can become depression, and it can even turn out that the person you are really angry with is God. Don't continue hiding it from Him — He already knows! Talk to Him about it and keep walking in the light as you learn and apply these biblical principles. He will give you the victory!

Processing Anger Like Jesus

Anger should only be expressed inwardly to motivate us to work through conflict individually by surrendering the issue and moving forward in faith.

And it should only be expressed outwardly to confront others biblically with the goal of reconciling relationships. Anger drove Jesus to grief, then to heal a man in need (Mark 3:5). To process anger like Jesus did, we should acknowledge it, grieve the injustice, then consider forbearing and reconciling by surrendering to the Lord. If we are not able to forbear, our anger should drive us to rectify, resolve, and reconcile conflict by bringing it to our brethren.

> **Mark 3:5** And when he had looked round about on them with anger, being grieved for the hardness of their hearts, he saith unto the man, Stretch forth thine hand. And he stretched it out: and his hand was restored whole as the other.

Another example of Jesus expressing anger biblically can be found in John:

> **John 2:13-16** And the Jews' passover was at hand, and Jesus went up to Jerusalem, And found in the temple those that sold oxen and sheep and doves, and the changers of money sitting: And when he had made a scourge of small cords, he drove them all out of the temple, and the sheep, and the oxen; and poured out the changers' money, and overthrew the tables; And said unto them that sold doves, Take these things hence; make not my Father's house an house of merchandise.

We see first of all that Jesus was responding, not reacting — he saw the people's sin in polluting the temple, and he then took the time to think about it and craft a scourge out of cords to methodically drive them out.

> **Hebrews 4:15** For we have not an high priest which cannot be touched with the feeling of our infirmities; but was in all points tempted like as we are, yet without sin.

Hebrews also tells us that Jesus was tempted but still without sin. In this situation, He may have been tempted to react sinfully out of outrage, but He was able to choose instead a biblical, sinless response. This can also be a comfort to us — Jesus understands what we're going through! He experienced anger and temptation just as we do, and when half of our frustration comes from being misunderstood, we can find solace in the fact that He has been in our shoes. A third thing to notice is in John 2:17 — Jesus' response wasn't a product of him being offended or even just emotional. Instead, it was a response directed by His deep passion for God and God's house. When we love the things of God and we love God Himself, we'll be submitted to His Word and how He says to respond. Processing our emotions through God's Word is how we express anger in biblical and sinless ways.

Redirecting Anger and Bitterness

When we identify the real enemy (the world, our flesh, and the devil), we can redirect our anger away from internalizing and externalizing to work through our anger God's way. The redirection process is to put off the old way, renew our mind by seeing the truth, and put on the new way.

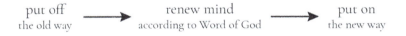

put off → renew mind → put on
the old way   according to Word of God   the new way

Ephesians 4:22-24 That ye put off concerning the former conversation the old man, which is corrupt according to the deceitful lusts; and be renewed in the spirit of your mind; and that ye put on the new man, which after God is created in righteousness and true holiness.

Overcoming a Pattern of Exploding and/or Stuffing

If you recall from my testimony, I had developed patterns of both stuffing and exploding my anger. In this lesson we have walked through biblical ways of dealing with our anger, but if you or someone you're working with have a pattern or stronghold of exploding and/or stuffing anger, you may need to break down the steps further. Here is a chart that might help.

Exploders need to:	Stuffers need to:
1. Redirect to slow to anger (Proverbs 15:18)	1. Redirect to root of bitterness (Hebrews 12:15)
2. Find where anger is coming from	2. Find out where anger is coming from
3. Validate the violation	3. Validate the violation
4. See how their anger is misplaced & that exploding is a sinful reaction	4. See how their anger is misplaced & that stuffing is a sinful reaction

Casting down your thoughts and replacing them with God's is the key to victory (2 Corinthians 10:3-5; Ephesians 4:22-24; Romans 12:2). Here are more memory verses on anger to help you through this process:

> **Proverbs 15:1** *A soft answer turneth away wrath: but grievous words stir up anger.*

> **Proverbs 15:18** *A wrathful man stirreth up strife: but he that is slow to anger appeaseth strife.*

> **Proverbs 16:32** *He that is slow to anger is better than the mighty; and he that ruleth his spirit than he that taketh a city.*

> **Proverbs 19:11** *The discretion of a man deferreth his anger; and it is his glory to pass over a transgression.*

> **Proverbs 22:24-25** *Make no friendship with an angry man; and with a furious man thou shalt not go, lest thou learn his ways, and get a snare to thy soul.*

> **Proverbs 29:22** *An angry man stirreth up strife, and a furious man aboundeth in transgression.*

> **Ecclesiastes 7:9** *Be not hasty in thy spirit to be angry: for anger resteth in the bosom of fools.*

James 1:19-20 *Wherefore, my beloved brethren, let every man be swift to hear, slow to speak, slow to wrath: for the wrath of man worketh not the righteousness of God.*

God made us and gave us our emotions, but it's essential that we don't allow them to control us and turn into sin. Anger is one emotion that can often swing dangerously close to sin because it prompts us to react instead of respond with biblical thought patterns. Anger can also easily feed into more serious problems, such as bitterness or even division in the church body. Fortunately, we can learn from Jesus' example and lean into His grace to understand how to properly deal with anger and how to trust Him to overcome our unbiblical ways of coping with it.

Questions to Consider:

1. How are you walking? Are you in the light with God, or do you have sin in your life that you need to deal with?

2. When you find yourself in sin, do you usually run to the light or hide in the dark? *hide*

3. Would those around you describe you as someone who handles their anger well? *no*

4. Are you someone who puts off dealing with anger, or do you deal with it the same day? Which is better? How can you improve?

5. Is anger sin? When is anger sin? *wrath?*

6. What is the key to not sinning when angry? *finding the root & renewing my perspective by my thoughts*

7. How soon should you deal with anger? *immediately*

8. What can wrath easily turn into? *bitterness, sin*

9. What are the two sorrows we all can face, and which is good? *godly sorrow & worldly*

10. What does repentance mean? *turning in how we think & act*

11. Write down one of the memory verses here and commit to memorizing it this week.

HEB 4:15 & 16 "For we do not have a high priest who is unable to empathize with our weaknesses, but we have one that has been tempted in every way, just as we are - yet he did not sin.

Let's then approach God's throne of grace with confidence, so that we may recieve mercy & find grace to help us in our time of need."

8

How to Love and Forgive

Love and forgiveness go hand in hand, and unfortunately, this is a lesson that I had to learn the hard way. It happened within the first six months after I started going to church. I was offended by someone, and I honestly don't even remember what it was all about now. Back then, our discipleship lessons weren't as developed, and I had not yet learned how to deal properly with my sin. After she offended me, she began to really get on my nerves. Our class fellowship wasn't that big at the time, so I'd see her often. Every time I would see her, my frustration grew and grew until just the sight of her really bothered me. Because of this, I would try to avoid her at all costs — I'd see her coming and I'd turn around and go somewhere else. It got worse and worse until I just hated her! It was finally so bad that I didn't even want to go to church because I knew I would see her. Now that is festered anger and hatred! Through this experience, God taught me that I had a deep root of bitterness that needed to be dealt with and that my emotions had turned into a huge sin problem. I wasn't dealing with these things correctly.

This chapter contains the verses and principles that the Lord used to help me recognize and acknowledge my sin and understand more about what was going on in my life. Before we look at these biblical principles, please ask yourself up front if there is anyone in your life right now that you cannot love or that you feel you cannot forgive. And even though you may immediately say no, please realize that if someone just popped into your mind, they might be someone you are holding a grudge against. Search out your heart attitude and see if any unforgiveness dwells there.

First, you need to realize that the person that popped into your mind isn't your enemy, even if you think that they are. We're going to clearly see that your real enemy here is the devil. The Bible even goes on to say that unforgiveness is a device or trick of the devil. Paul only gives us two clear warnings about the devil's arsenal — one is a warning of anger turning to wrath, and the other is unforgiveness (Ephesians 4:26; 2 Corinthians 2:10-11). The devil wants to get you so upset with someone that it ends up destroying your relationship with the Lord. That's all he's after — to get you disconnected from God. This is important, because the thing that Jesus prayed for in John 17 the night before He was crucified was that we as the body of Christ would be unified. Satan doesn't want a unified church sharing the gospel across the whole world, so he seeks to divide and destroy. There were two commandments Jesus gave us in the gospels: love God and love others.

> **Mark 12:28-34** *And one of the scribes came, and having heard them reasoning together, and perceiving that he had answered them well, asked him, Which is the first commandment of all? And Jesus answered him, The first of all the commandments is, Hear, O Israel; the Lord our God is one Lord: and thou shalt love the Lord thy God with all thy heart, and with all thy soul, and with all thy mind, and with all thy strength: this is the first commandment. And the second is like, namely this, Thou shalt love thy neighbour as thyself. There is none other commandment greater than these. And the scribe said unto him, Well, Master, thou hast said the truth: for there is one God; and there is none other but he: and to love him with all the heart, and with all the understanding, and with all the soul, and with all the strength, and to love his neighbour as himself, is more than all whole burnt offerings and sacrifices. And when Jesus saw that he*

answered discreetly, he said unto him, Thou art not far from the kingdom of God. And no man after that durst ask him any question.

Take notice as you read and meditate on those verses that there is another instruction of love that says to love "as thyself." We are to love our neighbor as we love ourselves. In other words, we must receive the love of Jesus for ourselves. Only then can we give it back to God and to others. We will learn step-by-step instructions from the Word of God about how to do that. Receive it for yourself first and then you can share it with those around you.

> *1 John 3:18* My little children, let us not love in word, neither in tongue; but in deed and in truth.

First, we must understand that biblical love is not about what you say. My second husband, the guy who was beating me up, used to tell me he loved me about twenty times a day. Over and over he would tell me that, and he would usually say it even more after a beating. Looking back, I wonder why he did that. Did he do it out of guilt and shame for what he had done? I don't know, but I do know one thing: he did not truly love me. Not at all. Now, there is nothing wrong with telling people you love them, but understand that our words don't prove our love. This verse says we love in deed *and* in truth. There are only two things the Word of God says are the truth: Jesus and the Word. So, we love through deeds, through Jesus, and through the Word of God. In other words, true love exhibits itself through deeds (works) and the truth (Word); it has nothing to do with your feelings. For example, John 3 says he that doeth TRUTH cometh to the LIGHT that his DEEDS may be manifest that they are wrought in God. We're going to see in this lesson that biblical love has little and even nothing to do with our feelings, but it has everything to do with our actions. The Bible also says that people will know whether you love God by looking at your life, so do not say you love Jesus without first examining your life.

> *1 Corinthians 8:3* But if any man love God, the same is known of him.

Our natural attitude in our flesh is to judge others rather than to love them. We judge amongst ourselves and we accuse some and excuse others, like it says in Romans 2. We pretend we're God! God is clear that He wants us to overcome this judging by loving. If we want to judge, let's judge ourselves against Jesus' example. We will fall short every time, so why do we spend so much time judging others?

God says in Romans 14 that Jesus is our brother's judge, not us. Yes, He does say in 1 Corinthians 2 that we that are spiritual can judge all THINGS because we have the mind of Christ, which is the Word of God. That Word became flesh and dwelt among us, and we hold the Word's mind through the Bible. So as we make choices and decisions, we can judge things according to what the Word of God says. The key is comparing scripture with scripture and allowing it to build a safety net of boundaries around our lives. We aren't the judge; God and His Word are.

> **Romans 15:1** *We then that are strong ought to bear the infirmities of the weak, and not to please ourselves.*

Yes, we can judge what someone is doing based on the Word of God. But at the same time, God wants us to love them and show them the right way. We are to hate the sin but love the sinner. This is exactly how the Lord approached us and this is how we are to approach others. Instead of immediately jumping to conclusions, we should love and help others, realizing that we are no better than they are. Meet them where they are at and give them the benefit of the doubt.

> **Galatians 6:1** *Brethren, if a man be overtaken in a fault, ye which are spiritual, restore such an one in the spirit of meekness; considering thyself, lest thou also be tempted.*

This verse gives us clear guidelines for when we see someone in a fault or sin issue. If we decide to approach them, we must make sure we are approaching them in a spirit of meekness. Be very careful here! This verse says that if you're not walking in the Spirit and addressing them with meekness, whatever is attacking them or going on in their life could very well end up on your back. We don't know what cross they are bearing or what demon is chasing them, and we also haven't walked in their shoes and seen the problem from their point of view. Be careful and let the Lord work it out. Sometimes we can help them, but we must do it in a spirit of meekness, considering ourselves.

As I was having this problem with this girl at my church, I was sitting at my house feeling really upset when I read 1 John 4:18 where it says that "perfect love casteth out fear." The whole chapter of 1 John 4 is about the perfect love of Jesus and how it casts out all the fear in our lives. I remember the day like it was yesterday — I was struggling with the thoughts of hating her and also struggling with so much fear inside. I latched onto 1 John 4:18 and wrote the verse down, trying to memorize it in the hopes of overcoming my fear and hatred. I finally crinkled up the paper and threw it in the trash can. I gave up and came to the conclusion it just wasn't going to work. Fortunately God did not give up on me, even though I gave up on His promise. He kept bringing me back to these verses. He kept breaking me, showing me my wrong, and helping me see His instructions on how to make it right. It was through this process that God started showing me how to apply the verses in 1 John 4 to my life. Here are four principles He showed me about how to love and forgive.

> *1 John 4:7-21* *Beloved, let us love one another: for love is of God; and every one that loveth is born of God, and knoweth God. He that loveth not knoweth not God; for God is love. In this was manifested the love of God toward us, because that God sent his only begotten Son into the world, that we might live through him. Herein is love, not that we loved God, but that he loved us, and sent his Son to be the propitiation for our sins. Beloved, if God so loved us, we ought also to love one another. No man hath seen God at any time. If we love one another, God dwelleth in us, and his love is perfected in us. Hereby know we that we dwell in him, and he in us, because he hath given us of his Spirit. And we have seen and do testify that the Father sent the Son to be the Saviour of the world.*

> *Whosoever shall confess that Jesus is the Son of God, God dwelleth in him, and he in God. And we have known and believed the love that God hath to us. God is love; and he that dwelleth in love dwelleth in God, and God in him. Herein is our love made perfect, that we may have boldness in the day of judgment: because as he is, so are we in this world. There is no fear in love; but perfect love casteth out fear: because fear hath torment. He that feareth is not made perfect in love. We love him, because he first loved us. If a man say, I love God, and hateth his brother, he is a liar: for he that loveth not his brother whom he hath seen, how can he love God whom he hath not seen? And this commandment have we from him, that he who loveth God love his brother also.*

The **first step** is found in verse 7, and it is to recognize that the love that we need is the love of God. This is a love that only saved people have. Before we were saved, we didn't have access to this love because it is the unconditional love of Jesus Christ and it's not found in the world. It has nothing to do with our feelings or infatuation. Rather, it is found in what Christ did for us on the cross.

The **second step** we see is in verse 10, and it is to recognize who God is and His love for you. God clearly demonstrated His love for us in Jesus Christ — we can clearly see this in John 3:16. God's love for us was displayed on the cross. Love is seen in action and not in words, and God's actions in sending Jesus spoke loudly of His love for us.

The **third step** is seen in verse 19, which says, "We love Him, because He first loved us." Personal illustrations are good tools to illuminate a point, but biblical illustrations are the best. Here's a great biblical example of this step:

> *Luke 7:36-50 And one of the Pharisees desired him that he would eat with him. And he went into the Pharisee's house, and sat down to meat. And, behold, a woman in the city, which was a sinner, when she knew that Jesus sat at meat in the Pharisee's house, brought an alabaster box of ointment, and stood at his feet behind him weeping, and began to wash his feet with tears, and did wipe*

them with the hairs of her head, and kissed his feet, and anointed them with the ointment. Now when the Pharisee which had bidden him saw it, he spake within himself, saying, This man, if he were a prophet, would have known who and what manner of woman this is that toucheth him: for she is a sinner. And Jesus answering said unto him, Simon, I have somewhat to say unto thee. And he saith, Master, say on. There was a certain creditor which had two debtors: the one owed five hundred pence, and the other fifty. And when they had nothing to pay, he frankly forgave them both. Tell me therefore, which of them will love him most? Simon answered and said, I suppose that he, to whom he forgave most. And he said unto him, Thou hast rightly judged. And he turned to the woman, and said unto Simon, Seest thou this woman? I entered into thine house, thou gavest me no water for my feet: but she hath washed my feet with tears, and wiped them with the hairs of her head. Thou gavest me no kiss: but this woman since the time I came in hath not ceased to kiss my feet. My head with oil thou didst not anoint: but this woman hath anointed my feet with ointment. Wherefore I say unto thee, Her sins, which are many, are forgiven; for she loved much: but to whom little is forgiven, the same loveth little. And he said unto her, Thy sins are forgiven. And they that sat at meat with him began to say within themselves, Who is this that forgiveth sins also? And he said to the woman, Thy faith hath saved thee; go in peace.

Notice that the Pharisee spoke within himself. This Pharisee was having lunch with Jesus and was internally judging Jesus. It was his heart attitude that was judgmental while his outward actions looked like he loved God. This is a great example of attitude versus action — his words said one thing, but his heart attitude showed no love. His actions are contrasted with the actions of the woman in this passage who bowed at Jesus' feet and asked for forgiveness. She didn't wickedly judge Him; she saw Jesus for who He really was. Her actions showed her love, unlike the Pharisee's. Her love and humility allowed her to get a glimpse of God and caused her to bow down and worship. The Pharisee, clothed in his religion and self-righteousness, didn't have a clear picture of himself or his flesh. He didn't see Jesus for who He was, and as a result he did not worship or love.

As you see who God really is and His love for you, you are naturally going to love Him. There isn't anyone in this world who really gets a glimpse of the Lord and doesn't want to bow down and worship Him for who He truly is and love Him. The challenge is getting people to see God for who He really is. Unfortunately, our pride and self-righteousness can cause us to be blind and totally miss Him. That's what was happening to the Pharisee, and that's what caused him to miss Jesus, God in the flesh. But the more the woman saw Jesus, the more she was able to see herself more clearly and the more she realized her own sin. The more we look to Him and His goodness, love, and glory, the more our sin is revealed. And the more we see our sin, the more we ask for forgiveness from our Savior. The more we see Him, the more we move toward Him and away from our sin. That is repentance. The beautiful thing is that the more she asked forgiveness and saw His forgiveness, the more she loved Him! What a beautiful picture.

In order to love Him back, you have to personally see His love for you! Let your glimpse of Jesus be greater than your glimpse of others or of yourself. Compare yourself with Jesus. We will always fall way short — after all, we were made out of dirt. We have flesh, and that flesh sins.

> *1 Timothy 1:15* This is a faithful saying, and worthy of all acceptation, that Christ Jesus came into the world to save sinners; of whom I am chief.

Now, the illustration of the Pharisee and the woman might cause you to think that seeing and learning to love Jesus is about understanding our degree of sin, but 1 Timothy 1:15 makes it clear that that is not the case. Here Paul, who followed the law blamelessly according to Philippians 3, said he was chief of all sinners. How could he say that? How could this righteous man, blameless concerning the law, claim to be the worst of all sinners? He was able to claim this because he got a glimpse of God. Seeing God and then seeing ourselves magnifies how much we fall short of the glory of God. That's how Job, the most righteous man on earth in his time, knew that he was vile! He recognized his flesh. Comparing our sinful flesh to our holy God will always result in a drastic change in perspective. We need to gain this proper point of view: ALL flesh is sinful. We were ALL made out of dirt. When we compare ourselves to the Lord instead of to other sinners, we will see how much we need Him. Paul, Job, and the woman in Luke 7 all saw that and responded accordingly.

That takes us to the **fourth step**, which is found in verse 21 of 1 John 4. The more that we see who God is, the more love we have for Him. As we receive God's love for ourselves and grow in our relationship with Him, the more we can turn around and give that love to others. Until we understand God's love and see it for ourselves — until we receive and experience God's love personally — we can't love Him back or give it to someone else! We can't give someone something we don't have.

I love to mentor and disciple, but as much as I love the girls that I work with, I cannot help them or love them the way that God can. When I start working with a girl, I surrender to God and ask Him to love her through me. I don't know what's going on in her life, and I don't know what she needs. My love and care won't grow her up in Christ, but His will! That's how we need to be with others. We don't need to love them in our flesh. Loving people in our flesh can lead to great feelings, but we need to choose to let God love people through us instead. If we love God, we're going to love our brother (or sister). If we have a problem with our brother, we need to deal with that because we love God.

The book of 1 Corinthians was written to a church that was all messed up. There was someone in the church who had fallen into terrible fornication and was sleeping with his father's wife. Everyone in the church was aware of his sin, but no one was correcting him. Paul confronts him and the whole church, saying that this man needed to be put outside the church and that the church needed to step up and correct him. Then, as Paul began writing 2 Corinthians, the man who was caught in fornication in 1 Corinthians had repented and was wanting entrance back into the church. Paul tells the church to forgive him. This forgiveness was hard to offer, and sometimes we, too, simply cannot forgive someone in our flesh. There are just going to be some things that hurt you so badly that you don't want to forgive them. That's what happened in Corinth, and that's what happened to me with the girl at my church all those years ago. Thankfully Paul used this circumstance to go over how to overcome the sin of unforgiveness, and the bottom line is letting Christ do it for and through us. Let's meditate on and step through what Paul said to the church in Corinth.

> **2 Corinthians 2:9-11** *For to this end also did I write, that I might know the proof of you, whether ye be obedient in all things. To whom ye forgive any thing, I forgive also: for if I forgave any thing, to whom I forgave it, for your sakes forgave I it in the person of Christ; lest Satan should get an advantage of us: for we are not ignorant of his devices.*

This passage is a little bit of a tongue twister, but it says that we have to forgive through "the person of Christ." Maybe we can't do it ourselves, but we can do it through Christ. Jesus Christ lives inside you and He can forgive them through you. He can give you the power and ability to forgive. Love and forgiveness go together — if you find it hard to love someone, it is usually because you can't forgive them. Though we usually focus on their sins, we need to realize that we are also in sin when we do not forgive. This takes surrendering to the Lord and admitting that we also have sinned against Him in our attitude and response to the offending person.

When you think someone does you wrong, it is very hard to turn around and admit your own sin and surrender. It's difficult because we are seeing them through our self-righteousness and pride and we are comparing ourselves to them. We are judging them by our expectations, and we are looking at them instead of looking at God. But what we need is to get refocused on God, His love, and His person. Some people are very easy to love and forgive and some are not. God gives us opportunities to love and forgive all kinds of people because He wants us to learn that we need His help and power, not the power of our own flesh.

According to verse 11 of 2 Corinthians 2, we see that unforgiveness is a device of the devil. He's the one that is your real enemy. He has a plan to mess you up by getting you to hate your brother or sister in full unforgiveness. He wants that because he wants your relationship with God to be damaged. After all, Matthew 6:14-15 says that if you do not forgive, then God will not forgive you (note that this is in terms of our daily fellowship with God, not our eternal standing if we have been saved; refer back to Chapters 1–3 for a refresher on salvation and eternal security). Remember that the devil is your enemy, not the person who offended you, and the devil wants you to disobey God by not forgiving or loving someone.

When I was upset with this girl, my connection with the Lord became completely cut off because of the sin of unforgiveness in my life. This is what the Lord showed me to get right with Him and right with my sister, and this is what we have to do to maintain our connection with God: we have to get on our knees and ask Him to do it through us. You must get on your knees and ask God to forgive you first for your unforgiveness and lack of love. Be honest with God — get it all out in the light and then ask Him to love and forgive them through you. This is the biblical way to deal with unforgiveness, and it is the only way that works. It is a willing heart that God wants, and when He sees your willingness to let Him do it through you, a transformation in your heart will take place.

Now, you might have a stain. If you get a grass stain on your clothes, you have to wash it over and over. Sometimes we can get stained with sin, and this sin might be a stronghold. All those years ago, I got stained with the sin of unforgiveness, and it was such a bad stain that even though I followed these steps and forgave her, I was still often tempted with unforgiveness whenever I saw her. This meant that I had to continually choose to forgive her and go to the Lord time after time for help. With strongholds, you might have let it go, but you're so stained with it that it comes back up. If this is true of you, keep going back over and over the biblical principles and don't stop! This girl eventually became a very good friend of mine. It is possible to forgive when you are relying on God to do it through you.

Next, know that forgiveness is free, but trust is earned. Just because you forgave someone doesn't mean that you will be a doormat for them. One of the greatest illustrations I've read about forgiveness is about Corrie ten Boom. She and her family were Dutch Christians who helped Jews escape from Nazis during the Holocaust of World War II. Six months before the end of the war, they were betrayed and arrested. Corrie, her sister Betsie, and their father were thrown into a concentration camp, and her father got sick and died within the first weeks of their imprisonment. Corrie and Betsie managed to stay together and clung to their faith in God throughout all of the horrific experiences in the camp. A few months later, Betsie died, and shortly thereafter, Corrie was released by mistake. She later found out that all the women in her barracks were murdered within days of her dismissal.

After the war she became a great speaker testifying of what God did in her life. At one of her conferences about love, she spotted in the audience the man who was instrumental in her sister's death. It terrified her to see his face, but she continued her speech while praying to the Lord for help. After she was finished speaking, he approached her. He introduced himself, saying that he didn't know if she remembered him, but that he had become a Christian after the war and wanted to ask for her forgiveness. He put his hand out, and she was caught in internal struggle. She wanted to hate him for what he had done, but she knew that God desired forgiveness. As she prayed, the Lord miraculously lifted her arm by His grace so that she could shake his hand. She couldn't forgive him by herself, but by asking for forgiveness from God and then asking Him to love the man through her, she forgave that man. She was able to let Jesus forgive him through her. This is the forgiveness that is spoken about in 2 Corinthians 2, and it is the forgiveness that is only found in surrendering to God and allowing Him to forgive through you.

Our forgiveness comes from our love for the Lord, but how do we know if we love the Lord? According to John 14:15 and Mark 12:28-34, we know that we love the Lord if we keep His commandments! We also feed God's sheep — spiritual babes in Christ. That's what He says in John 21:15-17.

> *John 21:15-17 So when they had dined, Jesus saith to Simon Peter, Simon, son of Jonas, lovest thou me more than these? He saith unto him, Yea, Lord; thou knowest that I love thee. He saith unto him, Feed my lambs. He saith to him again the second time, Simon, son of Jonas, lovest thou me? He saith unto him, Yea, Lord; thou knowest that I love thee. He saith unto him, Feed my sheep. He saith unto him the third time, Simon, son of Jonas, lovest thou me? Peter was grieved because he said unto him the third time, Lovest thou me? And he said unto him, Lord, thou knowest all things; thou knowest that I love thee. Jesus saith unto him, Feed my sheep.*

This passage is where Peter gets his heart right with the Lord after he denied him three times. Jesus keeps asking him, "Peter, do you love Me?" Three times he asks this, and three times Peter says yes. But what does Jesus say in response? "Feed My sheep." He could have said many things back to him, but what He said was that if Peter loved Him, then he would feed His sheep. If we love God, we feed His sheep, imparting to them what was imparted unto us. This looks like discipleship, mentorship, and fulfilling the needs of the brethren as we are able. And we can't forget about Psalm 119:165, which says: "Great peace have they which love thy law: and nothing shall offend them." People who love God's Word will have peace and nothing will offend them. Choosing not to be offended is a great way to deal with forgiveness!

1 Corinthians 13 details what true love and charity look like. It is another great chapter to read when struggling with love and forgiveness. Read it every day as you work through all the above principles when learning how to love and forgive. I would like to close this chapter with a brief testimony regarding these next verses.

> *John 13:34-35 A new commandment I give unto you, that ye love one another; as I have loved you, that ye also love one another. By this shall all men know that ye are my disciples, if ye have love one to another.*

A number of years ago I told my mother that I couldn't go to her family event because church was at the same time. She was very disappointed and distraught. She explained that she had watched my life over the years after getting saved, and it seemed to her and Daddy that I loved my church friends more than I loved them. I was cut to the heart by her remark and told them that I loved them and that I was sorry. I decided to set aside my plans and join them Sunday morning for the family event. After hearing her complaint, I began making a prayerful and concentrated effort to show them how much I loved them. I began spending more time with them and loving on them.

One afternoon while I was visiting, my dad, who was a great man and loved by many, asked me a serious question: "Debbie, what exactly is this thing called the rapture?" He was in his mid-sixties at that time and was genuinely interested (and somewhat perplexed) about this event. His question began one of the most memorable and blessed moments of my life! Growing up, my dad and I weren't very close. He had adopted me at the age of six, and for whatever reason, there was some distance between us. However, during my thirties and forties — which was after my salvation — we had grown close, and by the time he asked me this question, I could tell he'd been thinking about it for quite a while. For a brief moment I was in shock and was not sure that I had heard him correctly. In the past, he and my mother had slammed shut any doors to talk about God and the gospel, but after years of seeing God transform me, they were finally ready to hear. I also believe God was using my concentrated effort of love toward them after mom had noticed my love for my friends at church. What happened next was a two hour-long conversation about Jesus Christ: why He came, what He did, how to personally know Him, and that He is coming back someday!

Then I asked my dad if he wanted to know Him. He said yes, and my mom, who was sitting in the same room and listening, said that she did too! And there we were, all three bowing before the Father as my parents accepted Christ as their Lord and Savior. This was one of the most glorious moments of my life, and it didn't end there. They had a million questions, and over the following years, they began growing in their relationships with the Lord. They eventually found a church and were both baptized in obedience to the Lord.

How to Love and Forgive

My dad could barely walk then and needed assistance getting to the tank. Mom's brother had drowned when she was young and she always had trouble putting her head under water. Yet there they were — both in their sixties and proclaiming to the world that they were believers in Jesus as they followed through in baptism. Now they're both with our Lord Jesus in Heaven, and all I can say is, "Soon and very soon, we are going to see the King!"

Our love is what shows the world that we are Jesus' disciples, and it is often what draws people to ask questions about Christ. Similarly, when we do not walk in love, it means that our relationship with God is not what it needs to be. A lack of love allows unforgiveness to fester, and unforgiveness is one of the major desires that the devil has for Christians. He wants us to be made useless and divided, and there is no better tool for this than unforgiveness. Though unforgiveness can be a stronghold that needs constant reproof and redirection toward biblical thinking in our lives, God gives us the ability to love and to forgive as we draw near to Him, understand His love, and ask for Him to do all of this through us.

Questions to Consider:

1. Do you struggle with love or forgiveness?

2. Think over your relationships, past and present. Do you hold any grudges or unforgiveness against anyone? What does the Bible say to do?

3. Are you easily offended by people?

4. We are to love our neighbors as "_____."

5. Do words prove love? If not, what proves love?

6. Do you often judge others? What is the only way that we are supposed to judge each other?

7. With what spirit should we approach people who are in a sin issue?

8. Have you personally seen God's love for you? Do you believe that He loves you?

9. What should we do if we find that we are struggling to forgive someone?

10. How does your forgiveness of others affect God's forgiveness of you?

11. How do we know whether or not we love the Lord?

12. Do you think that your family feels loved by you?

9

Job's Example of Overcoming Fear
(An Application of Love and Forgiveness)

In this chapter we will be looking at the story of Job to see a biblical application of overcoming fear in our lives. We are also going to be able to see an application of love and forgiveness! We will see many of our previous lessons about fear, love, and forgiveness collide because it is fear that often holds us back from loving and forgiving. They are all tied together and connected — in order to deal with my fear, I had to learn to biblically deal with love and forgiveness. It isn't a strange or coincidental thing that the lessons on fear, love, and forgiveness all build upon each other, and we'll see that all of the upcoming lessons build upon one another in similar fashion. Each one is another stepping stone to growing in confidence, security, and our relationship with God. The ultimate key to all of this is knowing God and knowing what He says, and it's a process of abandoning ourselves to Him and His principles. In this lesson, we are going to see how to deal with the devil's tricks, how to deal with sin, and an application of love and forgiveness. All of this hinges on the ability to say, "I'm wrong" and "I surrender." However, before looking at Job, I want us to look at Luke 15:11-32.

Luke 15:11-32 *And he said, A certain man had two sons: and the younger of them said to his father, Father, give me the portion of goods that falleth to me. And he divided unto them his living. And not many days after the younger son gathered all together, and took his journey into a far country, and there wasted his substance with riotous living. And when he had spent all, there arose a mighty famine in that land; and he began to be in want. And he went and joined himself to a citizen of that country; and he sent him into his fields to feed swine. And he would fain have filled his belly with the husks that the swine did eat: and no man gave unto him. And when he came to himself, he said, How many hired servants of my father's have bread enough and to spare, and I perish with hunger! I will arise and go to my father, and will say unto him, Father, I have sinned against heaven, and before thee, And am no more worthy to be called thy son: make me as one of thy hired servants. And he arose, and came to his father. But when he was yet a great way off, his father saw him, and had compassion, and ran, and fell on his neck, and kissed him. And the son said unto him, Father, I have sinned against heaven, and in thy sight, and am no more worthy to be called thy son. But the father said to his servants, Bring forth the best robe, and put it on him; and put a ring on his hand, and shoes on his feet: and bring hither the fatted calf, and kill it; and let us eat, and be merry: for this my son was dead, and is alive again; he was lost, and is found. And they began to be merry. Now his elder son was in the field: and as he came and drew nigh to the house, he heard musick and dancing. And he called one of the servants, and asked what these things meant. And he said unto him, Thy brother is come; and thy father hath killed the fatted calf, because he hath received him safe and sound. And he was angry, and would not go in: therefore came his father out, and intreated him. And he answering said to his father, Lo, these many years do I serve thee, neither transgressed I at any time thy commandment: and yet thou never gavest me a kid, that I might make merry with my friends: but as soon as this thy son was come, which hath devoured thy living with harlots, thou hast killed for him the fatted calf. And he said unto him, Son, thou art ever with me, and all that I have is thine. It was meet that we should make merry, and be glad: for this thy brother was dead, and is alive again; and was lost, and is found.*

Here we see two sons: the younger, who is the prodigal son, and the older. The younger brother ran off to the world, squandered all of his inheritance, and finally returned home in humility and repentance. His father threw him a party and everybody was excited about the son's return. But the older brother who never left his father was angry at his father's reception of his younger brother. He was upset that his father blessed his brother with a party and a fatted calf while he — who had always obeyed — never received a celebration like this. To which son do you relate most?

For me, when I first was saved and accepted the Lord as my Savior at 26, I could greatly identify with the prodigal son. But when I was reading this story maybe 15 years later, I found myself relating to the older brother and empathizing with his complaint. Inside I was thinking that it just wasn't fair how the older brother was being treated. And as I studied these thoughts and attitudes out, it dawned on me that the older son had fallen into a performance-based relationship with his father.

He thought that what he was doing for the father was what brought him merit — it was no longer about His relationship with his loving father. Instead, it had turned into him thinking the father owed him something. This is why he was so upset when the younger brother — who had done nothing but sin — was given such a warm reception, and he — who had always played by the rules — received no recognition. Deep down he thought that he was better than his younger brother. This is exactly what we saw in the lesson on grace (Chapter 6) when we learned the results of resting on our works or ministry rather than resting in our love relationship with the Lord. As I began to understand this, I saw that I was just like the older son. My thoughts were similar to those of the older son — to him, it was about what he was doing for the father, not who he was in the relationship to the father: a son.

The Lord began challenging me to think about the two brothers and compare them both to Jesus. What would Jesus have done here? With whom would He have identified? Of course, He would have been like the older brother in that He would have stayed with the father. But would He have gotten upset when the younger brother came back? No! Most likely the Lord would have gone after the prodigal son Himself, driven by His love for and relationship with the father. He would have wanted to please the father so much, and He would have understood the heart of His father so well that He would have gone out to rescue His little brother. That's what Jesus would have done, and, actually, that is exactly what Jesus did! He came to the world to seek and to save that which was lost, bringing many sons unto glory with the Father (Luke 19:10; Hebrews 2:10).

However, the older son was not like Jesus. Instead of pursuing his prodigal brother, he stayed with the father and performed tasks which he thought would give him favor with the father. He developed the attitude that he was better than his little brother, and all the while disregarded the heart of the father and how much it was broken over his little brother's departure. The older son became the center of his own life instead of his relationship with his father being at the core. Ladies, we can do this too! We can become so involved in works and ministry that we begin to rest on what God is doing through us instead of who God is to us. We can slowly begin resting on our own rightness. Our flesh, the old man, is so sneaky and deceptive that we can become convinced that blessings in our life are a direct result of our works and not because of the grace and goodness of God.

We start thinking that it's about us being right, so we start trusting in our rightness rather than Christ's righteousness. Our "rightness" becomes our self-righteousness. This difference is so subtle that we can be convinced our rightness is our righteousness, just like the older brother. His reasoning seems very logical, but it is all wrong. Eventually, resting on this attitude will let us down and fear will begin creeping in. This is because this reasoning is not based on the perfect love of Christ which casts out fear. If we believe that God's blessings for us and God's view of us are based on our own performance, then we will always be afraid of losing them and we will always be striving in our flesh to be right in His eyes. This is a fearful and unstable place to be.

> **Romans 10:3** *For they being ignorant of God's righteousness, and going about to establish their own righteousness, have not submitted themselves unto the righteousness of God.*

This verse shows us what happened to Israel, and the same thing can happen to us without us even realizing it. When we are living right and doing right, we can start relying on our good works and forget that our flesh is still as sinful as it ever was. We forget our need for Christ. Our righteousness and God's righteousness are very, very different. We know this intellectually, but it is a different matter making sure that our hearts know it, too. These principles and boundaries are what we're going to look at in the life of Job.

Job was a very righteous man, and it is clear from what is written about him that God loved him very much. Romans 8:28 tells us that when we love God, all things work together for good. Get that down and rest on this principle! All things work together for good if you love God, even the bad things (or the things that seem bad), because they are all going to help us be conformed to the image of the Lord Jesus Christ. This principle applies to Job too. We see that some things are going to happen to him that are going to look bad, but they will actually be for his good in the end.

> **Job 1:8** *And the LORD said unto Satan, Hast thou considered my servant Job, that there is none like him in the earth, a perfect and an upright man, one that feareth God, and escheweth evil?*

In Job 1:8 we see that it was actually God who brought Job's name up to the devil for consideration! God did this because had a plan. God told Satan that Job was one of His faithful servants who feared Him and eschewed (avoided) evil. He said that Job was blameless, and he challenged the devil to check out this great man! The next thing we see is the devil going after him with everything he could attack him with — even Job's secret, hidden fears (Job 3:25). The important thing to remember is that the Lord allowed it all, and it was all within God's limits.

Emotional Victory

Everything was destroyed in Job's life: his family, his home, his wealth, and his health. It even messed with his marriage. Regardless of what you have been through, you have never had it this bad. It's a picture of the tribulation, and it's also a picture of some of what our Lord and Savior Jesus endured when our sin was placed upon Him at Calvary. Job was in a horrible, horrible predicament. We see in Job 2 that his friends came to speak with him and sought to comfort him, mourn with him, and pray for him. Their intentions seemed to be pure, as they wanted to sit with him in his misery and help in any way that they could. They waited seven whole days before they said a word, and after those seven days, Job opened his mouth. He slowly began his defense, explaining how his tribulations were not the result of his own sin. This began a debate between him and his friends for the next twenty chapters as they discussed his sin, their thoughts on the cause of his misfortune, and God's character.

These were friends around the same spiritual age as Job, and they were his good friends. They were trying to help, but as Job continued, he mentioned that he had a great fear buried deep inside that only God knew about. We will talk about this fear a little later in this chapter.

I've often heard people say that Job's friends were bad friends. They said a lot of "right" things, but they said them at the wrong time, and they were oftentimes things that didn't necessarily apply to what Job was going through. As the debate went on, Job was also justifying and defending himself. Not only did he have to battle his own emotions and understanding of his situation, he also had to defend himself against their accusations.

Couldn't God have interrupted his friends during this twenty-chapter debate? Why did He let them continue with their accusations? Who was actually in control here? Could God have given them insight into what was really going on? Of course the Lord could have revealed the truth! Many times when I'm working with someone, God will reveal the truth and help us find a way out. But with Job and his friends, God is quiet throughout their entire debate. They end up going back and forth, each defending their own position. This slow torture goes on for twenty chapters as these friends tell Job what they think is wrong, and Job continues defending himself, becoming more and more miserable as they go.

Finally Elihu, the one writing the book, spoke up. He was the youngest of the friends and he blasted them all, asserting that none of them knew what they were talking about. These guys were all elders to him, but he finally voiced his opinion and corrected them all. This would be like if you were married for twenty-five years and going through a rough patch, and someone who has been married six months knocks on your door and wants to tell you what's wrong with your marriage! And yet the Lord still allowed all of this to happen.

It's not until the end of all this that Job finally gave up and stopped defending himself. He stopped trying to justify, defend, and explain what it is going on. He stopped saying that he was right. He finally gave up and died to himself, just like in John 12:24:

> **John 12:24** *Verily, verily, I say unto you, Except a corn of wheat fall into the ground and die, it abideth alone: but if it die, it bringeth forth much fruit.*

It's as though Job was being peeled like an onion, being stripped little by little of his own right doing. Our righteousness can be like clothing, and God says our own righteousnesses are as filthy rags compared to His (Isaiah 64:6). We are to be adorned in the Lord's righteousness instead, and in the Lord's righteousness, we do not have to defend ourselves. In the Lord's righteousness He is our defender. It took twenty chapters for Job to get to the place of surrender where his own righteousness was fully peeled away. This is similar to John 21 when Peter was naked in the boat and heard Jesus was on the shore. His nakedness represented how his self-righteousness had been stripped away after he denied the Lord in John 18. That's what we are seeing happen to Job — after all of his debating and justifying, he was finally naked before the Lord. All his righteousness was gone, and he was totally dead to his own defense and justifications.

Interestingly, once he comes to the end, stops trying to defend himself, and stops explaining the reasons why this is all going on, God shows up! And ladies, that's a good thing to remember. If you are trying to justify the problem or defend yourself, you need to watch out! You might be (and probably are) defending your own righteousness. God will wait until you have thrown off your own righteousness. He will allow you to go through that trial, just as He did in Job's life.

Let's look at some verses where Job is declaring his own righteousness. Job wasn't wrong — he was a righteous man. The thing is, we can't lean on our own righteousness. Here are just a few examples:

> *Job 27:6* My *righteousness I hold fast, and will not let it go: my heart shall not reproach me so long as I live.*
>
> *Job 29:14 I put on righteousness, and it clothed me: my judgment was as a robe and a diadem.*
>
> *Job 13:15 Though he slay me, yet will I trust in him: but I will maintain* mine *own ways before him.*
>
> *Job 32:1 So these three men ceased to answer Job, because he was righteous* in his own eyes.

Many people quote Job 13:15, but they only quote the first part. That second part says: "but I will maintain mine own ways before him." We are either going to maintain our ways or God's ways. Yes, Job was following the Lord and he was righteous, but there were still elements of his righteousness that he had surrounded himself with in place of God's righteousness. We know this is the case because there was a hidden fear inside of Job, and fear surfaces when we are relying in any way on our own righteousness to obtain the favor of God. Perfect love casts out fear, but Job had his fear hidden deep inside.

As we study what God said to Job, we start seeing that God was perfecting Job. His friends spouted biblical truths with incorrect applications, and God let them continue. As long as Job was trying to defend himself, God didn't step in to defend him. God was taking Job through a really rough valley to help him grow up and to trust in God's righteousness rather than his own. As we grow, we will all go through a Gethsemane or an "evil day," so to speak. We all have to learn to totally die to self (our flesh) so that God can do His work through us. Job had to be completely dead to his flesh and efforts in order for God to reveal His righteousness. The Lord was taking him through this hard time to teach him this lesson and to grow him up in it.

> ***Job 38:1-3*** *Then the LORD answered Job out of the whirlwind, and said, Who is this that darkeneth counsel by words without knowledge? Gird up now thy loins like a man; for I will demand of thee, and answer thou me.*

Interestingly and ironically, when God first showed up, he didn't excuse Job's behavior. God didn't come and say, "Poor, Job! Let me comfort you and make everything right again." Instead, he asked Job why he was questioning Him. Realize that only Job and God were in the conversation now. God didn't even acknowledge or talk to his friends. It was just Him and Job, and God just went on to explain in the next couple chapters how awesome His power is. In other words, God was saying, "Job, who do you think you are? You can't compare to Me. You don't come anywhere close." We all need to remember that the Bible compares us to grasshoppers, worms, the grass of the field, and dirt.

> ***Job 40:1-5*** *Moreover the LORD answered Job, and said, Shall he that contendeth with the Almighty instruct him? he that reproveth God, let him answer it. Then Job answered the LORD, and said, Behold, I am vile; what shall I answer thee? I will lay mine hand upon my mouth. Once have I spoken; but I will not answer: yea, twice; but I will proceed no further.*

In this passage Job began acknowledging how feeble he was, and God didn't miss a beat. He went on to explain to him the devil's power, which is far greater than ours, and said that even the devil is nothing compared to Him. He wanted to get Job to the place where he recognized the difference between who God was and who he was. We might compare ourselves with each other — which is not wise — but when we compare ourselves to God and we think that our righteousness has some similarities to God's, we are way off. Of course, we know that in our minds, but sometimes it takes difficult moments to clearly understand it. What we are going to see is that it took a glimpse of God for Job to truly understand this.

> **Job 42:1-6** Then Job answered the LORD, and said, I know that thou canst do every thing, and that no thought can be withholden from thee. Who is he that hideth counsel without knowledge? therefore have I uttered that I understood not; things too wonderful for me, which I knew not. Hear, I beseech thee, and I will speak: I will demand of thee, and declare thou unto me. I have heard of thee by the hearing of the ear: but now mine eye seeth thee. Wherefore I abhor myself, and repent in dust and ashes.

Job finally asked for total forgiveness! This is where Job was getting a clear glimpse of God, but this only happened after he was totally and completely broken. When he got this glimpse of God, he saw that his righteousness was absolutely nothing! When we get a real glimpse of the Lord, we see that we are dirt — after all, that's where our flesh comes from. We can't bring God down to our size by thinking that our righteousness is anything compared to His. This passage is similar to what we see in Romans 7 with Paul's internal battle with his flesh. He says, "Oh wretched man that I am!" when he got a glimpse of God (Romans 7:24). Job repented, and that's when everything changed for him.

Let me ask you something: do you think that those guys were still Job's friends? God did, and He called them that. Once Job had a good glimpse of God, he experienced God's perfect love which casteth out fear. This is a good example of what we went over in the previous lesson — the more that you see God, the more you see His love! And once we receive it, we can give it back to Him and to others. So Job was glimpsing God, experiencing this unconditional love, and was being covered in God's righteousness. The fear was gone and the unconditional love of God now lived inside him after he truly got a glimpse of the Lord. After that, God went on to justify Job to his friends in Job 42:7-8, telling them that they were all wrong and Job was right. God told Job to pray for his "friends." God knew the hurt that they had caused Job, but He wanted Job to forgive them and pray for them. You can't pray for someone unless your heart is in it and right with God. And Job prayed for his friends! Then, look at what God said in Job 42:10. God turned his captivity and gave him way more than what he started out with. But the greatest thing Job now had was a stronger relationship with the Lord!

> ***Job 42:10*** *And the LORD turned the captivity of Job, when he prayed for his friends: also the LORD gave Job twice as much as he had before.*

We all have a cross to bear, and we're all learning how to die to self. It is through this process that we allow God's unconditional love to flow through us. When you get a glimpse of God and focus on that, there is not going to be any fear in your life. Instead, God will take up residency, both inside and out. We no longer have to defend ourselves, just like Jesus when He was accused by so many people. He gave no defense or justification at the cross. He let God the Father defend Him, and that's what we're after. God walked Job through his fear, and God's perfect love cast it out.

If you find that you are struggling with this perfect love, read 1 Corinthians 13, which outlines unconditional love. If you are struggling with letting go of your own righteousness, read Philippians 3, which explains how Paul let go of his own righteousness and learned to hold onto and rest in God's. We all have to learn this lesson, and it can often be a difficult trial of our faith. God will allow us to be taken down low so that we can see just how lifted up and on high He is. Once we see who He is, we can rest in His righteousness alone. If we do that, forgiveness will never be an issue in our lives.

Questions to Consider:

1. Do you often struggle with fear?

2. What is the one thing that, when we focus on it, casts out all fear?

3. Do you base your relationship with God on your performance?

4. To which son from Luke 15 do you relate?

5. What was the prodigal son's sin, and what was the older brother's sin?

6. Do you ever forget how sinful your flesh is?

7. How does God feel about self-righteousness, and what does self-righteousness look like in your life?

8. What was Job's great fear?

9. What is the thing that God addresses when He finally answers Job?

10. How does glimpsing God allow Job to forgive his friends?

10

Conquering Fear and Finding the Secret Place

In this lesson, I'm going to try to explain something God calls "the secret place." But to be up front with you, this place is actually quite unexplainable — there are just no words that I can find to fully define everything about it. It's a place that is better experienced than explained, so with that in mind, let me try to help you to find and experience the secret place for yourself if you haven't already. If you have been there, let me encourage you to go back often.

We began discussing how to overcome insecurity and anxiety in Chapter 2, and in almost every chapter since, we have touched on additional biblical principles about conquering fear that need to be added to our foundation in Jesus Christ. The Bible teaches that growing in Christ requires balancing and building biblical principle upon principle — "precept upon precept; line upon line," just like Isaiah 28:9-10 says. This chapter is about conquering fear, but we can't just start here. In order to thoroughly begin overcoming our fears, we must build upon basic precepts that we've already covered in order to continue moving forward. This is why it is so important that you seek to apply the principles outlined in previous chapters of this book instead of just moving through. These lessons all work together to build up the biblical growth process of discipleship.

How did David kill Goliath? How did this kid fight this giant that the whole nation of Israel would not go and fight? The answer is that he had a relationship with the living God! He had a track record with his Heavenly Father who had helped him to slay the bear and the lion when he was keeping his father's sheep (1 Samuel 17:34-37). God had come through for him then, and he knew God would come through again because of their personal relationship. Each time the Lord came through and revealed something new about His nature, their relationship grew.

Our relationship with the Lord is like an iceberg: you only see the top because the bulk of the iceberg is underwater and you can't see its depth or foundation. What people see God doing in and through you should just be the tip of the iceberg. The unseen portion of the iceberg that's beneath the water should be a vast amount of personal, intimate time you've spent building your relationship with Him.

And that's what was happening here with David. When he was out keeping his father's sheep, he was spending lots of quality time with the Lord. He knew that God was bigger than the giant, and he knew that God was bigger than the fear. How did he know that? Because he spent tons of time with God! He had gotten a glimpse of God, and he knew God and what His Word said!

Another thing to remember about fear is that many times, our greatest fears can be the place where God wants to bless us the most. The enemy sees that and tries to stop us or stop God by throwing fear at us. Remember, fear is a spirit, and God has not given us a spirit of fear (2 Timothy 1:7). Fear only comes from the world, the flesh, or the devil.

Fear is the source of most of the struggles in my life. Growing up I was always plagued by fears, and I learned at an early age that I couldn't trust anything

100%. I learned that everything was eventually going to let me down, and the more that things let you down, the more fear is going to creep in. There are only two things that won't let us down and only two things that are 100% flawless: the Word of God and God Himself. I didn't know anything about either of those things while I was growing up, so fear had its way in my life.

Looking back, my two greatest fears at the time I got saved were being single and public speaking. Talking in front of others was horrifying to me — the anxiety was so bad that I would get terrible stomach aches in high school any time that I had to talk in front of others. My parents took me to the doctor, but nothing was found to be wrong with me besides my fears. My parents even sent me to this course called "Dale Carnegie" to try to help me through these fears. It cost them a lot of money, and it was money they didn't have to spare. I went one time and ended up telling my parents that I just couldn't go back and that I would pay them back their money. I got a part-time job and paid them back every penny. In college I didn't get my degree because I wouldn't take a speech class! The classes I loved were accounting and data processing (which is what they called computer programming back then), and I would ace them with very little study. My accounting teacher kept calling on me during class because he said he knew I knew the answers. I told him if he kept calling on me that I would have to drop his class. He said, "No, no. You know the answers. I'm going to keep calling on you so you can get over this fear." He continued calling on me and I dropped the class! This ended up happening twice — two different teachers did the exact same thing.

Speaking in front of people was one of my greatest fears. I hated it. After I got saved, the Lord slowly started dealing with me about that. Not right away, but gradually. At first, if I thought I was going to get called on in a group to pray or say something, I would sneak out the back. If I saw someone who needed to be prayed out loud over, I would leave the room. I would figure out all kinds of ways to get out of speaking up during the first couple of years after salvation. The Lord let me slide at first, but eventually He began dealing with me on it. He started by giving me one-on-one relationships that required me to speak up. I knew that He wanted me to disciple, but the idea of teaching another individual terrified me. The first time I met with someone to go through the first discipleship lesson, I was literally on my knees at the edge of my bed for over an hour before she arrived. I was terrified by the idea of discipling.

Then I was asked to speak in front of people — people asked for prayer or they asked me to give a devotion. It was clear that God was starting to deal with me on this and wasn't going to let me slide any more. He eventually got me in a corner to face my fear through a ministry called "Gospel in the Stars," which is where we'd go out to Smithville Lake with a presentation about the stars and use it as a way to reach people with the gospel! Sometimes I think I got more out of it than our visitors. One year at our annual adult Bible camp, the leadership asked our ministry group to share about Gospel in the Stars one night. They decided that each person would take a constellation and tell the gospel story behind that constellation to the whole retreat group. From the very first week that they announced this to us, I was praying and seeking a way to get out of it! I knew I couldn't lie to them and say I was sick, and I finally came to the conclusion that there was no way out. It was terrible!

The night before the presentation I didn't sleep at all and tried to figure out what I was going to do. In the afternoon before the presentation, I went on a walk. It was a beautiful and hot, sunny day. There was a pond at the retreat site and I headed that direction. I walked and talked with the Lord, begging Him to not make me do this. After the second time around the pond, it was very clear that this was an area I needed to give up and surrender to Him. Again, this is what we've been going over throughout this book — you're going to have struggles in your life where you're going to have to let it go. You have to abandon yourself and tell Him, "Lord, I don't want it this way, but I am willing and I surrender. Not my will, but Thy will."

All He wanted was for me to be willing. 2 Corinthians 8:12 says that all He wants is a willing mind. 2 Corinthians 9:8 says that He is able. He doesn't ask us to be able because He is able for us. So I finally surrendered it all. I knew that He was greater than this fear that I had, and even though I knew that I wasn't able to do it, I knew that He was. I knew that He could slay this giant of fear in my life just like He slew Goliath. I just had to be willing to let Him use me and do it through me.

> **2 Corinthians 8:12** For if there be first a willing mind, it is accepted according to that a man hath, and not according to that he hath not.
>
> **2 Corinthians 9:8** And God is able to make all grace abound toward you; that ye, always having all sufficiency in all things, may abound to every good work:

After I let it go and surrendered to His will, I walked back to join everyone at the camp center. We were getting ready for dinner and the line was very long inside the large barn-like cafeteria. When I went in, there wasn't a cloud in the sky and no prediction of bad weather coming. But by the time I came out an hour later, the clouds were rolling in. It poured and poured and poured down rain, and they ended up having to cancel the Gospel in the Stars presentation that night. God had put me in a corner to surrender, and then after all that struggle, He didn't make me go through with the presentation that night. This was good because though I was willing to speak, I was not yet equipped to talk in front of hundreds of people.

The moral of the story is that before they cancelled it, God had taken me to a place of willing surrender. The ironic thing is that I was asked to do a devotion in our small group the very next week. This time I had to follow through with my commitment to surrender. The first devotion was only with two other ladies, but it was very terrible for me at the time. The fear was still there, but the Lord walked me through the fear! He began showing me that He could do it through me. All I had to do was be willing. He was able!

I'm just giving you one illustration from my life of how the Lord began conquering my fears. I had to surrender each of my fears to Him step by step. There will be many times when you will come to this crossroads and need to surrender to the Lord. This is when He began showing me that He wanted to use me more in speaking and sharing with others publicly. This is still not my comfort zone, but God can change us little by little to become more like the Lord Jesus Christ.

The Bible is like a gold mine! There is buried treasure in this Book. We are looking at some of these promises, and for every broken heart, every difficulty, every obstacle, and every fear, there is a promise in there that God wants to give you. But the only way that we're going to get to these promises is by spending time with Him. As He brings us to those crossroads — whether they be fear or difficulty — we must abandon and surrender to Him and His Word, step by step and little by little.

In this chapter we are going to talk about the secret place of the living God. We all have access to this place! Just like with grace, I don't have more access than you do, and David didn't have more access than we do. The question isn't whether you have access, because we all do through the pages of the Word of God. The questions are whether you believe what God says and whether you take Him up on His invitation to access this place. That's the key: how much do you choose to access this secret place? How much do you believe His words about this secret place?

> **Acts 4:13** *Now when they saw the boldness of Peter and John, and perceived that they were unlearned and ignorant men, they marvelled; and they took knowledge of them, that they had been with Jesus.*

This verse shows the thing that can never let us down and the thing that will give us true confidence in our faith. It's all about how much time you're spending with the true source of power: Jesus Christ. How much time are you spending with God in His Word? David spent hours upon hours with the living God as he tended the sheep. Just read Psalms and you'll see it — the book is all about David's love relationship with his Heavenly Father! He was a man after God's own heart, and to discover God's heart, David spent time in His Word getting to know the facts of His words. He knew God because he knew His Word. He had a relationship with the living God, and he took everything to the Lord!

We began learning about how to get this kind of confidence from a relationship with God in His Word back in Chapter 2, and this is the only thing that true confidence should stem from. This is where we're going to conquer our fears. Let's look at some facts about fear that we've already addressed. We saw Job struggling with fear in Job 3:25 — he may have sometimes been motivated by fear of circumstances rather than fear of God. At the beginning, he had a great fear hidden inside, and rather than being 100% motivated by perfect love, he was sometimes motivated by that fear. God wants us to fear Him more than we fear other things and other people, not because we are afraid to be with Him, but because we've been with Him so much, we know that He is bigger than any fear we ever have! We know that He is God!

In order to get Job to fear Him above all else, He had to show up and let Job have a glimpse of Him. That's how we learn the same thing — after we get a glimpse of God, we're going to fear Him when we see how awesome and big and glorious He is. When that happens, we're going to better understand how much bigger He is than any of our fears.

In our society we are fueled by fear. We're fearful of rejection, we're fearful of man, we're fearful of failure, and we're fearful of getting old. Hospitals are full of people with fears. Our spirit and soul and body all ripple together, and even though we might have a spiritual problem, we end up with physical ailments because of it. We saw in Chapter 2 that all of our fears begin with a fear of death (Hebrews 2:14-15). From a very young age, we become afraid to die! That fear is deep-seated within our flesh. From there our fears just spread out and build upon that. We've already talked about how fear is a spirit (2 Timothy 1:7) and that perfect love casts out fear (1 John 4:18). In the end, it really boils down to who is sitting on the throne of our heart. Faith is believing the Spirit of God and letting Him control, and fear is believing the spirit of fear and letting it control. There's no in-between — we're either going to have faith or we're going to have fear. We need to lift the shield of faith in Ephesians 6:16 and let the Word protect us from the spirit of fear.

> **2 Timothy 1:7** *For God hath not given us the spirit of fear; but of power, and of love, and of a sound mind.*

> **Ephesians 6:16** *Above all, taking the shield of faith, wherewith ye shall be able to quench all the fiery darts of the wicked.*

Our faith needs to be selective — we can't have faith in just anything. Faith — real, biblical faith — must stem from the Word of God. After all, "faith cometh by hearing, and hearing by the word of God" (Romans 10:17). When you sit in a chair, you have to first have faith that the chair will hold you up. Biblical faith is having faith in the words of the living God, and you can do that by taking a verse and stepping out in faith that God's Word will direct and preserve you. That's difficult, but it's what we have to do. Courage is not the absence of fear! Courage is walking through fear with the living God who is greater and bigger than all our fears. However, you won't know this until you grow in your relationship with Him. David walked with God when he went out to meet Goliath because he knew God was bigger.

David overcame fear by finding the secret place of God, which is the spiritual place where he communed with the living God, but David wasn't the one that wrote about it. Psalm 91 tells us about the secret place of God, and it's the key text for this chapter as well as the ammunition for conquering fear. This psalm was written by Moses after the mobile tabernacle was finished. The tabernacle was a picture of the coming temple of God and was the place where God met with His people. Inside it was the Holy of Holies — the most sacred place of the temple that allowed the high priest to experience nearness with God (Exodus 26:33-34)! Now, as church-age believers, our bodies become the temple of the Holy Spirit of God at salvation (1 Corinthians 6:19-20). We, too, have the ability to find the Holy of Holies — the spiritual secret place where we meet with the living God!

If you're struggling with fear, this is a great chapter to meditate on as you build your relationship with Him.

> **Psalm 91** *He that dwelleth in the secret place of the most High shall abide under the shadow of the Almighty. I will say of the Lord, He is my refuge and my fortress: my God; in him will I trust. Surely he shall deliver thee from the snare of the fowler, and from the noisome pestilence. He shall cover thee with his feathers, and under his wings shalt thou trust: his truth shall be thy shield and buckler. Thou shalt not be afraid for the terror by night; nor for the arrow that flieth by day; nor for the pestilence that walketh in darkness; nor for the destruction that wasteth at noonday. A thousand shall fall at thy side, and ten thousand at thy right hand; but it shall not come nigh thee. Only with thine eyes shalt thou behold and see the reward of the wicked. Because thou hast made the Lord, which is my refuge, even the most High, thy habitation; there shall no evil befall thee, neither shall any plague come nigh thy dwelling. For he shall give his angels charge over thee, to keep thee in all thy ways. They shall bear thee up in their hands, lest thou dash thy foot against a stone. Thou shalt tread upon the lion and adder: the young lion and the dragon shalt thou trample under feet. Because he hath set his love upon me, therefore will I deliver him: I will set him on high, because he hath known my name. He shall call upon me, and I will answer him: I will be with him in trouble; I will deliver him, and honour him. With long life will I satisfy him, and shew him my salvation.*

Let's break down this psalm verse by verse and see what we can learn about growing in this secret place. Verse 1 starts out by immediately talking about the secret place. What and where is the secret place? To answer this question, we must first understand that we're not talking about a feeling. In addition to that, for us in the church age, we must understand that we are not talking about a physical location or outward surroundings like those described in the Old Testament. You may have a certain place in your home where you like to pray (I do!), but that's not the secret place. Even Jacob used to return to Bethel to get right with God, but that wasn't the secret place. The reason it's not a physical location is because it is a spiritual one.

> **1 Corinthians 6:19** What? know ye not that your body is the temple of the Holy Ghost which is in you, which ye have of God, and ye are not your own?

> **John 14:23** Jesus answered and said unto him, If a man love me, he will keep my words: and my Father will love him, and we will come unto him, and make our abode with him.

We have a secret place to meet with the living God! We all have access to the Holy of Holies — the place of God's presence — through the blood of Jesus Christ! The secret place of God is found in the Kingdom of God which, as we mentioned before, is a spiritual kingdom.

> **Matthew 6:33** But seek ye first the kingdom of God, and his righteousness; and all these things shall be added unto you.

> **Luke 17:21** Neither shall they say, Lo here! or, lo there! for, behold, the kingdom of God is within you.

The Kingdom of God exists in a spiritual dimension, and the portal to this place is the Bible.

> **Ephesians 3:17-19** That Christ may dwell in your hearts by faith; that ye, being rooted and grounded in love, may be able to comprehend with all saints what is the breadth, and length, and depth, and height; and to know the love of Christ, which passeth knowledge, that ye might be filled with all the fulness of God.

Notice here the mention of the breadth, the length, the depth, and the height. We talk in three dimensions, but God is talking about four dimensions! Again, we have the spiritual realm that we've been talking about and all know about, and this realm has four dimensions. The relationship we have with God exists within this realm.

When I was a young Christian, I went to an all-night prayer service. They turned out all of the lights in the auditorium and there were no windows there, so it was pitch black. All of a sudden, they played an audio of bombs, artillery, and other noises of warfare. It went on for about 60 seconds or longer, and that's a long time when you're sitting in the dark. They finally turned off the audio and turned on the lights. The leader of the prayer meeting got up on stage and said, "I just want you all to realize what's really going on all around us in the spiritual realm. Folks, there's a war zone everywhere we go, and one of our most powerful weapons is prayer!"

Here's another illustration that I share a lot because there are many biblical principles in it. It's the movie *The Matrix*. The characters think that they're living in reality, but they aren't! Where they live is not the real world, and that's exactly how it is for us, too. This temporal world we see is not the real world! There is another whole reality going on in the spiritual realm, so we must get our focus off this temporal world and learn to put it on the eternal one. We need to enter into that spiritual realm. Here's another great biblical example where a prophet of God explains to his disciple to see the things of God, not the things of this world.

> ***2 Kings 6:15-17*** *And when the servant of the man of God was risen early, and gone forth, behold, an host compassed the city both with horses and chariots. And his servant said unto him, Alas, my master! how shall we do? And he answered, Fear not: for they that be with us are more than they that be with them. And Elisha prayed, and said, Lord, I pray thee, open his eyes, that he may see. And the Lord opened the eyes of the young man; and he saw: and, behold, the mountain was full of horses and chariots of fire round about Elisha.*

Our church is a battleship, not a cruise liner. There are spiritual battles going on all around us. This tumultuous spiritual reality is the real world, and spiritual battles for the souls of men are happening around us everywhere we go.

The Old Testament tabernacle, established around the time Psalm 91 was written, is a picture for us of the secret place. Think about how the tabernacle was set up: there was the outer court, which was a picture of fellowship. The inner court represented ministry, and then there was the most holy place, the Holy of Holies, which represented intimacy. In the Old Testament, the only person who could go there was the high priest once a year. That was it! That was a picture for us so that we could better understand the reality of the secret place as a spiritual location. That is why the Old Testament saints, like David and Moses, were able to find the same secret place as we New Testament believers do!

Now we operate in a spiritual reality and not a physical one like they did in the Old Testament. They had the Kingdom of Heaven, which is physical; we have the Kingdom of God, which is spiritual. God's throne room is in us through another dimension. Once we are saved, this is where we find our secret place. Our bodies are the temple of God, so we have access to the Holy of Holies with our Lord. Jesus is our great high priest and can be touched by our feelings! Just like the high priest who went into the physical Holy of Holies, Jesus enters into God the Father's presence in intercession for us. But unlike the Old Testament priests who only went there once a year, Jesus is there continually (Hebrews 9:7, 11-12)!

> **Hebrews 4:14-16** *Seeing then that we have a great high priest, that is passed into the heavens, Jesus the Son of God, let us hold fast our profession. For we have not an high priest which cannot be touched with the feeling of our infirmities; but was in all points tempted like as we are, yet without sin. Let us therefore come boldly unto the throne of grace, that we may obtain mercy, and find grace to help in time of need.*

This is an awesome and spectacular promise to us New Testament believers! It says that Jesus can literally be touched by what we're going through. When you think no one else cares, remember that God does! He invites us to come to Him and tell Him about what we are going through and ask for His help. This is what the Prayer Exercise (Chapter 3) is all about: connecting with the Lord in the Holy of Holies. When the veil was torn, we were given full access to the spiritual Holy of Holies and to full intimacy with God. This secret place is accessed through prayer!

We've discussed what and where, and now we are going to talk about who. Whom will we find in this miraculous secret place, in the Holy of Holies? Well, I think it is pretty obvious!

> **Psalm 91:1** *He that dwelleth in the secret place of the most High shall abide under the shadow of the Almighty.*

We find the Most High, the Almighty. We find the High One (Isaiah 57:15) under whose shadow we can hide (Psalm 57:1). He's our Father (2 Corinthians 6:17-18), and He's our refuge, our fortress, our deliverer, our bodyguard, our complete and total protection (Isaiah 25:4)! If you're saved, you are a child of the King!

> **Psalm 91:2-4** *I will say of the Lord, He is my refuge and my fortress: my God; in him will I trust. Surely he shall deliver thee from the snare of the fowler, and from the noisome pestilence. He shall cover thee with his feathers, and under his wings shalt thou trust: his truth shall be thy shield and buckler.*

> **Psalm 91:11-12** *For he shall give his angels charge over thee, to keep thee in all thy ways. They shall bear thee up in their hands, lest thou dash thy foot against a stone.*

Do you really believe that? Have you been spending time with Him? Have you been getting to know Him? Don't forget, you must see past your earthly father. If you had a difficult relationship with your earthly father or no relationship at all, like me, then you have to look past that and not let that hurdle stop you. Your Heavenly Father says He is the Father to the fatherless! Oh my, what a great promise for us to lay our naked souls upon.

If you are in somebody's shadow, you are very close to them. If you dwell in the secret place of the Most High, you're going to abide under His shadow.

That is intimate, and that's the place I want to be! That's the place we should all want to be. He is our shield and our buckler — do you believe that? Again, this is what it boils down to. As you spend time with Him, you see all the ways that He has come through for you. You begin to understand the surety of His promises. Both the Father and the Son are there in the secret place. Remember that Jesus is our Knight in Shining Armor and that He ever liveth to make intercession for us.

> **Hebrews 7:24-25** *But this man, because he continueth ever, hath an unchangeable priesthood. Wherefore he is able also to save them to the uttermost that come unto God by him, seeing he ever liveth to make intercession for them.*

What do we find in this secret place? We don't find anyone else but Him. If you have been walking with the Lord for very long, you have found this place. You know it well. It's where nothing else matters, and it's where you're on your knees before the Lord. It is the throne room of God, and once you've been there, you want to go back! It is so spectacular. Unfortunately, we don't always go there as often as we should. We have to learn to keep going there and eventually live or dwell there. We find the fruit of the Spirit in this secret place. And though the world gives us tribulations, the secret place gives peace.

> **Romans 14:17** *For the kingdom of God is not meat and drink; but righteousness, and peace, and joy in the Holy Ghost.*

> **John 16:33** *These things I have spoken unto you, that in me ye might have peace. In the world ye shall have tribulation: but be of good cheer; I have overcome the world.*

To find this secret place, we have to reckon ourselves in Christ. We have to die to ourselves and live unto Him. Again, getting back to the cover of this book, we need to keep asking ourselves who is on the throne of our hearts. Are you walking in the Kingdom of God today? It is a choice that we make every single day. Paul said, "I die daily." We need to do the same and let Jesus live His life through us. We have to stay connected to Him, and we have to decide this every moment of every day. We have to choose to follow the Spirit, and if we are not walking in the Spirit, there is no way for us to find this secret place.

It is easy to check ourselves to see if we are in the Spirit because the Lord clearly lists the works of the flesh and the fruit of the Spirit. If we are walking in the Spirit, it will be easy to see its fruit in our lives. In the same sense, if we have works of the flesh, then it's obvious what we need to do! We may have to go back to the chapter on dealing with sin and take care of it that way. Sometimes, like we discussed, we might be stained and have to wash our pattern of sin over and over until it's gone. But we are to check ourselves — in 2 Corinthians 13:5 the Bible says we have to examine ourselves. Galatians 5:16-26 and James 3:14-17 list the fruit of following the flesh and the fruit of following the Spirit.

> **Galatians 5:16-26** *This I say then, Walk in the Spirit, and ye shall not fulfil the lust of the flesh. For the flesh lusteth against the Spirit, and the Spirit against the flesh: and these are contrary the one to the other: so that ye cannot do the things that ye would. But if ye be led of the Spirit, ye are not under the law. Now the works of the flesh are manifest, which are these; adultery, fornication, uncleanness, lasciviousness, idolatry, witchcraft, hatred, variance, emulations, wrath, strife, seditions, heresies, envyings, murders, drunkenness, revellings, and such like: of the which I tell you before, as I have also told you in time past, that they which do such things shall not inherit the kingdom of God. But the fruit of the Spirit is love, joy, peace, longsuffering, gentleness, goodness, faith, meekness, temperance: against such there is no law. And they that are Christ's have crucified the flesh with the affections and lusts. If we live in the Spirit, let us also walk in the Spirit. Let us not be desirous of vain glory, provoking one another, envying one another.*

> **James 3:14-17** *But if ye have bitter envying and strife in your hearts, glory not, and lie not against the truth. This wisdom descendeth not from above, but is earthly, sensual, devilish. For where envying and strife is, there is confusion and every evil work. But the wisdom that is from above is first pure, then peaceable,*

> gentle, and easy to be intreated, full of mercy and good fruits, without partiality, and without hypocrisy.

Please take time to read these verses. They are key. Yes, these are some long lists, but it is good to go over them periodically. The more we go over them, the more the Lord will keep reminding us how to follow the Spirit. Using this list makes it very easy for us to tell what the fruit is in our life, and the fact that God put envy right next to murder in Galatians 5 shows us that we should take all works of the flesh very seriously, even ones that don't seem "that bad." If you find a work of the flesh, just put it under the blood and give it to the Lord. Wash it out in the water of the Word.

> **Romans 8:31** What shall we then say to these things? If God be for us, who can be against us?

Another important thing about the secret place is that if the Lord has told you something through His Word, you can have confidence in what He has said. There is no fear there, and there is just no confidence that can come close to that! By getting in that secret place and hearing a word from God for ourselves, we can conquer fear. When we dwell in His Kingdom, we have His protection. Who's going to touch you if the Lord is next to you?

> **Isaiah 54:15-17** Behold, they shall surely gather together, but not by me: whosoever shall gather together against thee shall fall for thy sake. Behold, I have created the smith that bloweth the coals in the fire, and that bringeth forth an instrument for his work; and I have created the waster to destroy. No weapon that is formed against thee shall prosper; and every tongue that shall rise against thee in judgment thou shalt condemn. This is the heritage of the servants of the Lord, and their righteousness is of me, saith the Lord.

Are you serving the Lord right now? If you are, He says that His protection is the heritage of His servants. You have His protection. Claim that verse! That promise is yours.

Isaiah 51:12-13 *I, even I, am he that comforteth you: who art thou, that thou shouldest be afraid of a man that shall die, and of the son of man which shall be made as grass; and forgettest the Lord thy maker, that hath stretched forth the heavens, and laid the foundations of the earth; and hast feared continually every day because of the fury of the oppressor, as if he were ready to destroy? and where is the fury of the oppressor?*

Isaiah 51:12-13 says that when we fear, we forget God. Remember, you can't think about two things at the same time. These verses are basically saying that we ourselves get in the way. Don't forget who God is. If you find fear in your life, go back and remember what He's done for you. Set that track record. There is no confidence in the world like knowing that you're doing what God has told you to do and that you're letting Him do it through you. This is not a feeling, it's an awareness of the person of the living God. It's a relationship. It's the greatest confidence you can have, and it's the only real confidence that is attainable and sustainable. Who's bigger: your God or your fear? I remember one prayer I often prayed during my early walk when I feared man so much. I used to pray, "Lord, help me fear You more than I fear man." Praise God, He answered that prayer!

Once we find the secret place, the next hurdle is to learn how to stay or abide in the secret place. In Psalm 91:1 and 9 He talks about abiding in this secret place. He doesn't want us to just visit like we do when we're desperate. He wants us to learn how to abide there — to live and rest in the secret place of God. This means that you have to make another conscious choice! Again, just like you get up every day and die to self and let the Lord live His life through you, your spiritual habitat must be with Him as well — it's a conscious choice. David was a man after God's own heart, and he chose. He was king of Israel, but he said he would rather be a door keeper for the Lord.

Psalm 91:1 *He that dwelleth in the secret place of the most High shall abide under the shadow of the Almighty.*

> **Psalm 91:9** *Because thou hast made the Lord, which is my refuge, even the most High, thy habitation;*

> **Psalm 84:10-12** *For a day in thy courts is better than a thousand. I had rather be a doorkeeper in the house of my God, than to dwell in the tents of wickedness. For the Lord God is a sun and shield: the Lord will give grace and glory: no good thing will he withhold from them that walk uprightly. O Lord of hosts, blessed is the man that trusteth in thee.*

David's attitude was that he wanted to remain in God's presence, even just as a door keeper. In order to stay in God's presence, we have to make an intentional choice to do so. We need to be mindful and aware of Him and of our actions. Are you consciously aware of God's presence in your life? Like walking after the Spirit, this is also sometimes just a switch inside us based on our decisions and heart attitude.

Back when I was so fearful, I had a lot of stomach aches and a lot of pain. This led me to be constantly talking to the Lord, which kept me constantly aware of Him. Sometimes as things got easier and some my fears were overcome, there were moments when I let my guard down and was no longer thinking about the Lord as much as I should have been. But that's not what David did. He stayed constantly aware, and that's what we need to do. We have to work at our relationship with God by spending time with Him. We have to balance our time so that He is always the priority.

We often hear about tithing our income, but we rarely hear about tithing our time. In one week, we have 168 hours. If we get 7 hours of sleep a night, we are left with 119 hours. If we work 40 hours a week, then we are left with 79 hours. Now we know that a good place to start is always the tithe, or 10%. So you can either tithe off of your gross or net time. If it's gross, it's off 168 hours a week, giving 16.8 hours to God. If it's off the net, then we tithe off 79 hours, giving 7.9 hours with God. Do you spend 10% of your time with God? If you just start with tithing your time, it's between 7.9 and 16.8 hours a week you should be spending with Him. However, if you've really gotten a glimpse of the living God, you'll find that you make it much more than that.

Another good thing to consider is who you spend the most time talking with each week. Again, God is with you always, and if we stay consciously aware of that, it changes everything! Who wouldn't want to walk with the Creator of the Universe, the King of kings, and the Lord of lords? But when we aren't having a rough time, we can sometimes forget God. You must set your priorities and set apart time with Him.

Think about how much time you spend doing your hobbies or how much time you spend watching TV. Nothing is necessarily wrong with those things, but just make sure that you're not doing that more than you're spending time with the Lord. Because we live in a comfortable world, we can all fall into misprioritizing the way that we spend our time.

Psalm 91:14 says to set your love on Him. Way back when I was younger, we used to "set" our hair — we would wrap strands of wet hair around curlers and leave them in all night. In the morning we would take out the curlers and our hair would be set in curls! Similarly, God says to set your love on Him! Set it there and make it stay there. John 14:23 says that if you love the Lord then you're going to keep His words and He will fellowship with you!

Have you ever been in love? Do you remember the first time you fell head-over-heels in love? Think about that time. If you're smiling right now, I'm sure you can remember what it was like to be in love like that. It's the same way with the Lord! As believers, we are called the bride of Christ, and as His bride, we need to be in love with Him as our Groom. Are you in love with the Lord? If so, are you staying in love with Him? Or have you lost your first love? Even our marriages to our spouses can inadvertently become more focused on the kids or the job or so many other things that we forget about one other. In those situations, married couples need to get away from all the distractions and spend focused time with each other. This quality time is the cure, and it is how we address our love with the Lord as well.

Just like how marriages produce the kids that distract the spouses from each other, the only reason we have ministry is because of our relationship with our Lord! We want to maintain that. We can't get so focused on our ministry or discipleship that we lose focus on our Groom, Jesus. He gives us clear directions on how to get back to our first love, which is the love we had when we were first saved.

> ***Revelation 2:2-4*** *I know thy works, and thy labour, and thy patience, and how thou canst not bear them which are evil: and thou hast tried them which say they are apostles, and are not, and hast found them liars: And hast borne, and hast patience, and for my name's sake hast laboured, and hast not fainted. Nevertheless I have somewhat against thee, because thou hast left thy first love.*

He's talking to the church at Ephesus, which was a good church! They loved the Lord and they had a solid ministry, but they had left their first love. The Lord gives them (and us) a clear way to return to our first love in Revelation 2:5.

> ***Revelation 2:5*** *Remember therefore from whence thou art fallen, and repent, and do the first works; or else I will come unto thee quickly, and will remove thy candlestick out of his place, except thou repent.*

First, He says to remember! Remember back when you had that first love with Jesus. Talk to someone about when you got saved or experienced that first love with the Lord. Share it and reminisce over it. We need to remember when we first started walking with the Lord. After we remember that, the next thing He tells us to do in Revelation 2:5 is to repent! We talked about repentance in earlier chapters. It's saying, "I'm wrong, and you're right, Lord. Forgive me for forgetting that first love!" Then He says, "Repent and do the first works." This means to go back and do what we did when we were head over heels in love with Him (like spending hours in prayer and the Word, being zealous about sharing the gospel, and being content to just sit at His feet). He says remember, repent, and do. So walk with Him and be joyous! We've got to be in love with the Lord. One other thing I like to do is begin consciously sharing my testimony and telling others all about times when I walked in that first love. It's amazing how those thoughts begin bringing me into sweet fellowship with Jesus!

He also says in Psalm 91:14 that we must know His name. There are numerous names of God that we can find in the Word. We get to know His name and all the names He goes by in the Word as we spend time with Him. Know who He is. Know Him better than you know anyone else, and know His Word more than any other hobbies or interests.

Fellowship with Him in the secret place. He is your father, protector, provider, and bridegroom! Think about who He is to you and then call on Him. We can find full confidence in the secret place, but we have to be constantly choosing to spend time with Him there. As we meditate on His Word and spend time in prayer with Him, we will begin to better understand this quiet place. And as we go about our day, our thoughts must be centered on Him. We must choose to enter the secret place, and spending time there is the only way to overcome fear.

In these chapters are a number of foundational verses and passages for overcoming fear. Keep reading and spending time with Him. Collect more of the promises He gives you though His Word. Another good book and companion to this study is *Hinds' Feet on High Places* by Hannah Hurnard. This book is an allegory that is so helpful in understanding how to overcome fear, and I encourage you to read it if that's something you struggle with.

Questions to Consider:

1. How is your relationship with God like an iceberg?

2. What is the secret place? How do you access it?

3. How often do you access the secret place? What do you find there?

4. Why is there confidence in the secret place?

5. How does the secret place allow us to overcome fear?

6. Where does true faith stem from?

7. When God is calling us to do something impossible for us, what is the only thing that He asks from us in 2 Corinthians 8:12?

8. How much time do you spend on entertainment a day? How much time do you spend in ministry, reading the Word, and praying?

9. How do we operate from a spiritual reality and not a physical one?

10. Did you realize that there are constant spiritual battles raging around you? How did that make you feel? What will you do differently now?

11. Do you feel like you have lost your First Love? What do you need to do to get it back?

11

How to Keep from Being Deceived

In this chapter we're going to look at God's hierarchical structure of authority and lay out reasons why our emotions can cause us so many difficulties. We will also see how to apply soberness and discretion in order to overcome the obstacles that our emotions create.

When I see the word "deception," it makes me think of something very elusive or mysterious, but in reality, it really only means to be tricked into believing a lie. That's the bottom line: you've been tricked, and your foundation is a lie. The mysterious part of deception is actually in how it was carried out. Do most people want to intentionally believe a lie? No! That's absurd. Most of us like to think that we don't believe lies... but we often do.

I hate to make this reference again, but *The Matrix* is such a great example! Just like in that movie, our current world system has allowed us to believe a reality that is only partially true. We must learn to see everything through the filter of the Word of God. That is the key, because truth is the only thing that can expose deception. Just like how we can believe all of the nice things that an unsaved man says to us in order to win our hearts, and just like we can believe what we see on TV, Twitter, and Facebook throughout the day, we can easily be pulled into lies. An easy way to identify lies is if they don't line up with what's in the Bible! It might only be a "little" lie, but even if it's 97% true, it's still a lie and will create a faulty foundation.

> **2 Corinthians 4:4** *In whom the god of this world hath blinded the minds of them which believe not, lest the light of the glorious gospel of Christ, who is the image of God, should shine unto them.*

This verse says that the god of this world, Satan, blinds us when we choose to not believe the truth, and this can even happen to those of us who are saved! We can all have blind spots. In my car, there's a spot on the rear right side where a car could be and I wouldn't even know it. Just like that, we Christians can have blind spots in our lives if we don't understand what the Word of God says about something. It is only going to be through the truth that a lie is going to be exposed! So we need to get the truth. Our world questions truth and says that each person has their own truth. "Everything is truth," and because everything is truth, nothing is truth. John 17:17 says, "Thy word is truth." God says that His Word is truth. Jesus says, "I am the way, the truth, and the life" (John 14:6). Truth is the Word of God, and Jesus is the Word of God. Only God's light exposes the darkness, and only His Word can discern truth from lies.

This is a key verse of this chapter:

> **1 Corinthians 10:13** *There hath no temptation taken you but such as is common to man: but God is faithful, who will not suffer you to be tempted above that ye are able; but will with the temptation also make a way to escape, that ye may be able to bear it.*

What this verse tells us is that God will always give you a way out. It lines up with what David wrote in Psalm 119:11: "Thy word I have hid in my heart, that I might not sin against thee." Through His Word, God gives us a way out of both temptation and deception, so when we go through those storms, we have to find the verses that we can hold on to. They will be the anchors for our souls. But also in this verse it says that, "There hath no temptation taken you but such as is common to man," so realize that whatever storm you may be facing or getting ready to face, it is a storm that others also face. A lot of times we want to think that we are the only ones in the world who are going through what we're going through and we can get into a big pity party. But God says right there in this verse that every temptation you go through is common to man! Other people are going through or have gone through the same thing. You may not know who they are, but often there are others in our own church body who are enduring the same things and we don't even know it! We must keep going back to the verses and remember what God says about how to keep from being deceived. God says other people are going through this, and He also says that He is going to give us a way out! Therefore we need to approach Him in faith, knowing that He is more than familiar with our crisis and that He has already provided us a way out (Hebrews 4:15-16).

In my day, the way a bank teller could tell a counterfeit dollar bill from a real one was through experience. In other words, they were so familiar with the real deal that when the fake showed up, it was obvious! The same principle applies with us. The more familiar we become with the real deal — the Word of God — the less we can be deceived. God doesn't change. The more we learn His principles and the way He does things, the more we can tell when it is a fake deal. It begins to get easier as we learn to identify "book, chapter, verse" — what does God say about it in His Word? When I was younger and unsaved, I was often deceived. I pretty much believed everything anyone told me. That got me into so much trouble and my life was a wreck. We must first believe God and let His Word prove out what others say. It is the truth of the Word of God that helps us turn our lives around. I know I've said this over and over again, but it is knowing the principles of the Word of God and studying to "shew thyself approved" (2 Timothy 2:15) that will give you victory in your life with anything that you might face.

Now, let's look at how we get deceived in the first place. One way that we as women can be deceived is by our own hearts — through our feelings, emotions, perceptions, sensitivities, preconceived notions, and intuitions — that we often let run our life instead of running things through the Word of God. We can get easily messed up by our heart, which the Bible says is so deceitful. This is why the Bible says that "He that hath no rule over his own spirit is like a city that is broken down, and without walls." (Proverbs 25:28). That's our own spirit running things, not the Spirit of God. When we are taken over by our carnal heart or our own spirit, then we get into trouble.

> *Jeremiah 17:9* *The heart is deceitful above all things, and desperately wicked: who can know it?*

We need to be very familiar with this verse — after all, it tells us that we can be deceived by our very own hearts. I have written "You are your own worst enemy" next to Romans 7 in my Bible, because I am! My heart often keeps me from walking in obedience to the things that God has called me to. Our flesh works with the devil and deceives us. Yes, our perceptions, feelings, preconceived notions, and our sensitivities can all be good things, but they can also be very bad. This is especially true if we are trusting and resting on these things instead of on the Word of God. Let me give you some examples. There were times when I was younger in the Lord that I would go to church and wave at a friend, only to be put in a state of distress when they looked right through me and walked away without waving back. I got caught up in thinking about all of the things that I must have done wrong, and then I would begin to think about how unfair and unfriendly they were. I would begin to defame their character and think evil of them, but all along what I didn't know was that they were too caught up in the storm in their personal lives to have even seen me. That, or they honestly did not see me wave at them! I didn't have the full picture and my heart deceived me. We build a whole case in our minds, and the next time we see them, our resentment continues to grow.

Remember: fact, faith, feeling. Don't let your imagination run wild when you do not have the facts. It's easy to do! It could be because of a guilty conscience on your own part, or it could just be because they are having a bad day or you're having a bad day. Give people the benefit of the doubt and go by the facts. We cannot let our perceptions run wild.

Another thing is sensitivities. Our culture is a Laodicean culture. Laodicea means "rights of the people," which means that the rights of God are completely ignored. We are a sue-happy culture that is always seeking to defend our personal rights regardless of the cost to ourselves or others. Everyone is busy trying to make sure no one gets offended, but all the while they're offending God. Everybody has rights in our society — except God. "You can't do that to me! You're violating my rights!" That's what happens in Laodicea Land, and sensitivities can be enveloped within all of that. Psalm 119:165 says, "Great peace have they which love thy law: and nothing shall offend them." Our world is full of people taking offense at the smallest things because they do not love God's Word. This does not mean that God calls us to be inconsiderate of others or unkind. We do need to be kind, but let's get a proper definition of kindness. I'm going to give you two examples of our Lord and ask you if Jesus was kind or if He sinned.

> *Luke 9:59-60* And he said unto another, Follow me. But he said, Lord, suffer me first to go and bury my father. Jesus said unto him, Let the dead bury their dead: but go thou and preach the kingdom of God.

This passage talks about a young man that comes to Jesus but wants to first bury his father who had just passed away. Do you know what Jesus said? "Let the dead bury the dead." Can you imagine someone in our culture saying that to someone? Though it may sound insensitive, that's what Jesus said to this man! He wanted to get the point across for him to look at the spiritual and not the physical. Our culture would just go crazy over a response like this! Be careful! Jesus was kind, and Jesus never sinned. His response was righteous.

Another example is in Matthew 15:

> *Matthew 15:22-28* And, behold, a woman of Canaan came out of the same coasts, and cried unto him, saying, Have mercy on me, O Lord, thou son of

> *David; my daughter is grievously vexed with a devil. But he answered her not a word. And his disciples came and besought him, saying, Send her away; for she crieth after us. But he answered and said, I am not sent but unto the lost sheep of the house of Israel. Then came she and worshipped him, saying, Lord, help me. But he answered and said, It is not meet to take the children's bread, and to cast it to dogs. And she said, Truth, Lord: yet the dogs eat of the crumbs which fall from their masters' table. Then Jesus answered and said unto her, O woman, great is thy faith: be it unto thee even as thou wilt. And her daughter was made whole from that very hour.*

At this point in Jesus' ministry He was reaching the Jews, because that was the work that God the Father had given Him. So when this Samaritan (Gentile) woman comes to Him and asks for help with her demon-possessed daughter, do you know what He said to her? "I'm not here for the dogs." Was Jesus kind? You know He was! Did Jesus sin? You know He didn't! He was testing her, and her response was, "Truth, Lord. But even the dogs eat the crumbs at the master's feet." In other words, she accepted that He was focused on the Jews at that time, but she still asked for His help. So He blessed her and rescued her daughter! There are other stories like that in the Word of God. Again, we need to let the Bible define for us what truth is and what kindness is, like in Ephesians 4:32. Jesus was the epitome of everything in this Book, including kindness, but He sometimes confronted people with the truth in a fashion that seems unkind to us in our culture.

All of this shows us that our sensitivities can get in the way of God working in our lives. We can get easily offended at God, at messages, and even at the Bible itself! But we are told to "endure hardness, as a good soldier of Jesus Christ" (2 Timothy 2:3)! In order for God to teach us how to be soldiers, we are going to have to go through "basic training" and not say, "You're encroaching on my rights!" Our American society is rich with goods and has a need for nothing, and we're all about protecting our comfort zones. We need to confront ourselves on some of these issues and realize that we can't be Laodicean. We must put on the armor of God and remember our church is to be a battleship, not a cruise liner.

Even our preconceived notions can deceive us. A preconceived notion is defining a situation by something you've already determined to be true in your mind. In other words, your mind is made up and it's not open to God. In Ezekiel 14:2-11, God says that if you come to Him with a preconceived notion (an "idol"), He will give you a lie to believe! We have to come to this Book with an open heart and an open mind and be seeking God's definitions. We have to have the humility to ask Him to help us replace our preconceived notions with truth from His Word. Isaiah 43 says that if we have other gods on the throne of our hearts then God will not reveal Himself to us. He holds back and waits until we ask Him. It is our job to clear out the idols and things that get between us and God, including our own feelings and perceptions.

Another way our heart can deceive us is found in Ecclesiastes 7:

> *Ecclesiastes 7:21-22 Also take no heed unto all words that are spoken; lest thou hear thy servant curse thee: for oftentimes also thine own heart knoweth that thou thyself likewise hast cursed others.*

These verses bring up an important area of deception. Satan is always looking to trick us, and our flesh is always looking to fulfill its own way. When we hear others talking about us, it is very easy for us to be deceived. We can take ourselves too seriously or begin to desire the praise of others, which means taking our eyes off God. We can also be deceived by sin! We just went over in Chapter 9 how self-righteousness can sometimes get in our way — we can lean on the good things that we're doing and deceive ourselves into thinking that it is by our works that we earn favor with God or exalt ourselves over others. We can become performance-based and begin thinking that our works earn us merit with God. That can become sin.

> *Romans 7:11 For sin, taking occasion by the commandment, deceived me, and by it slew me.*

Your heart can deceive you, and your sin can deceive you through pride and self-righteousness. Another interesting thing is how sin can deceive us for our own oath's sake.

> **Matthew 14:9** *And the king was sorry: nevertheless for the oath's sake, and them which sat with him at meat, he commanded it to be given her.*

This verse talks about how sorry King Herod was for promising to cut off John the Baptist's head after he was pleased with his daughter-in-law's dance. However, for his oath's sake (because he promised), he goes through with it. That's self-righteousness! These are all ways we can deceive ourselves. Herod was keeping his own word, but he was killing God's man. He was deceived by his self-righteous intentions in thinking that keeping a promise was better than sparing God's prophet.

We can also be deceived by our own ignorance. That's why it's important to study to show yourself approved, and this is why it is so important to go to a church that will teach you how to learn the Word of God for yourself. The more you learn about the Lord, the more it's going to protect you from being deceived. Fact, faith, feeling — the facts have to be the foundation. When you start to let your imagination go wild and think of all kinds of things without one fact to back them up, stop! You're going to get yourself way out of line. Mix faith with the facts and you may have a feeling, but don't let the feeling become the foundation. Always let the facts be the foundation.

So who is behind this deception? We have three enemies in this world: the world, the flesh, and the devil. Your own flesh is included in that. The devil is the god of this world (2 Corinthians 4:3-4), and he is a liar and the father of lies (John 8:44). He is an imitator of God and of godliness (2 Corinthians 11:13-15). He is not going to come at you with red horns, pitchfork, and tail. He is going to come to you pretending to be the real God and claiming to have God's words. He is coming to you to deceive you, and he is going to use carnal means to do that — he is going to use your own heart. Job 40-41 talks about Leviathan and Behemoth, and these creatures are actually pictures of Satan and the Antichrist.

These chapters go over how Satan is the chief of the ways of God (Job 40:19), so don't think that you're going to be smarter than the devil. He can outsmart any of us — he's been here a lot longer and he knows the Bible inside and out, but his pride keeps him from surrendering and submitting to God. He is headed for the lake of fire and wants to take all of us with him.

We see the first deception in Genesis 3. The Law of First Mention is an important Bible study principle — in most cases, the first time something is mentioned in the Bible, God will define it and teach us a lot about it. In Genesis 3 we have the first woman who is the first to be deceived by Satan. In looking at this passage we can see a lot about how Satan will seek to deceive us, and what we see is that his attack is first and foremost on the Word of God. Now this shouldn't come as a surprise. If we think about it, all of Satan's deceptions throughout time stem from the same basic maneuver: get someone to believe a lie instead of God's Word. Unfortunately, through ignorance, Eve also misquoted God's Word in response.

> **Genesis 3:1-7** *Now the serpent was more subtil than any beast of the field which the Lord God had made. And he said unto the woman, Yea, hath God said, Ye shall not eat of every tree of the garden? And the woman said unto the serpent, We may eat of the fruit of the trees of the garden: But of the fruit of the tree which is in the midst of the garden, God hath said, Ye shall not eat of it, neither shall ye touch it, lest ye die. And the serpent said unto the woman, Ye shall not surely die: for God doth know that in the day ye eat thereof, then your eyes shall be opened, and ye shall be as gods, knowing good and evil. And when the woman saw that the tree was good for food, and that it was pleasant to the eyes, and a tree to be desired to make one wise, she took of the fruit thereof, and did eat, and gave also unto her husband with her; and he did eat. And the eyes of them both were opened, and they knew that they were naked; and they sewed fig leaves together, and made themselves aprons.*

When Satan came to Eve, he was very agreeable. His first word was "Yea" — that's a positive way to approach anyone. 2 Corinthians 11:3 says that he beguiled her, and it also says in verse 14 that he often shows up as an angel of light (and an angel of light looks like Jesus)! So, when Satan came to Eve, he came across as a good guy and a smooth talker asking about the Word of God. We can see by the question mark at the end of verse 1 that he already was trying to sow a seed of doubt in her mind. "Yea, hath God said?" Did He really say that? This is exactly what Satan tries to do when he comes to us to deceive — he tries to get us to doubt the Word of God.

In verse 2 we see that Eve added to the Word of God and switched around the words. Satan's ploy worked — she couldn't remember exactly what God said. We must both know God's Word and keep it pure from any additions or deletions on our side. Ignorance and tampering are both roads to deception.

Let's say that you're on a missions trip and there is someone on the trip that has a brand new bottle of water, but this person has a bad illness that can spread easily through saliva. You're both thirsty and he takes a long drink from the bottle first, then offers you a drink. The bottle probably only contains a little bit of his spit and the rest of the water is mostly pure. Would you drink it? Probably not! It is the same way with your Bible — you've got hundreds of translations nowadays that change just a few things here and there. Are they all correct? Can they all be correct if they disagree with each other? How much truth is true, and how much must be added or taken away to make the product no longer be full truth?

Think about that a while. That's all that Satan was doing with Eve. He was causing her to doubt and to question what God said. She didn't know exactly what He said and began adding to it because she didn't have the verse memorized, or she added a little bit here and there to make it more palatable or desirable. She had her own translation. Think about the spit — you might have a different translation that is only 1-5% wrong, but which 1-5% is wrong? That in and of itself causes one to begin doubting the whole. God promised us that He has preserved His Word (Psalm 12:6-7), and He promised us we can have the certainty of the Word of God (Proverbs 22:20-

21). Our job is to find out exactly what He says and hold on to it so the devil can't deceive us.

In verse 3 Eve was still quoting her version, and then in verse 4 the enemy came in to flat out deny the Word. This is the same for us. Trust me, if you get around a carnal guy, you might become like that too. He might deny what God has said, and if you like him enough and they are a smooth talker, you might just believe him.

Satan then went further and began to interpret the Word of God for Eve to tell her that God's intentions were to keep her from becoming like Him. Don't let someone else interpret the Bible for you — let the Spirit of God interpret it for you through the Word of God as you compare scripture with scripture (1 Corinthians 2:13). Be like the Bereans who searched the scriptures daily to make sure everything that Paul said was true (Acts 17:11). Make sure you see it from the Lord — let God be true and every man a liar (Romans 3:4). Just run it by the Lord in His Word. All Eve had to do was to investigate it herself by going straight to God or by discussing it with Adam. So many times we doubt God or come up with these imaginations in our mind when all we really have to do is just go ask someone about it. We often neglect to ask ourselves or others, "What does God say about this?" If you don't know the answer, get counsel, but not from just anyone. Go to someone who can help you see what the Bible says about the issue.

All Eve had to do was to give God the benefit of the doubt. He loved her, He created her, and she could have easily found out what God said instead of staying there debating with the enemy. Unfortunately, we see that she immediately jumped to conclusions before searching out all of the facts, and her conclusion ultimately fell out to what her own desires were. She believed Satan and she wanted to be just like God as Satan had said. That's what we do, especially when we follow our emotions. Don't jump to conclusions and don't go with your feelings. Go with God. Most problems stem from miscommunications and not knowing all the facts, or from taking things personally based on emotions. In the end we often chose the truth that we wish to believe, just as Eve did.

Eve didn't understand God's motivations. He wasn't trying to be mean to her or to hold anything good back from her. He was trying to protect her, and He was testing her to see if she would use her free will to trust and believe Him. But that's not what the enemy said, and the enemy got her to believe him instead of the Lord. The enemy succeeded in making her trust him and doubt God because she didn't know or believe what God actually said.

Another good illustration about just changing a little bit of the Word of God is if you are shooting a gun at a target that is 100 yards away. If you are just 1 millimeter off, by the time the bullet reaches the target, it'll be way off! We are building a foundation on the words of truth, and if you don't know whether you have the absolute words of truth, your whole building could be just so slightly off that the whole structure is affected. Even if you're off by one millimeter starting out, by the time you get to the third story, it's going to be leaning. Make sure you have the Word of God. After all, why would you replace your thoughts with the Word of God if it has errors? Why would you hide it in your heart if it's only "mostly true"?

If you don't know whether you have the absolute Word of God, that is something that you need to search out for yourself. You need to make sure you know that you have the infallible, perfect, preserved, authoritative words of the living God. God's Word is preserved and He has made it accessible to us, but this is only of use to us if we know about it. We need to be certain that we have the absolute words of truth.

Now that we've established that, let's learn why the first attack was on a woman.

> ***Genesis 1:27-28** So God created man in his own image, in the image of God created he him; male and female created he them. And God blessed them, and*

God said unto them, Be fruitful, and multiply, and replenish the earth, and subdue it: and have dominion over the fish of the sea, and over the fowl of the air, and over every living thing that moveth upon the earth.

Genesis 2:18 *And the Lord God said, It is not good that the man should be alone; I will make him an help meet for him.*

Genesis 1:27-28 and Genesis 2:18 say that Eve was made from the rib of a man. Adam was made from the ground and she was made from his rib. The Bible also says that she was to be his help meet, meaning that she was there to help him meet the needs of the commission that God had given them in Genesis 1:28. God gave Adam a commission of replenishing the earth, and Eve was an essential part in helping him fulfill that commission. There is just so much here that we need to understand about our makeup, but let's focus on why the enemy came to her specifically. 1 Timothy 2 and 1 Peter 3 give us some insight on that:

1 Timothy 2:13-14 *For Adam was first formed, then Eve. And Adam was not deceived, but the woman being deceived was in the transgression.*

1 Peter 3:7 *Likewise, ye husbands, dwell with them according to knowledge, giving honour unto the wife, as unto the weaker vessel, and as being heirs together of the grace of life; that your prayers be not hindered.*

1 Peter 3 uses the example of Sarah and Abraham to illustrate some biblical principles on marriage. Verse 7 of that chapter mentions that the wife is the weaker vessel, meaning that she is weaker than the husband is. In your home, there are all kinds of vessels you can use. There is a skillet and there is fine china. One isn't necessarily better than the other, but they are very different in their structure and function. We as ladies are different than guys! Realize that God had a different thing in mind when He created Eve than what He had in mind when He created Adam. This doesn't mean that Adam was better than Eve or that Eve was better than Adam. It just means that they were different. They each had a different job description and different ways to fulfill God's purpose.

This is why we must be careful and sober when we talk about women's equality movements. In truth, we are not equal with men because we are very different. We are equitable, but we are not equal. The way we process information is not equal and our hormonal structure is not equal. 1 Timothy 2 clearly says that Adam sinned when they fell, but Eve was deceived. She was tricked! We are women, so we have the same susceptibility that Eve had for being deceived. That's why this lesson is so important! She was there to help Adam fulfill the commission — she was to help bear and raise the children, which is something that only a woman can do. A man can't give birth to a child because that is a beautiful role that God gave only to women. There are all kinds of things that can cause problems for a woman because of what is going on in her body. Her hormones can really mess with her, and not only that, but her emotional makeup is there to attend to and raise children more effectively. That was God's purpose for women. We're not saying that one is better than the other, only that God has a different purpose for each.

The first commission to mankind in the Old Testament was physical: to replenish the earth with humans. Our commission in the New Testament, however, is spiritual! We are here to make disciples — spiritual babies in Christ that we train up to be spiritually mature in Christ. That means that as the bride of Christ and as women, we are good disciple-makers. We are here to raise babies, both physically and spiritually! Let God use you. As a woman, your first ministry is always to the Lord and your own household if you're a wife. Next (and if you're single), it's to minister to the local church. Lastly, it's to reach out to the lost — that includes those God has placed in your life outside of church, such as families, neighbors, coworkers, and even strangers.

Now let's talk about the consequences of the curse.

> *Genesis 3:16 Unto the woman he said, I will greatly multiply thy sorrow and thy conception; in sorrow thou shalt bring forth children; and thy desire shall be to thy husband, and he shall rule over thee.*

Realize that Eve was not yet under a curse when she was deceived — the curse didn't come until afterwards. However, we are under a curse, and that means that we can be deceived more easily than she was. Before the curse, childbearing must not have been sorrowful or hurtful because it was the curse that brought the pain! This difficulty in childbirth is all connected with our hormones and monthly cycle, and all of these things come from the fall. Think about it: PMS, menstrual cycle, postpartum depression, hormonal imbalance, pregnancy brains, menopause brains... all of this is connected to childbearing. I've been through menopause, and while PMS is rough, menopause is really bad. It just goes on and on. Our hormones get all messed up and can really screw things up in our life. Now I will note that taking care of your body can really help with these things, but the key is going to be submission. According to 1 Timothy 2, surrender and submission are essential.

> *1 Timothy 2:13-15* For Adam was first formed, then Eve. And Adam was not deceived, but the woman being deceived was in the transgression. Notwithstanding she shall be saved in childbearing, if they continue in faith and charity and holiness with sobriety.

I once heard someone say that this passage means that you have to have a baby to be saved! Oh my, how ridiculous. Now, I've worked with a lot of pregnant ladies and have seen how the effects of the curse on women (PMS, pregnancy, and menopause) do a whammy on our bodies. What Paul was actually saying in these verses was that the woman is easily deceived because of her hormonal structure for childbearing, but she can be saved from that deception if she continues in sobriety and faith! That's a promise! Be under the structure and be under submission. If Eve had been under the structure of Adam, she might not have been deceived. However, Satan purposefully overran that by going to Eve first instead of Adam.

The curse also says the desire of her flesh is now to please her husband. She didn't have that before, but this was added by God after the curse in response to what had happened. This source of protection wasn't there before, but now she really needed protection from future deception. She needed a covering, so God built this desire in her to protect her from being deceived by her emotions. Our desire to please a husband, father, or authority figure is a built-in protector from deception.

God protects us from deception through structure and order. We often think that God is being mean to us when we see some of these boundaries laid out, but that's not what God says! We were made differently — we need a covering, and we need to stay under this umbrella of protection for our own safety. Always remember, God is not the author of confusion.

> *1 Corinthians 14:33* For God is not the author of confusion, but of peace, as in all churches of the saints.

If you are confused about something, stop and wait. Waiting is the best thing that you can do. God is not the author of confusion and He has a structure of authority that He works through. This means that He has roles for the sexes. When we aren't surrendered and submitting under this structure, we can be just like Eve and get into big trouble. Paul explains this to us in 1 Corinthians 11, and the church he was writing to was all messed up on submission and following the leader that God had given them.

> *1 Corinthians 11:1* Be ye followers of me, even as I also am of Christ.

Paul says, "Follow me as I follow Christ." Don't ever let someone tell you not to follow a man. Just make sure that the man you're following is following Christ. God lays out the hierarchical structure for us: God, then Jesus, then man, then woman. God the Father and Jesus are part of the trinity, yet even within that there exists a hierarchy. No one would argue that Jesus was oppressed or "less than" God the Father, yet He told us that He is completely submitted to the Father (Luke 22:42). It is the same with us — you are hierarchically under a man's authority, whether it be your husband, your father, or your pastor. He is your covering. God put that desire in Eve to protect her from the enemy, and God had good reason to put it here. Remember that Adam wasn't deceived — Eve was because she was more emotional. This authority is to help protect us.

> **1 Corinthians 11:7** *For a man indeed ought not to cover his head, forasmuch as he is the image and glory of God: but the woman is the glory of the man.*

Later on in 1 Corinthians 11, Paul talks about a covering. He uses hair as an example, but he's really talking about this authority covering over us. Remember when you were a kid and you hid under your covers? You thought everything was safe there! Well, that's a biblical principle — remember to stay under the cover of authority! You have to remember that there is evil in the world, like evil men and evil angels. One-third of the angelic host fell with Satan, and those same evil spirits can deceive us, so we need a covering for protection. We can fall into the same deception as Eve did because we are weaker and our emotional makeup allows it to happen, so this biblical structure provides protection. Yes, men can be deceived, but not as easily as women. Our makeup and hormonal structure are so different, and as a result we are weaker and need protecting.

Always remember that structure provides protection and we are to submit to the powers that be. In the world, that means submitting to the government as long as it is not leading us to go against what the Bible says (Romans 13:1-6). In the family, the father or the husband is the leader (Ephesians 5:21-33, 6:1-4). In the church, the pastor is the authority (Hebrews 13:17), and in the workplace, it's our boss that we need to submit to (Ephesians 6:5-8). This doesn't mean they are always right, but it means that if we trust God, He can change our authority. It's not up to us to change our authority. Instead, we are called to just let go and let God — to surrender and submit. This is the foundation for learning how to trust and obey. I know that's not popular in our culture, but learning to submit is essential for our peace and well being. Sure, those in authority over us aren't perfect. So what do we do? We let God change them and we pray for them. We see that principle so clearly in both 1 Peter 3:1 and Jeremiah 3:12-15.

1 Peter 3:1 Likewise, ye wives, be in subjection to your own husbands; that, if any obey not the word, they also may without the word be won by the conversation of the wives;

Jeremiah 3:12-15 Go and proclaim these words toward the north, and say, Return, thou backsliding Israel, saith the Lord; and I will not cause mine anger to fall upon you: for I am merciful, saith the Lord, and I will not keep anger for ever. Only acknowledge thine iniquity, that thou hast transgressed against the Lord thy God, and hast scattered thy ways to the strangers under every green tree, and ye have not obeyed my voice, saith the Lord. Turn, O backsliding children, saith the Lord; for I am married unto you: and I will take you one of a city, and two of a family, and I will bring you to Zion: and I will give you pastors according to mine heart, which shall feed you with knowledge and understanding.

So what are we protected from? Why do we need all this protection? The answer is that we are protected from spiritual wickedness.

1 John 4:1 Beloved, believe not every spirit, but try the spirits whether they are of God: because many false prophets are gone out into the world.

1 Corinthians 11:10 For this cause ought the woman to have power on her head because of the angels.

You won't be deceived if you know the Bible and run everything through what it says. You can't just believe everything you hear. You have to run it through the Word of God — try the spirits and prove them out. Get under your covering and you will be under God's protection. Always remember there are wicked spirits and wicked angels out there, and we need an authority to be protected from them.

2 Corinthians 11:1-4 Would to God ye could bear with me a little in my folly: and indeed bear with me. For I am jealous over you with godly jealousy: for I have espoused you to one husband, that I may present you as a chaste virgin to

Christ. But I fear, lest by any means, as the serpent beguiled Eve through his subtilty, so your minds should be corrupted from the simplicity that is in Christ. For if he that cometh preacheth another Jesus, whom we have not preached, or if ye receive another spirit, which ye have not received, or another gospel, which ye have not accepted, ye might well bear with him.

There is someone out there trying to get you to believe something else instead of believing God, and they are trying to beguile and trick you. Eve was deceived and tricked, and that is exactly how Satan is going to come at us. His plans haven't changed since the garden, and neither have his methods.

2 Corinthians 11:13-15 *For such are false apostles, deceitful workers, transforming themselves into the apostles of Christ. And no marvel; for Satan himself is transformed into an angel of light. Therefore it is no great thing if his ministers also be transformed as the ministers of righteousness; whose end shall be according to their works.*

Satan will come to us as an angel of light, and that's how he came to Eve. Prove all things; hold fast to that which is good (1 Thessalonians 5:21). Remember, just because it's spiritual does not mean that it is of the Lord. We want to be biblical, and not everything that is spiritual is biblical. Channeling, wicca, white magic, horoscopes, ghost whispering, astrology, and divination are all spiritual things that are really quite wicked and have only gotten worse in the past few years. Splankna is now in churches, and it is actually just divination and witchcraft, which God clearly rejects (Galatians 5:19-20). Spiritualism is so popular in our culture, but just because it is spiritual doesn't mean that it is of God. It needs to be biblical — always look for "book, chapter, verse"!

Just as we can be deceived by these spiritual agents, we are also vulnerable to the deceptions of men. There are many girls that I have ministered to over the years who are no longer in church because they were introduced to a smooth talker and mistook their own feelings for God's words to them. Run your big decisions by your spiritual authorities, including your choice on who to date.

Your male authority isn't as easily deceived, and God says that that authority is there not to harm us, but to protect us.

We're also protected from false teachers and false disciples (2 Peter 2:1-3; 2 Timothy 3:1-9). Beware, too, of philosophy and false science (Colossians 2:8; 1 Timothy 6:20). The idols in our hearts can also deceive us, according to Ezekiel 14:3-4. If you come to God with your mind already made up saying, "I'm going to believe this no matter what," then God will allow the deception to move forward. Be careful — there is a lot out there that can deceive you if you don't know your Bible. Get in a good local church, get discipled, and grow. Identify your authority, work under it, and submit to it.

Another very important thing to remember is that just because the Lord uses the man as the authority figure doesn't mean that we ladies don't have our own relationship with the Lord. We should never hide behind a man's spirituality — we can go directly to God! Submitting to a male figure is in obedience to our own personal walk with the Lord, but a male figure does not determine our spiritual walk with God. Galatians 3:28 says in Christ there is neither Jew nor Gentile, male nor female — we can all have a relationship with the Lord.

James 1:8 *A double minded man is unstable in all his ways.*

Instability in our lives comes from being double-minded, so we need to be single-minded about submitting to the Lord, especially when it comes to admitting our faults, failures, and weaknesses. If there is any instability, confusion, or question as to whether God is in something you are facing, that is when you have to ask Him to help you be single-minded. In the multitude of counsellors there is safety (Proverbs 11:14). I'm an accountant and I like to have everything lined up, so I'll often wait and ask, "Lord, is this really of You?" Below are four things that are good protectors for you if you're at a crossroads. These are ways to prove something (or someone) out and make sure you have a green light over a decision:

1. **Peace.** You should have peace about the decision. God is not the author of confusion, He is the author of peace. If you don't have peace about something, wait!

2. **A word from the Lord.** What does the Bible say about it? Has God spoken to you personally about it? Be careful not to conjure something up to fit your own desires, and don't take things out of context. Don't be looking and searching for something to back up your agenda, and make sure it's actually from God. Nothing God tells you to do will ever be in conflict with anything else He has told us in the Bible.

3. **Authority's approval.** This is huge, and it ties back to everything that we have spoken about in this chapter. If there is a big decision in your life like a job, a move, or a guy, then it is good to ask for counsel. Ask your discipler, your mentor, or even your pastor. In the multitude of counselors there is safety. They will have wisdom that you do not have, and they might even know or see something about the situation that you don't.

4. **Circumstances lining up.** Again, whether it's a big decision about a job, a move, or a guy, stay under the covering of authority and let God line it up for you. Don't be deceived. This is commonly my prayer when I am at a big decision: "If You are in this, I need these things to line up and have a green light in all of them. No yellows, no reds. Either way, Lord, I want Your perfect will. Can You give me a green light in all of these steps if You want me to move forward?"

In closing, realize that no matter where you are in life, you can be deceived. That's why we always have to stay humble before the Lord and ask Him to show us what His Word says about whatever situation we come across. We must constantly trust God and His principles to help and guide us. This is why the phrases "I surrender" and "I'm wrong" are so important in our walk with God. Find your authority, submit to it, and trust God to do amazing things through you that you never thought possible. God will use us far more effectively when we are submitted than He could when we're on our own and tossed about with waves of deception. Find your authority and submit to it.

Questions to Consider:

1. What is deception and how is it accomplished?

2. What are some of the ways we can be deceived?

3. What is the only thing that can expose deception?

4. What happens when we build our thinking or lives upon the foundation of a lie?

5. How does God define truth?

6. In Psalm 12:7 God promises to preserve His Word. Do you know you have the absolute Word of God?

7. What is the "way of escape" through trials and temptations, as laid out in 1 Corinthians 10:13?

8. When you're confused, what do you usually do? What is the best thing to do when you're confused? Who is the source of confusion?

9. What is the authority structure laid out in 1 Corinthians 11? What is God's purpose for it?

10. Who are the authorities in your life right now? Are you submitted to them?

11. What are the four "green lights" needed when facing a crossroads or making a decision? Is there a situation in your life to which you can apply this approach today?

12

Romantic Relationships

Corinthians 7 is one of the greatest New Testament chapters on the subjects of marriage, divorce, and remarriage, as it gives us clear instructions and insights into each of these areas. In this chapter Paul gives us added revelation to the New Testament believer that was not in the Old Testament. The Corinthians were all messed up regarding doctrines of the church and had been asking Paul about how to be sanctified and mature in Christ, so Paul wrote the book of 1 Corinthians in response and elaboration to these serious doctrinal issues. If you ever have a question about marriage, divorce, and remarriage, start in 1 Corinthians 7. This lesson can also go hand in hand with learning to be chaste, especially for those of us who are single. 1 Corinthians 7 was a chapter I used to read over and over and over again because it was so contrary to what I'd learned about relationships in the world. I, like the Corinthians, was so messed up in my knowledge of romantic relationships, as I had grown up believing the complete opposite to what was written there. And that was over 30 years ago, which was nothing compared to the world's philosophy about sex today. If you are going to help someone with marriage, divorce, and remarriage, or even just counsel yourself in these areas, you must become familiar with 1 Corinthians 7, which builds upon and completes what was given in the Old Testament. Take some time here to read through and meditate on the entire chapter of 1 Corinthians 7 to lay a good foundation for marriage, divorce, and remarriage.

> **1 Corinthians 7** *Now concerning the things whereof ye wrote unto me: It is good for a man not to touch a woman. Nevertheless, to avoid fornication, let every man have his own wife, and let every woman have her own husband. Let the husband render unto the wife due benevolence: and likewise also the wife unto the husband. The wife hath not power of her own body, but the husband: and likewise also the husband hath not power of his own body, but the wife. Defraud ye not one the other, except it be with consent for a time, that ye may give yourselves to fasting and prayer; and come together again, that Satan tempt you not for your incontinency. But I speak this by permission, and not of commandment. For I would that all men were even as I myself. But every man hath his proper gift of God, one after this manner, and another after that. I say therefore to the unmarried and widows, it is good for them if they abide even as I. But if they cannot contain, let them marry: for it is better to marry than to burn. And unto the married I command, yet not I, but the Lord, Let not the wife depart from her husband: but and if she depart, let her remain unmarried or be reconciled to her husband: and let not the husband put away his wife. But to the rest speak I, not the Lord: If any brother hath a wife that believeth not, and she be pleased to dwell with him, let him not put her away. And the woman which hath an husband that believeth not, and if he be pleased to dwell with her, let her not leave him. For the unbelieving husband is sanctified by the wife, and the unbelieving wife is sanctified by the husband: else were your children unclean; but now are they holy. But if the unbelieving depart, let him depart. A brother or a sister is not under bondage in such cases: but God hath called us to peace. For what knowest thou, O wife, whether thou shalt save thy husband? or how knowest thou, O man, whether thou shalt save thy wife? But as God hath distributed to every man, as the Lord hath called every one, so let him walk. And so ordain I in all churches. Is any man called being circumcised? let him not become uncircumcised. Is any called in uncircumcision? let him not be circumcised. Circumcision is nothing, and uncircumcision is nothing, but*

the keeping of the commandments of God. Let every man abide in the same calling wherein he was called. Art thou called being a servant? care not for it: but if thou mayest be made free, use it rather. For he that is called in the Lord, being a servant, is the Lord's freeman: likewise also he that is called, being free, is Christ's servant. Ye are bought with a price; be not ye the servants of men. Brethren, let every man, wherein he is called, therein abide with God. Now concerning virgins I have no commandment of the Lord: yet I give my judgment, as one that hath obtained mercy of the Lord to be faithful. I suppose therefore that this is good for the present distress, I say, that it is good for a man so to be. Art thou bound unto a wife? seek not to be loosed. Art thou loosed from a wife? seek not a wife. But and if thou marry, thou hast not sinned; and if a virgin marry, she hath not sinned. Nevertheless such shall have trouble in the flesh: but I spare you. But this I say, brethren, the time is short: it remaineth, that both they that have wives be as though they had none; and they that weep, as though they wept not; and they that rejoice, as though they rejoiced not; and they that buy, as though they possessed not; And they that use this world, as not abusing it: for the fashion of this world passeth away. But I would have you without carefulness. He that is unmarried careth for the things that belong to the Lord, how he may please the Lord: but he that is married careth for the things that are of the world, how he may please his wife. There is difference also between a wife and a virgin. The unmarried woman careth for the things of the Lord, that she may be holy both in body and in spirit: but she that is married careth for the things of the world, how she may please her husband. And this I speak for your own profit; not that I may cast a snare upon you, but for that which is comely, and that ye may attend upon the Lord without distraction. But if any man think that he behaveth himself uncomely toward his virgin, if she pass the flower of her age, and need so require, let him do what he will, he sinneth not: let them marry. Nevertheless he that standeth stedfast in his heart, having no necessity, but hath power over his own will, and hath so decreed in his heart that he will keep his virgin, doeth well. So then he that giveth her in marriage doeth well; but he that giveth her not in marriage doeth better. The wife is bound by the law as long as her husband liveth; but if her husband be dead, she is at liberty to be married to whom she will; only in the Lord. But *she is happier if she so abide, after my judgment: and I think also that I have the Spirit of God.*

In this chapter we will lay out and overview some basic biblical boundaries for romantic relationships. We are also going to talk a lot about sex and what the Bible says about it, as we are bombarded in our culture with wrong ideas regarding this beautiful part of intimacy.

Realize that your marital difficulties can mean that there are other, deeper issues in your relationship with God. We've gone over 1 John 1:7 and how if we walk in the light by bringing everything to God, He will make our relationships right. So if you are experiencing marital issues, focus first on your relationship with the Lord. Get out of the way and let God be in charge. The key is always learning to be content, whether you're single or married and whether you're going through good times or bad. In any situation, learn to be content (Philippians 4:11).

Before we get into this subject, I want to go ahead and give some great resources regarding romantic relationships because there is no way that this chapter could be exhaustive on the subject. There is no need to reinvent the wheel if there are great resources available. If you are married and are having marital difficulties, the next thing you need to read after 1 Corinthians 7 is *The Power of a Praying Wife* by Stormie Omartian. I have seen God use this book to put marriages back together! The prayer principles laid out in that book are fabulous, and it's a great resource on surrendering and submitting to authority, especially to that of your husband. Another great resource for married ladies is the "Woman to Woman" or "Blueprints" study on Titus 2:3-5 that we have at our local church, Midtown Baptist Temple. This is a mentor-driven study that helps younger wives learn how to be biblical wives. Finally, another helpful resource is a class I teach at Midtown Baptist Temple on "Being Single with Joy and Purity." It goes a little deeper over the following principles, and I hope to put it in book form soon. The series is also available on the online sermon archive through the MBT website.

Titus 2:3-5 *The aged women likewise, that they be in behaviour as becometh holiness, not false accusers, not given to much wine, teachers of good things; that they may teach the young women to be sober, to love their husbands, to love their children, to be discreet, chaste, keepers at home, good, obedient to their own husbands, that the word of God be not blasphemed.*

Thinking back, our culture began trashing God's principles on the subject of romantic relationships during the freedom movement of the 1960s. I was raised in the '60s and '70s. When I was in junior high, I didn't even really understand much about sex. But kids today? They're knowing all about it in elementary school — it's terrible! There is so much exposure to sinful relationships on TV and on the internet that is constantly being laid before our children's eyes. Though we're grown women, it's still essential that we guard our minds and are intentional about avoiding exposure to this kind of content. For example, when you see things like this, you need to close your eyes, mute the TV, and fast forward. You don't need to sit there and watch it! When you put it in your mind, it's just going to get stuck there and hinder you at some point. Filter it out, and don't let it get in to begin with. It's just sad what our culture is faced with these days, and it's only going to get worse.

For many people, premarital sex is the norm, but let's see what the Bible says on this subject. We see the first marriage defined in Genesis, and when we see marriage defined throughout the Bible we see that when a man took or "knew" a woman, they had the intimacy of sexual relations (Genesis 4:1; Deuteronomy 20:7; Matthew 1:18, 24-25). "Knowing" was an intimate thing; for example, Joseph didn't "know" Mary until after she had Jesus. In other words, there was no sexual relationship between them even though she was called his wife. Hebrews 13:4 says that the marriage bed is undefiled — this means that sex outside of marriage defiles, but sex between a husband and wife is undefiled. As you can see in 1 Corinthians 7, God lays out how marriage takes care of these strong desires in our flesh! God lays out His boundaries by showing that the privilege of sex is given to married people only. Unfortunately, this is so far from today's mindset that some of the people reading this chapter might think that I'm crazy.

Ladies, if you aren't married and you're involved in sexual relationships, you are not only not in a right relationship with the Lord, but as we will see later in this chapter, you are destroying your body. That's the boundary that the Lord clearly has given us in His Word — a New Testament marriage clearly involves commitment, ceremony, and consummation. And before you get to that place, you want to obey God by abstaining from sex.

Not abstaining leads to adultery, which is when a married person gets involved in a sexual relationship outside of their marriage. We've already talked about how everything starts with thoughts and the heart. In Matthew 5:28, Jesus even told the Pharisees that adultery starts when someone looks on a woman and lusts after her in their heart. So adultery is not just when a married person gets outside of the marriage boundary and has sex with another person, it is also when anyone has those lustful thoughts in their minds. Adultery is the mindset that then results in sex outside of marriage. Remember, thoughts drive our heart attitude, and our heart attitude drives our actions.

A lesson we can learn from this is to be careful with your imagination! My imagination can take me places my body would never go. Wicked imaginations can be very dangerous, so we must learn to use our imagination for good. We have the ability to see amazing things like Revelation 19, which depicts Jesus on a white horse splitting open the heavens! You can see so many awesome things in your mind's eye through Bible verses, and God paints us so many awesome places and things to see. But we can also be very carnal through our imaginations and observe and visualize a lot of other things we should never look at. In Ezekiel 8, God is looking at the nation of Israel and its leaders. He asks, "Do you see what I see on the wall of their hearts?" They were imagining wicked things in their hearts and minds, and God said it was being painted on a wall for Him to see. The next time you start using your imaginations incorrectly, remember Ezekiel 8:7-13. As the Israelites were imagining it, God and Ezekiel were seeing it on a wall in heaven. So keep that in your mind instead of whatever carnal thing you were wanting to place there instead!

Whereas adultery is a married person having sex outside marriage, fornication is a single person involved in sexual relationships. When we are single, we aren't "married" in the eyes of God just because we have sex. I mention this because that's what I was once taught, but that is not what the Bible teaches. Fornication is getting involved with sex and not being married. We need to be familiar with what God says about fornication, because He says it is very, very dangerous for us. It can literally destroy your body.

> *1 Corinthians 6:13-20 Meats for the belly, and the belly for meats: but God shall destroy both it and them. Now the body is not for fornication, but for the Lord; and the Lord for the body. And God hath both raised up the Lord, and will also raise up us by his own power. Know ye not that your bodies are the members of Christ? shall I then take the members of Christ, and make them the members of an harlot? God forbid. What? know ye not that he which is joined to an harlot is one body? for two, saith he, shall be one flesh. But he that is joined unto the Lord is one spirit. Flee fornication. Every sin that a man doeth is without the body; but he that committeth fornication sinneth against his own body. What? know ye not that your body is the temple of the Holy Ghost which is in you, which ye have of God, and ye are not your own? For ye are bought with a price: therefore glorify God in your body, and in your spirit, which are God's.*

God uses the example of eating a meal to demonstrate the principle of avoiding fornication. I ate a delicious lunch from Whole Foods today. My body was made to take in and chew up that food and distribute it for nutrition throughout my body, and my belly was made to process that food. So God says that meat is for the belly, and the belly for meat, but neither are going to last because they are physical and temporal. He goes on to say that the body is not for fornication but for the Lord, and the Lord for the body. We're the temple of the Holy Spirit, and our body is not for fornication — we are actually told to flee it in verse 14. If you're tempted, God warns you to flee because fornication is a double whammy — it is against both our spirit and our body. He's giving us single women a very important warning: "he that committeth fornication sinneth against his own body." The consequences of fornication include physical afflictions, like STDs, but they are worsened by the fact that they also bleed into our spiritual state.

If you have a problem in this area, get help to overcome it. Nowadays we think it's no big deal, but again, this is how the enemy deceives us. We think that having sex, thinking about it, watching all these sexual movies, or going to porn sites on the internet is no big deal, but God is saying that is not the case! Don't fall for the enemy's tricks here. Get help in your local church and ask your discipler or mentor to help you overcome these temptations. Don't let a carnal or unsaved man destroy your testimony by trying to convince you otherwise. Be careful — remember that your spirit, soul, and body are all connected, and that sex outside of biblical principles is a weapon the devil has greatly used in our society.

Interestingly enough, the first four works of the flesh listed in Galatians 5:19-21 are sexual sins. There are a lot of other fleshly temptations we are bombarded by in our culture, but this is one place where we are hit hard. We have left this door wide open. Many coming out of the world and learning to become a part of the church body have no idea what the Bible teaches on this subject and must begin learning these boundaries for their own protection. Another great place to see the contrast between the world's system and God's system is to compare the strange woman of Proverbs 7:5-27 with the virtuous woman in Proverbs 31:10-31.

Another area of sexual temptation is homosexuality, and there are many verses in the Bible that clearly define this as a sin. The best place in the New Testament to see this biblical boundary is Romans 1:24-28. Since we are living in Laodicea Land, everything is all about the rights of people rather than rights of God, and this is why we hear a lot about the rights of those who want to be protected in their pursuit of sinful lifestyles. Now let me say up front that homosexuality is not the "abominable sin." It is no worse than any other sin, but it is a sin. I often hear the argument that those who practice homosexuality cannot help it because they were born that way, and yes, I agree on that point — I was born a sinner too! As we have clearly laid out in the book, we were all born sinners (Romans 3:23). We all have different weaknesses and temptations of sin depending on what influenced our parents and what influenced us.

Throughout the Old Testament we see that a son often repeated the sins of the father. The things you see growing up, such as the sins that your parents or your peers struggled with, will often be the temptations that you face. Or it may even be something that you took in and opened yourself up to at an early age and never dealt with biblically.

The key is to realize that sin is sin. It is not about the rights of people, it is about the rights of God. God has given us that boundary for our protection, and we can learn to overcome it the same way we learn to overcome other sins. Homosexuality is only different from other sins because, as fornication, it has that double whammy on your spirit and body. But sin is sin, and it is to be dealt with in the same manner. Everybody sins, and dealing with sin is what discipleship and mentorship are all about: helping younger Christians grow up and learn to overcome their sin, whether it is hate, unforgiveness, adultery, porn, anger, or alcoholism — the list goes on. There may be some tendency in your body to fall into this particular sin, but God can get the victory. It really doesn't matter what your area of weakness is, because now that we have the Lord Jesus Christ living inside of us, there are no more excuses to continue in sin. He can overcome it through us if we let Him. This is where discipleship and mentorship help so much. A great read on this subject is *Gay Girl, Good God* by Jackie Hill Perry.

Now let's look at what the Bible says about finding a husband:

> **1 Corinthians 7:23-24, 27** *Ye are bought with a price; be not ye the servants of men. Brethren, let every man, wherein he is called, therein abide with God. [...] Art thou bound unto a wife? seek not to be loosed. Art thou loosed from a wife? seek not a wife.*

God tells us all throughout this chapter that marriage isn't something you should be looking for. Yes, it may very well be part of God's plan for your life, but He makes it very clear that we shouldn't be out looking for a husband. Instead, we must learn to wait on God's timing through contentment. Yes, it is very likely that you will one day get married, but you have to understand that your life is not on hold until that day. Don't make marriage and finding a husband the main thing. He says here and in so many other places in your Bible to "seek ye first the kingdom of God" (Matthew 6:33). Seek God first! Don't make a guy the priority — let it go and let God. This is why I used to read 1 Corinthians 7 over and over. My life had been so screwed up in the area of guys before I was saved. When I was a young Christian, the Lord was showing me that He wanted me to put a hold on dating and learn to have a relationship with Him first, and God gave me contentment as I grew.

I did date some, but at the same time it just wasn't a priority for me anymore. Then all of a sudden, everybody was trying to fix me up with some guy they knew, including my family (who were still unsaved). One time my mom even called me early in the morning and said, "I just wish one time that I would call over there and a guy would answer." She was wishing I would have some guy over for the night! As you seek the Lord, you too will face pressure to be married or have a boyfriend. The Lord was clearly showing me that I needed to surrender it fully to Him and let it go. It wasn't easy, but I just decided that He was God and that He knew what was best for me. I made the decision to be content with singleness. There were times of intense struggle, and when those struggles happened, I would just spend more time in 1 Corinthians 7. That became my refuge — I would read it over and over again and pray to God for help. When a guy would ask me out, I would fall back on that structure of authority. I knew I could easily be deceived, so I would ask my pastor about him or have him go to my pastor. My pastor became like a father figure to me. My dad was not saved yet, so I used many of the principles we have already covered in this book to help protect me here. That's a good plan, especially when it comes to an unsaved or carnal guy. Remember to stay under the cover of a biblical authority.

Matthew 6:33 *But seek ye first the kingdom of God, and his righteousness; and all these things shall be added unto you.*

Keep your priorities straight. I have learned over the years that many people in our culture, including Christians, think you cannot be fulfilled unless you get married. Often they have found great joy in their marriage and, consequently, they think that that's the only way to find this great joy. Remember, contentment is found in Jesus, not in marriage. Our joy, too, ultimately comes from God. God's perfect will for your life may very well be to be married, and should the Lord tarry, most reading this will probably be married someday! That's great, but at the same time, it's not where your soul's fulfillment or joy will ultimately come from. These things only come in the person of Jesus. You must learn to wait on God, even when others are pressuring you. Be prepared — this pressure can come from yourself, your family, your friends, or even from your leaders. Throughout this, let God be true but every man a liar (Romans 3:4). If this is a huge weakness in your flesh, the temptation will be to cave in and to not wait on God. Unfortunately, I don't think that some happily-married couples realize the pressure they add to single ladies' choices when they make innocent comments like, "It will happen soon" or "Let me fix you up," especially if we are still struggling with the subject ourselves. Regardless, we must learn to listen to God more than we listen to others, and the foundation to overcome all this pressure is found in 1 Corinthians 7. You must learn to listen to Him, and always remember that being single does not mean there is something wrong with you. He says that singleness is a gift, and I can honestly attest that despite the difficulties and suffering of singleness, the Lord has been able to greatly use my singleness in the lives of so many ladies. He would not have been able to do that had I been married. We will talk more about that in our lesson on suffering.

For now, just be sure to learn to wait on God. One of the greatest illustrations of the benefits of waiting can be found in the example is Saul and David. Israel was demanding a king because they wanted to be like other kingdoms and nations (1 Samuel 8:19-20). This was all because they were not content to have

God as their King. God, on the other hand, had a king in mind for them, and that was David — a man after His own heart. God told them to wait, and He even told them if they got a king now, the king would hurt and hinder them (1 Samuel 8:11-18). Despite all His warnings they still wanted a king, so God gave them Saul. Oftentimes God will give us what we want only to show us that what He had planned was far better. I've seen many ladies that demanded a husband immediately who are now either not in church or who are far less connected to the church body than they were before, all because they couldn't wait on God's timing. Be careful, and remember too that an unsaved spouse is not even a consideration here. The man in your life needs to be your spiritual leader; you must also be connected emotionally and physically, but spiritual leadership is most important. Review the information we went over on God's authority structure. Prove him out, talk to your pastor and mentor, and seek counsel. Don't push God for the right thing at the wrong time.

Next, let's look at an excellent example of how God brought a man and a woman together in marriage. In Genesis 24, Abraham's servant, Eleazar, went out to find a bride for Abraham's son Isaac, and he ended up finding Rebekah. We see that their marriage was primarily to fulfill God's promise to expand His kingdom. This story also pictures God fetching a bride for His Son, as Abraham represents God the Father, the servant represents the Holy Spirit, and Isaac represents Jesus. For the New Testament believer, this pictures God working through the Holy Spirit to bring the church together to be the bride of Christ. Marriage is not about fulfilling your dreams, because you are already fulfilled and complete in Christ. Instead, it is about fulfilling God's commission. God wants to bring a couple together in His timing to accomplish His mission, not our own.

There might come a point in your life when God sees that He can be glorified through your life more as a married woman than as a single woman. But until that point, He is growing both you and your potential husband to get both of you to a certain point in your relationship with the Lord. Just let it happen the right way and let it happen in His timing. There might be something He wants to accomplish through and/or inside you before He puts you with the guy, and vice versa. During this process, you want to be totally in tune with God and wait on His timing. As hard as this is going to be, have a willing heart. Tell God that you're willing — willing to wait on His timing by forfeiting your own, and willing to wait on His perfect will. If you are willing, He is able.

Here is another thing to remember: it may be one year, five years, or even ten years before His plan for you for marriage is revealed. I can't tell you what the timing is, but I can guarantee you one thing: God does not have your life on hold until that time. He wants to use you today, so make *Him* the center, not a guy or an idea of what's coming down the road. He might have something very big He wants to accomplish through you today before the guy shows up, and He might have to hold off on bringing the guy into your life until that is accomplished. He might have something that is being perfected in you before that time gets here, or the guy might not be ready yet!

Another thing that often happens with carnal or unsaved men is that they will say that God told them that you were the right girl for them. Don't think that you have to be pressured into listening to him. Talk to your pastor, your mentor, or your discipler. This guy may have many things going for him, but if he is not saved, then this is not God's will for your life.

Let's walk through the 18 principles we see in Genesis 24 about how God brings a man and woman together. These are things you should meditate on, especially if you're single. Realize that if you're married, this process is a big struggle for most single ladies, so use these principles to help your single friends or disciples. Remind them that God has a purpose for their life today — their life is not on hold!

In Genesis 24, note how the Holy Spirit is the key player, not emotions. Now, you should have a spark — when God brings two people together, a spark should be there! That spark is what many girls go off of, but be careful not to let that be the foundation — instead, the first thing you should look for is whether this man is saved. This is very clear and can be seen in 2 Corinthians 6:14-17. After that, you must watch to see if there is a willingness to submit to the Lord and His mission. The only way you're going to be able to see these two things is to watch him in ministry, because the Bible says that by their fruits you shall know them (Matthew 7:20). We see Rebekah's willingness in verses 7-8, 18-20, and 58. You've got to watch and wait, proving all things (1 Thessalonians 5:21), and you can do this watching at the well (ministry) to observe who is involved and going the extra mile to serve and give people water (the Word of God). A person's character is seen in how they minister. Ministering the Word and giving without receiving are qualities that are developed in ministry and are necessary for marriage.

You're also looking for purity. Now, all of us have some kind of baggage, and some have more than others. But God can get rid of that baggage through His Word, and you can develop purity through the Scriptures no matter what kind of background you've come from. God wants to make you spiritually pure in your relationship with Him.

A prospective spouse should be able to go over and above what's asked of them. Also, they must not be vain or proud or only serve to get recognition from those around them. You should watch to see how they handle both anger and authority — what happens when their authority tells them "no"? They should also be charitable and hospitable, and there should be prayer during every step of the process, which we can see in verses 12-14 and verse 27. Abraham's servant, Eleazar, states: "I being in the way, the LORD led." He put himself in God's way and God was faithful to lead him. If you're in God's way, He will lead you — let that be the focus.

In verses 34-38 we see that the servant's plans are communicated to the bride's family. It's always a good idea for the guy to ask permission from the bride's father, pastor, or male authority. A potential husband should be clear about his intentions from the very start. When you're dating, you should be thinking about marriage. Dating is not about having fun and having a man in your life

— dating is intentional. It's about selecting a prospective marriage partner, so enter it with prayer and be very careful about it.

You should know how to be friends with men and women, but there are guidelines and boundaries. You want to be careful and remember these principles so that you can be blameless. Rebekah knew where the water (Word) was and what to do with it. A potential spouse should be willing and exuberant when it comes to the things of the Lord. After everything, including the above guidelines, is proved out, a proposal is made, and then the bride ceases to go her own way. She becomes his help meet and follows him (v. 61). His burden becomes hers.

No matter what stage of life you might find yourself in — single or dating, married or divorced — the Bible gives clear guidelines about romantic relationships. Because marriage is two becoming one, we must be very careful about who we let into our hearts. An unsaved man is never an option, but also be careful that your Christian man isn't carnal. Choose a man who will be your spiritual leader — one who serves the Lord fully and with pure motivations. Run it by your leaders and trust God to provide the right man at the right time. If you focus on the field God has given you to work, who knows what kind of Boaz He will prepare for you! But you must always wait on Him. Finally, always flee temptation — remember we are Christ's bride, and He wants a bride that is chaste, pure, and serving Him with focus and contentment.

18 Principles from Genesis 24

1. The Holy Spirit is the key player, not emotions (vv. 1-6).

2. Lost people are not marriage candidates (vv. 3, 37).

3. The first thing to look for is their willingness to submit to the Lord and His mission (vv. 7-8).

4. Prove all things (vv. 15-21, 25). The only way to prove a person out is to watch at the well (the ministry) and observe who is involved and going the extra mile to give people water (the Word of God) and to serve them. A person's character is defined in how they minister. Giving without receiving and ministering the Word of God are qualities that are grown in ministry and are necessary for marriage.

5. God wants you to have a partner as much as you do, but you must wait on His timing (v. 15).

6. Look for purity. The Word of God makes you pure. Most of us have some form of "baggage", but you must see if their baggage has been dealt with biblically (v. 16).

7. A spouse should go over and above what is asked and not do it to impress anyone (vv. 18-21).

8. They should have charity and hospitality (v. 25).

9. There should be prayer throughout the whole process (v. 26).

10. Get "in the way" of God and let Him carry you (v. 27). "I being in the way, the LORD led."

11. The man is in communication with the woman's family (vv. 34-36).

12. Again, the unsaved are not marriageable for the believer (v. 37).

13. The potential husband was clear about his intentions and nothing was kept secret from the family (vv. 43-44).

14. A marriage candidate should not be a novice. She knew where the water (Word) was and what to do with it (v. 45).

15. A potential spouse should be willing and exuberant when it comes to things of the Lord (v. 46).

16. Handles stubbornness well — camels are very stubborn (v. 46).

17. A proposal is made after all of the above principles are proved out (v. 58).

18. After they are betrothed, the two go the same way. The bride ceases going her way (v. 61).

Questions to Consider:

1. What is the key New Testament chapter about marriage, divorce, and remarriage?

2. What is the difference between adultery and fornication?

3. Why does God tell us to flee fornication? What are the "double whammy" consequences of this sin?

4. Take a moment to read Proverbs 7 and 31. Compare and contrast the women in these chapters. Who are you like, and who do you want to become?

5. We see in 1 Corinthians 7 that we are not to look for a husband. Does this statement surprise you? What does God want us to prioritize/seek instead?

6. When it comes to contentment in relationships, who are you finding contentment in?

7. True or false: Marriage is not about fulfilling your dreams, it is about fulfilling God's commission.

8. Which principle(s) from Genesis 24 stood out to you most and why?

9. What should be the foundation of our relationship with a man?

10. What is the best proving ground of the character of a potential spouse?

13

Depression

As we grow through the seven stages of spiritual growth, God uses valley and mountaintop experiences to teach us how to maintain our connection with Him. We will learn to be in His presence and make Him our foundation, but that process requires stretching. This stretching is invaluable, as it allows us experience in following the Spirit and not the flesh and shows us how to consistently be in the presence of God. Philippians 4 talks about this truth:

> **Philippians 4:11-13** *Not that I speak in respect of want: for I have learned, in whatsoever state I am, therewith to be content. I know both how to be abased, and I know how to abound: every where and in all things I am instructed both to be full and to be hungry, both to abound and to suffer need. I can do all things through Christ which strengtheneth me.*

Paul gives us the key on how to grow closer to God and maintain our connection with Him through any circumstance. Notice verse 12 — he knew how to be abased in the valley and how to abound on the mountaintop, how to be full on the top and how to be hungry down at the bottom. He knew how to both suffer and abound. The Lord was taking him through this extreme stretching because He wanted to teach him how to maintain a balanced, consistent connection to the Lord, NOT a connection that swings like a pendulum. The Lord wants to teach us the same thing. He doesn't want our experiences to dictate our walk with Him, and He doesn't want us to be controlled by our emotions. He wants us to learn how to do "all things through Christ which strengtheneth me."

Staying Connected with God

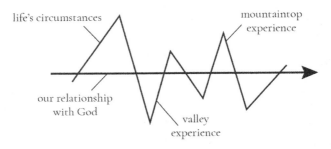

God stretches us to the heights and depths of life in order to teach us how to maintain our relationship with Him and focus on His presence at all times and in all things.

Those valleys and mountaintops begin to strengthen us each time we go through them and each time we get stretched a little more. The beautiful thing is that eventually we get the opportunity to teach others to do the same.

> *2 Corinthians 5:17-20 Therefore if any man be in Christ, he is a new creature: old things are passed away; behold, all things are become new. And all things are of God, who hath reconciled us to himself by Jesus Christ, and hath given to us the ministry of reconciliation; to wit, that God was in Christ, reconciling the world unto himself, not imputing their trespasses unto them; and hath committed unto us the word of reconciliation. Now then we are ambassadors for Christ, as though God did beseech you by us: we pray you in Christ's stead, be ye reconciled to God.*

2 Corinthians 5:17-20 says we are new creatures in Christ Jesus, old things are passed away, and all things are become new. Remember, at the moment of salvation, our soul and spirit were sealed by the Holy Spirit. We got all of Him, but He did not get all of us. So the more we go through the ups and downs of life, stay in the presence of God, and turn over complete control of our lives to Him, the more we are reconciled to God (Romans 5:10). Sanctification is a continual, present-tense process. Old things are passed away and all things are become new as we die to self. This passage also says we are ambassadors for Christ and have been given the ministry of reconciliation. God gave us this ministry and the Word of reconciliation to fulfill it, and the more we are reconciled, the more we can turn around and help others be reconciled. We keep getting stretched and sharing what He shows us. Therefore, be ye reconciled to God!

In 2 Corinthians 1:3-4, 9-10, God talks about how we go through difficult times so that we can help someone else who is going through a similar thing and comfort them with the comfort that we have received from Him. That's what it's all about! Just like how Jesus is a perfect high priest because He went through and felt the same infirmities that we did (Hebrews 4:15), when we go through hard times, we are better able to comfort others who are going through hard times with the same comfort that we received. Not only that, but as we go through hard times, we can also grow in sanctification and wisdom as we're conformed to the image of Christ. The more we look like Christ, the stronger our witness will become to those around us.

Deuteronomy 8 says that we will go through two types of trials: adversity and prosperity. During each season of trial we get to experience God's victory and presence, and we can share that bread with others. Deuteronomy 8 is a great place to turn to see God's heart during times of trial and also to have a sobering perspective of where our heart should be in all seasons.

It is important to note that through those ups and downs, we are all going to experience times of depression. There will be suffering involved in our walk with the Lord because we are called to join into the fellowship with His suffering (Philippians 3:10)! This suffering can lead us to times of depression and even burnout. To face depression is not to fail as a Christian — even King David faced many trials that led to depression. Instead, a season of depression is actually an opportunity to walk in victory as we apply God's Word to our lives (Philippians 4:13).

The foundation for this lesson is from something I heard way back in 1987 from our biblical counseling ministry. It's a story in 1 Kings 18-19 about the great prophet Elijah who fell into depression, and then how God brought him out of it and gave him victory. Let's start by understanding that depression is not unusual. Every person who is reading this book is going to experience times of depression, and those around you — including your disciple — will experience it too. Depending on what's going on in our life, depression can range from mild to severe. Unfortunately, depression often has a lot to do with our expectations or sense of entitlement instead of what the Bible says. In our Laodicean culture, we can feel entitled to our way and expect things that are contrary to biblical principles. We think it is all about our rights, when in fact, it is all about God's rights! This is His universe. and though He is a loving, awesome, and spectacular Father, He has a plan set up and in motion. It's our job to see that plan and jump on board.

We have to stop thinking that we are entitled to things contrary to biblical principles. For example, we can't have a difficult week and think the answer is to run to the doctor for a pill. Back when I was saved in 1984, we didn't have a cultural setup where we could just go to a doctor and get an antidepressant. Please don't misunderstand me — for some people, depression is the result of years of inappropriate brain levels of different chemicals. However, for many, the problem has a different source — such as inadequate vitamin D levels, irregular sleeping and eating habits, or lack of exercise — that could really be addressed without the use of medication. We are often quick to throw a pill at something without investigating the root issue. I have worked with so many girls over the past several years that say, "Well, I was depressed these past couple of weeks, so I just went into the clinic on campus and they gave me an antidepressant." The doctor didn't even run any tests or ask many questions. Many girls that I have worked with who had depression also had low vitamin D levels, and once they started taking vitamin D supplements, their depression quickly went away.

If you are on antidepressants, I am not telling you to throw them away or stop taking them. You should work with a doctor if you do choose to slowly get off them. I've even worked with some ladies who have been on them most of their lives and it's okay if they never stop taking them. What I am saying is that if you haven't already started taking a drug, then talk to a good biblical counselor first, because there is a good chance that biblical principles could help you greatly. It could also be that something along the lines of vitamin D, exercise, eating right, or getting enough sleep will solve the problem. The darker your skin is, the harder it is for you to absorb vitamin D from the sun, and if you put on sunscreen, you're not getting vitamin D from the sun. All of these things can affect our mood. It's so much easier to go get a pill, and there is a billion-dollar pharmaceutical industry that is trying its hardest to get us hooked on something. While biblical counseling is harder, it is the only process that actually can solve both the root issue and the symptoms.

Sometimes depression can be due to a true chemical imbalance in the brain, but oftentimes the foundational problem is a spiritual issue. If it's not your vitamin D level or the mishandling of your body, it usually originates from a spiritual issue. Remember that our spirit, soul, and body all work together, and if you spiritually grieve the Holy Spirit long enough, this will affect your body. And if this spiritual issue isn't fixed, no matter what medication you take, it's not going to solve the problem. It may help some, but the spiritual issue is what really needs to be addressed. That's why we've talked about forgiveness and anger in previous chapters, because the Bible says that those are some of the biggest things that can automatically get us messed up. We have an enemy, and his trick is to get you focused on yourself and not on the Lord. Focusing on yourself means that these spiritual issues begin to fester will eventually ripple and manifest through symptoms in your body. Then it becomes a heavier depression that will just keep progressing if the spiritual issue is not resolved. It can eventually become severe or radical depression where an individual has psychosis or is suicidal.

We are going to be looking in 1 Kings 18 at the man Elijah, who was a great prophet of God who also faced depression. We often think that the great prophets were strong mentally and emotionally despite all that they faced from the nation of Israel. However, what we see is that they struggled just as we would in the face of trial. They, too, faced depression.

> **James 5:17** *Elias was a man subject to like passions as we are, and he prayed earnestly that it might not rain: and it rained not on the earth by the space of three years and six months.*

This prophet had emotions that caused him to go up and down and fall out of fellowship with God. Elijah had "like passions as we are," meaning that he felt things the same way that we do. He faced trials just like we do, and he felt the same way about them that we do. This example shows how God's people can fall into a deep, severe depression but still come out of it.

We will begin the story in 1 Kings 18:17. Here we see that Elijah had previously prayed, in obedience to the Lord, that it would stop raining in the land for three years as a result of Israel's departure from God. The drought caught the nation's attention, and the wicked king, King Ahab, now had questions to ask Elijah. He asked Elijah why he caused this evil to fall upon Israel, but Elijah answered that it was the wickedness of King Ahab and the nation that caused this evil to happen because they had turned away from God. Elijah called all of Israel to Mount Carmel to watch a great contest between himself and Ahab's false prophets to reveal the one true God — Elijah's God, or Ahab's god Baal. He asked them how long they were going to halt between two opinions (1 Kings 18:21). In other words, who were they for — the Lord or the devil? Elijah challenged the prophets of Baal, whose power was of the devil, to prepare a sacrifice and lay it upon an altar. If fire came down from heaven, it would prove that Baal was greater than the LORD. All morning they called upon Baal and leaped upon the altar, trying to get their god to accept the sacrifice. At noon Elijah began mocking them, asking if Baal was too busy to help them — maybe he was talking, or away on a journey, or sleeping? His jokes made the 450 false prophets try even harder to get Baal to acknowledge them. All afternoon they cried louder and louder and even cut their own bodies until blood gushed out! But their god never showed up.

Then Elijah prepared his sacrifice and poured an abundance of water on it three times. Let's not forget that this really got Israel's attention since it hadn't rained for three years. Finally, Elijah called upon the Lord and asked Him to accept his sacrifice while acknowledging that he had done everything according to what God told him to do. God answered and fire fell from heaven and consumed the sacrifice and the wood, stones, and dust, and even licked up the water in the trench. After being faced with this show of power, the whole nation of Israel fell on their faces in surrender to the Lord and acknowledged that He alone is God. Then Elijah killed all 450 false prophets that had been deceiving Israel. After this, he climbed to the top of Mount Carmel and prayed seven times to the Lord asking for the rain to come, and it did! When the stormcloud appeared in the distance, he told his servant to warn wicked King Ahab to return to his palace in Jezreel and eat and drink because a storm was coming. Elijah then ran on foot back to Jezreel (a 15-18 mile journey), and all the while, there was no mention that he ate or drank anything during or after the showdown with the false prophets.

Elijah spent the whole day fighting this great battle for the Lord — he won all of Israel back to God and he killed all the false prophets. He even prayed for rain and it rained after three and a half years of drought, and he ran fifteen or more miles without eating and drinking anything throughout the day. Now, when word of Elijah's victories reached Ahab's wicked wife, Jezebel, she immediately sent a messenger to Elijah threatening to kill him by the next

Emotional Victory

day. What happened to this great man of God? What happened immediately after this tremendous victory for the Lord? Elijah got very afraid. He took his eyes off the Lord and focused on her threat. He got scared and ran for his life.

When he reached Beersheba, he left his servant behind so he could be alone and then traveled a day's journey into the wilderness. There he sat under a juniper tree, wished he was dead, and then fell asleep. Two times God mercifully sent an angel to feed him, and in the strength of that food he began a 40-day journey on foot to Mount Horeb in the hopes of finding God. Once he arrived, the Lord asked him several times why he was there. After all, the Lord never told him to go there. Elijah had a big pity party and explained how he was the only one serving the Lord in the land. He had had this great victory in obedience to God and he was doing everything the Lord had asked him to do, and what happened? Jezebel was out to kill him. God immediately answered him and showed him that he would not find a connection with the Lord in the big circumstances of life. God wasn't to be found in strong winds or earthquakes or fires. Elijah was looking at the physical — he was scared and ran to a particular place thinking he could only find God in the physical. He had been going helter-skelter, running like a chicken with his head cut off, trying to get to God and get God's attention. He did all of this when he could have just knelt his heart to the Lord as soon as Jezebel had spoken.

Finally, Elijah realized what he had been doing ever since Jezebel threatened to kill him: he had gotten his eyes off the Lord and he was following his flesh instead of the Spirit of God. He realized that God was not found in the physical, and as soon as he understood all of this, he heard the still, small voice of the Lord and surrendered himself. His surrender allowed him to connect with the Lord through the spiritual instead of the physical, and as he did that, God gave him a fresh vision. He had come to the end of his last assignment or burden from the Lord and got a new one. However, first the Lord tells him to get up and go back! Read through the chapter and afterward we will look at all the reasons why Elijah fell into depression and how he came out of it.

Depression

1 Kings 18:17-46 *And it came to pass, when Ahab saw Elijah, that Ahab said unto him, Art thou he that troubleth Israel? And he answered, I have not troubled Israel; but thou, and thy father's house, in that ye have forsaken the commandments of the Lord, and thou hast followed Baalim. Now therefore send, and gather to me all Israel unto mount Carmel, and the prophets of Baal four hundred and fifty, and the prophets of the groves four hundred, which eat at Jezebel's table. So Ahab sent unto all the children of Israel, and gathered the prophets together unto mount Carmel. And Elijah came unto all the people, and said, How long halt ye between two opinions? if the Lord be God, follow him: but if Baal, then follow him. And the people answered him not a word. Then said Elijah unto the people, I, even I only, remain a prophet of the Lord; but Baal's prophets are four hundred and fifty men. Let them therefore give us two bullocks; and let them choose one bullock for themselves, and cut it in pieces, and lay it on wood, and put no fire under: and I will dress the other bullock, and lay it on wood, and put no fire under: And call ye on the name of your gods, and I will call on the name of the Lord: and the God that answereth by fire, let him be God. And all the people answered and said, It is well spoken. And Elijah said unto the prophets of Baal, Choose you one bullock for yourselves, and dress it first; for ye are many; and call on the name of your gods, but put no fire under. And they took the bullock which was given them, and they dressed it, and called on the name of Baal from morning even until noon, saying, O Baal, hear us. But there was no voice, nor any that answered. And they leaped upon the altar which was made. And it came to pass at noon, that Elijah mocked them, and said, Cry aloud: for he is a god; either he is talking, or he is pursuing, or he is in a journey, or peradventure he sleepeth, and must be awaked. And they cried aloud, and cut themselves after their manner with knives and lancets, till the blood gushed out upon them. And it came to pass, when midday was past, and they prophesied until the time of the offering of the evening sacrifice, that there was neither voice, nor any to answer, nor any that regarded. And Elijah said unto all the people, Come near unto me. And all the people came near unto him. And he repaired the altar of the Lord that was broken down. And Elijah took twelve stones, according to the number of the tribes of the sons of Jacob, unto whom the word of the Lord came, saying,*

Israel shall be thy name: And with the stones he built an altar in the name of the Lord: and he made a trench about the altar, as great as would contain two measures of seed. And he put the wood in order, and cut the bullock in pieces, and laid him on the wood, and said, Fill four barrels with water, and pour it on the burnt sacrifice, and on the wood. And he said, Do it the second time. And they did it the second time. And he said, Do it the third time. And they did it the third time. And the water ran round about the altar; and he filled the trench also with water. And it came to pass at the time of the offering of the evening sacrifice, that Elijah the prophet came near, and said, Lord God of Abraham, Isaac, and of Israel, let it be known this day that thou art God in Israel, and that I am thy servant, and that I have done all these things at thy word. Hear me, O Lord, hear me, that this people may know that thou art the Lord God, and that thou hast turned their heart back again. Then the fire of the Lord fell, and consumed the burnt sacrifice, and the wood, and the stones, and the dust, and licked up the water that was in the trench. And when all the people saw it, they fell on their faces: and they said, The Lord, he is the God; the Lord, he is the God. And Elijah said unto them, Take the prophets of Baal; let not one of them escape. And they took them: and Elijah brought them down to the brook Kishon, and slew them there. And Elijah said unto Ahab, Get thee up, eat and drink; for there is a sound of abundance of rain. So Ahab went up to eat and to drink. And Elijah went up to the top of Carmel; and he cast himself down upon the earth, and put his face between his knees, And said to his servant, Go up now, look toward the sea. And he went up, and looked, and said, There is nothing. And he said, Go again seven times. And it came to pass at the seventh time, that he said, Behold, there ariseth a little cloud out of the sea, like a man's hand. And he said, Go up, say unto Ahab, Prepare thy chariot, and get thee down that the rain stop thee not. And it came to pass in the mean while, that the heaven was black with clouds and wind, and there was a great rain. And Ahab rode, and went to Jezreel. And the hand of the Lord was on Elijah; and he girded up his loins, and ran before Ahab to the entrance of Jezreel.

1 Kings 19:1-18 And Ahab told Jezebel all that Elijah had done, and withal how he had slain all the prophets with the sword. Then Jezebel sent a messenger unto

Elijah, saying, So let the gods do to me, and more also, if I make not thy life as the life of one of them by to morrow about this time. And when he saw that, he arose, and went for his life, and came to Beersheba, which belongeth to Judah, and left his servant there. But he himself went a day's journey into the wilderness, and came and sat down under a juniper tree: and he requested for himself that he might die; and said, It is enough; now, O Lord, take away my life; for I am not better than my fathers. And as he lay and slept under a juniper tree, behold, then an angel touched him, and said unto him, Arise and eat. And he looked, and, behold, there was a cake baken on the coals, and a cruse of water at his head. And he did eat and drink, and laid him down again. And the angel of the Lord came again the second time, and touched him, and said, Arise and eat; because the journey is too great for thee. And he arose, and did eat and drink, and went in the strength of that meat forty days and forty nights unto Horeb the mount of God. And he came thither unto a cave, and lodged there; and, behold, the word of the Lord came to him, and he said unto him, What doest thou here, Elijah? And he said, I have been very jealous for the Lord God of hosts: for the children of Israel have forsaken thy covenant, thrown down thine altars, and slain thy prophets with the sword; and I, even I only, am left; and they seek my life, to take it away. And he said, Go forth, and stand upon the mount before the Lord. And, behold, the Lord passed by, and a great and strong wind rent the mountains, and brake in pieces the rocks before the Lord; but the Lord was not in the wind: and after the wind an earthquake; but the Lord was not in the earthquake: and after the earthquake a fire; but the Lord was not in the fire: and after the fire a still small voice. And it was so, when Elijah heard it, that he wrapped his face in his mantle, and went out, and stood in the entering in of the cave. And, behold, there came a voice unto him, and said, What doest thou here, Elijah? And he said, I have been very jealous for the Lord God of hosts: because the children of Israel have forsaken thy covenant, thrown down thine altars, and slain thy prophets with the sword; and I, even I only, am left; and they seek my life, to take it away. And the Lord said unto him, Go, return on thy way to the wilderness of Damascus: and when thou comest, anoint Hazael to be king over Syria: and Jehu the son of Nimshi shalt thou anoint to be king over Israel: and Elisha the son of Shaphat of Abelmeholah shalt thou anoint to be prophet in thy room. And it shall come to pass, that him that

> *escapeth the sword of Hazael shall Jehu slay: and him that escapeth from the sword of Jehu shall Elisha slay. Yet I have left me seven thousand in Israel, all the knees which have not bowed unto Baal, and every mouth which hath not kissed him.*

There are three types of problems that come up against us that can cause us to fall into depression: organic or physical problems, sin issues, and satanic attack. We see that all three hit Elijah at the same time. Let's break down the causes one at a time and examine how they affected Elijah and how we can learn to diagnose these problems in our own lives.

First, it could be an organic problem. This means that it could be from lack of exercise, lack of sleep, not eating right, or low vitamin D, just to name a few. If you are having depression, make sure you are eating right and exercising and even have your vitamin D levels checked. Elijah had spent all day with Baal worshippers and was already emotionally and physically exhausted, and then he ran for 15-18 miles. When we get down in the dumps and let go of our body, it will affect us. Remember, our spirit, soul, and body all ripple into each other. We have to make sure to take care of ourselves. I know that there are times where we don't want to eat right and we don't want to exercise, but we must remember that our body is the temple of the living God and He wants to use us. We need to take care of His temple.

Secondly, it could be a sin issue. Elijah's sin started out so small, remember? He simply focused on what Jezebel said rather than what God told him, and as a result he reacted and became double-minded. His vision was distorted and he took the rejection personally. Instead of fearing God alone, he feared man, and instead of moving forward in serving God, he ran away. He feared Jezebel having him killed and started worrying about tomorrow. He began running helter-skelter to Horeb looking for God. This goes along with the chapter on deception and getting divided by our own heart. Did it matter that Jezebel didn't like him? Absolutely not. But a lot of times we take rejection personally, especially when we are already emotionally or physically worn down. We can start getting focused on a threat or a worry and make it out to be a big scene in our minds. We can let our imaginations run wild, and before we know it, we've forgotten God and His promises. That's what Elijah was doing — he was worrying about tomorrow and running to a place where God had not directed him to go. We see his depression in how he sought to be alone and sought to sleep. All of those things were a result of falling into sin. A simple threat from a woman caused him to take his eyes off God and fall, and this great prophet Elijah became like a me-monster. He was totally after the flesh and focused completely on himself and his fear. We all do the same thing, and the answer to this cause of depression is simple: deal with your sin biblically and promptly.

Finally, the third cause of depression is satanic attack. Whenever there is spiritual victory, Satan will try to counterattack. We must keep a balance in our connection with the Lord and not let our guard down. We must remember that a spiritual battle is constantly going on around us 24/7. The enemy will try to pull you down as soon as you reach a mountaintop, and there is a tendency for us to relax whenever we have a great victory. We may even start thinking that we had something to do with a victory that could've only come by God's hands. 2 Corinthians 12:9 reiterates that our victories come only by God's grace and that His grace is sufficient to get us through, not ourselves. This is where Satan tries to deceive us. "Wherefore let him that thinketh he standeth take heed lest he fall" (1 Corinthians 10:12). The answer to this source of depression is found in our relationship with the Word. We need to constantly be vigilant against spiritual attack and make sure to put on our armor of God every day (Ephesians 6:11-17). Establish a solid and consistent quiet time where you are meeting with God every day and applying what you are reading as truth in your life.

Look what happened to Joseph in the book of Genesis — his own brothers threw him into a pit and sold him into slavery. After he had so much success at Potiphar's house, he was thrown into jail. There were all of these terrible things, but the Bible repeatedly said that the Lord was with him, and that's because Joseph didn't walk away from the Lord. Sometimes we get away from God, but Joseph always maintained this relationship. No matter what horrible pit or circumstance he was in, he never gave up on God. This is what God is trying to teach us when He stretches us from the mountaintops to the valleys. He wants to keep us focused on Him and maintaining His presence — not on the valley and how terrible it is, and not on the mountain and how great it is. Joseph is a great example of what this looks like, as he maintained a good balance and consistency with the Lord no matter what was going on in his life. He's a great man to study about that balance, and we will look at him closer in our lesson on suffering. We also see him using the principles of Philippians 4 in learning to be content.

Unlike Joseph, Elijah allowed himself to feel defeated. We need to remember that we are always triumphant in the Lord (2 Corinthians 2:14). Whether we are coming out of depression or burnout or are in a beautiful season of life, we can always be triumphant. After all, the Bible says that we are more than conquerors through Christ (Romans 8:37).

If you have addressed all of these areas but still face depression, then be at peace. Sometimes depression truly is caused by an imbalance in the chemistry of the brain. However, if you have not prayed through and worked through these three areas — especially with your leaders — then I would encourage you to do so. These are most often the causes of our depression.

But what about burnout? Burnout is closely related to depression, and it happens when we become performance-driven and end up doing things in the flesh. In Luke 10:38-42 we see Martha fall into burnout. What are signs of burnout? Complaining, murmuring, looking at what everyone else is doing, and thinking that you're the only one doing anything are some common indicators, just like with Elijah. We, too, can become performance-driven and do things in the flesh. We all go through those phases, so just beware of burnout if you see yourself starting to complain or fear.

If you do start to notice complaining or fear in your life, take a time-out, get with the Lord, and actively maintain your relationship with Him and His presence. Reconnect with that small voice of His. That's what Elijah did, and that's also what Mary (Martha's sister) did in Luke 10:39. When Elijah reconnected with the Lord, he received a fresh, new vision. In Proverbs 29:18, it says, "Where there is no vision, the people perish." He was at the end of what God had told him to do and needed a new burden and new task, but instead of awaiting God's vision, he got caught up in his own problems. When we focus on our own problems we'll only find despair, but when we connect with God and trust Him for a vision to move forward, we'll often find ourselves rising out of our depression.

You can try to help someone come out of depression by helping them eat, exercise, go to the doctor, and take their vitamins. But at some point it all boils down to their choice to get up and get out, and you cannot do that part for them. That's why God told Elijah to go and return — we have to get up and get back. Encourage yourself with these principles when you fall into depression or burnout! Let this be a reminder to you immediately when you start to fall into depression. Get up, get out, and get a hold of these principles and verses. You have to hold to God's promises and maintain a connection to Him. Don't let the adversity or the bad circumstance pull you down, and don't let your prosperity pull you away. Usually those circumstances can drag our emotions in the wrong direction. Return to your First Love, like we discussed in earlier chapters. When David fell into sin, he prayed Psalm 51 and asked God to restore the joy of his salvation. Joy and our First Love go hand in hand.

Part of the vision that God gave Elijah was to go help Elisha — he was to take on a disciple and teach and mentor him. That's what we are here for and that is where you will find purpose. I started discipling ladies back in 1987, and since then, there hasn't been a time in my life where I haven't been mentoring. Discipling others actually helped me more than being discipled because it has helped me constantly review the basics and be reminded of the simplicity in Christ. It has helped me be transformed, and it has changed all the many ways I was screwed up in my mind and attitudes. As you help others and God uses you to help them, you will get convicted by the very words you share with them because you are held accountable to those words as well. Discipleship gets our focus off of ourselves by letting God use us and work through us. Elijah suffered as he grew, and even Jesus learned obedience by the things that he suffered (Hebrews 5:8). We will go through suffering. In Deuteronomy 8, God warns the nation of Israel that there are trials of tribulations and that there are trials of prosperity. He wants to teach us how to go through both and be victorious in Jesus.

Realize, too, that the wilderness that you go through is a proving process that God will take you through to help you connect to Him through the trial. That's what Deuteronomy 8 talks about! Also, as we continue growing, we move through seven stages of spiritual growth. This process of growth is preparing us for the evil day (Ephesians 6:13). The Bible clearly teaches that there is coming an evil day for all of us, and we must learn to prepare for that day. Remember Jesus praying in the garden of Gethsemane in Matthew 26:36-46? This was where Jesus had to fully surrender Himself to the Father's will as He faced the impending pain of the cross. This is where He was "very heavy" (v. 37) and "exceeding sorrowful" (v. 38) and even sweat "great drops of blood" (Luke 22:42) as He acknowledged the sacrifice He was about to make. This is where His obedience was at its highest testing point, and through submission to God's will and Word, Jesus passed the test. We all have a Gethsemane coming. We go through preparations and test after test in order to arrive at our Gethsemane, just like taking the training wheels off of a bicycle. The Lord will take us through these trials and teach us to hold onto Him and die to self. We will go through these really low, hard valleys with Jesus at our side, and all the while, we can experience the fellowship of His suffering. We go through the trial and learn how to stay in His presence. We are going to go through times of severe testing, and during those times we can choose to learn and to fellowship with the Lord's sufferings. That's what falling into depression and learning to come out of it is preparing us for.

Recommended Reading: For further study, I highly recommend *Self-Confrontation: A Manual for In-Depth Discipleship*. It's a 24-lesson reference book designed to direct you back to the Bible for daily living. Useful for personal growth and discipleship, *Self-Confrontation* will help you learn how the Bible is sufficient and applicable to produce lasting victory in every circumstance and relationship, no matter how difficult.

Emotional Victory

Questions to Consider:

1. Why does God stretch us to mountaintop and valley experiences?

2. According to 2 Corinthians 5:17-20, after we get saved, we are new creatures in Christ and are given what role and ministry? Why?

3. How do we become more reconciled to God?

4. Do you ever struggle with depression? How do you usually respond? What might be the root issue(s)?

5. What are the three categories of problems that can lead to depression?

6. How can we come out of depression biblically?

7. What happened after Elijah's day of great victory? Why did Elijah run to Mount Horeb? What could he have done instead?

8. What did God tell Elijah to do after he finally surrendered?

9. What is the difference between how Elijah and Joseph responded to their adversities?

10. Do you feel burned out? What are signs to look out for?

11. "Whether we are walking through a valley or on a mountaintop, coming out of depression or burnout or are in a beautiful season of life, we are always _____ in Christ."

12. Is there anything you can do today to help yourself falling into depression or burnout in the future?

14

Developing and Keeping a Positive Attitude

Is the cup in your life half full or half empty? Let's realize up front that we Christians have the privilege of having three enemies: the world, the flesh, and the devil. The devil is the god of this world, and he wants to stop us and everything we represent. He wants to take as many souls with him to hell as possible, which means that he wants to stop you from winning anyone to the Lord. He wants to make sure you never disciple or mentor anyone. With so many strong enemies, this seems impossible... but God! We have the Lord on our side — the Creator of the Universe, the King of kings, and the Lord of lords! Because we know Jesus, and because we have been freed from our sins, we are the only ones on the face of this earth that truly can say beyond a shadow of a doubt that the cup is always half full. In fact, the cup is completely full because we have all spiritual blessings in Christ (Ephesians 1:3; 2 Peter 1:3-4; Psalm 23:5). He is with us, and we have the good news of the gospel! It is therefore imperative that our attitude reflects our reality in Christ, because we have no reason to have a negative or bad attitude when God has given us so much.

Romans 8:28-29 *And we know that all things work together for good to them that love God, to them who are the called according to his purpose. For whom*

> he did foreknow, he also did predestinate to be conformed to the image of his Son, that he might be the firstborn among many brethren.

Anyone who has ever lived could easily agree that this world is tough. But God! We have the reality of the kingdom; we know the truth, and all we have to do is believe it and walk in it. Romans 8:28 says that "all things work together for good" — all things! I don't know what you're going through, but He says that all things will work for good, even the things that seem really tough or unbearable.

I've shared some of the things I have faced in my life, and they have often been very difficult things. Many of my mom's last years were extremely difficult, but I've also seen God use it to bring my brother back into my family. I've seen some good things happen from very bad-looking situations. With some of the challenging things in my life I still don't know all of what God was trying to do, but I do know that I love the Lord and that He gives me Romans 8:28 as a promise. Claim that verse! If we just believe that, we can begin seeing the cup as full. How? Romans 8 goes on to say that we are predestined from the day we get saved to become more like Jesus. Those rough things that we go through and those valleys are helping you to be conformed to the image of the Lord Jesus Christ. We could be raptured at any time, but as long as we're down here, there is still a purpose behind everything. When we get to the other side, that's eternity! In light of eternity, we shouldn't be too focused on what's going on down here — we have to get our focus off the physical and on the spiritual. When things look really bad, we must remember it's for our good. Again, I can't always explain it. I just believe it, because that's what He says.

> **1 Thessalonians 5:18** *In every thing give thanks: for this is the will of God in Christ Jesus concerning you.*

Give thanks in everything! This verse says that thankfulness is God's will in my life in every circumstance. We went over this principle thoroughly in the chapter on prayer. Hopefully you've already started developing this concept in your life. Sometimes you're going to hit up against things that you can't give thanks for in the moment, and during these times you need to ask God for the grace to give thanks. You must be honest and tell Him how you are feeling about it and then ask Him to help you to give thanks anyway.

> ***Ephesians 5:20*** *Giving thanks always for all things unto God and the Father in the name of our Lord Jesus Christ;*

Give thanks IN every situation, and give thanks FOR everything! The Prayer Exercise that we went over in Chapter 3 helps you build upon this foundational doctrine, and I encourage you to keep doing it. After all, this is how David was always able to say, "my cup runneth over" (Psalm 23:5)! We Christians are the only ones on this earth with the Good News, so how can the cup be empty when we stand on that foundation?

Like I've mentioned several times, our Laodicean culture is often the reason why this is so hard for us to embrace — we have a sense of entitlement rather than a heart of thankfulness. Check yourself: are you operating from a place of entitlement or from a place of thanksgiving? In the end, this will influence our relationship with Him and ability to be used by Him. If we are operating from a place of thanksgiving, acceptance, and contentment, then it will only be natural for us to be walking in the Spirit and allowing Him to work through us. We want to follow God because of who He is, but we cannot do that if we are not thankful. We have to remember that everything is about the heart attitude, and it is through the heart attitude that God will do anything in and through our lives.

> ***Proverbs 17:22*** *A merry heart doeth good like a medicine: but a broken spirit drieth the bones.*

Learning to have a merry heart is just like taking medicine! It brings health to our spirit, which will show in our countenance. It makes sense, then, that a heart that is not merry is like a poison that only damages us. A broken spirit dries the bones.

> **Proverbs 15:13** *A merry heart maketh a cheerful countenance: but by sorrow of the heart the spirit is broken.*

We must always guard our attitude of heart because a merry heart goes a long way. The state of our heart influences our attitudes and our actions.

> **Proverbs 4:20-23** *My son, attend to my words; incline thine ear unto my sayings. Let them not depart from thine eyes; keep them in the midst of thine heart. For they are life unto those that find them, and health to all their flesh. Keep thy heart with all diligence; for out of it are the issues of life.*

Protect your heart attitude and don't let your guard down. We can be deceived by our heart, so guard it and examine it more than just every once in a while. This should be a 24/7 job for each one of us! You don't have time to be focusing on someone else's heart, because you are to be guarding your own heart! If you can't be thankful, you can easily become just like Elijah in the last chapter. Out of your bad heart attitude are the issues of life, and today's issues that you're dealing with — whether good or bad — often stem from yesterday's attitude. Your heart attitude dictates where God is taking you and what you need to help you conform to the image of Jesus.

When we start to develop a bad attitude, it can begin snowballing if we don't do anything about it. If it can happen to the great prophet Elijah then it can happen to us, and this is why we have to guard our heart. To make matters worse, the enemy is constantly trying to get us to develop a bad attitude, just like he did with Job. God gave him permission to do this with Job because He knew where He was going to take Job through that trial. Similarly, He lets rough things happen to us all for our good so that we will become more like Jesus. There is no need to develop a bad attitude when these things happen because Romans 8 continues on to say that nothing can separate us from the love of God, not even trials of our faith.

Realize, too, that our attitude colors our world. That's how we can get a merry heart through a right heart attitude. Remember how you felt when you got saved? At that time, all you could think about was Jesus! You were in love with the Lord, and everything was awesome. When I was first saved, some of the most horrible circumstances of my life were happening to me. My husband was beating me, but my focus was so much on Jesus that it didn't hinder my attitude. Love does that — when you are in love with Jesus, you don't even mind that expectations aren't being met. When you are in love with God, it makes it seem like nothing else matters because you have fallen head over heels in love with your one True Love. That's where we need to stay with God — in a place of remembering who He is and all the things that He has done for us! But as life goes on, we can easily fall down into the dumps and get distracted. When our expectations aren't met we can lose sight of our love relationship with Jesus and our problems or difficulties become bigger to us than He is.

We must understand that our attitude not only colors our world, it is also contagious and colors the worlds of those around us. Think about it — when you're around someone with a joyous and merry attitude, it begins affecting you. On the other hand, the same happens when you're around someone with a scornful attitude. That's why we need to work on a merry heart.

Proverbs 16:9 *A man's heart deviseth his way: but the LORD directeth his steps.*

When our attitude is right, our steps are going to be right. When our attitude is wrong, our steps are going to be wrong. It is our attitude of heart that devises the way, but God is the one directing the steps that we take.

All of this is why it is so important that we safeguard our heart. The key is letting God sit on the throne of your heart attitude and your will. This holds true because if you are willing, then God is able. 2 Corinthians 8:12 says He accepts our willingness, and 2 Corinthians 9:8 says that He is able. Remember that you become what you think about (Proverbs 23:7). If it doesn't line up with biblical truth, then we will get messed up. We are what we think about — it's all about our thoughts becoming our attitudes and our attitudes becoming our actions. God is looking for our heart attitude to be right because that is what will produce the right fruit in our lives. The battle is in our mind and our heart needs to be transformed. That happens by the words and thoughts we take into it.

As contradictory as it sounds, gaining a right heart is a habit that can start with us doing right on the outside while we let the Lord begin changing us on the inside. That's what Naomi did — Naomi went back to Israel after suffering so many trials and losing her husband and sons. All of this led to her telling the people of Bethlehem to call her Mara, which means "bitter," instead of Naomi, "pleasant" (Ruth 1:19-21). She also lamented how she "went out full," but the Lord brought her "home again empty" (v. 21). It is obvious that her heart hadn't been transformed to where it needed to be. God was changing her heart, but it started with her obedience in returning to Israel. Once she was there and seeking the right things according to God's Word, God would turn her bitterness back into pleasantness.

"Do the next right thing" is a famous quote and practice by Elisabeth Elliot. Do what you know is right and let God begin working on your heart attitude in the meantime. Let Him start working even if you don't feel like it. Many times we don't feel like it, and this is what the devil wants to use to stop us. If you are saved, he can't stop you from going to heaven, but he knows that he can mess up your life so much that he can keep you from taking anyone else to heaven with you. A Christian who is serving themselves is not a threat to the enemy, but if you decide to follow the Lord, then you had better believe that everything and the kitchen sink will be thrown at you. When that happens, begin an attitude adjustment by choosing to be joyful. John 14:1 says, "Let not your heart be troubled." That means that we have a choice. In the world we will have tribulation, but in Christ we have peace because He has overcome the world. We have to learn how to let not our heart be troubled by focusing on God's promises instead of our circumstances. We have to choose peace by looking unto Jesus and not this world. We have to choose joy by seeing the eternal joy that is ahead and looking past the temporal pain, just like Jesus did on the cross.

Hebrews 12:2-3 *Looking unto Jesus the author and finisher of our faith; who for the joy that was set before him endured the cross, despising the shame, and is set down at the right hand of the throne of God. For consider him that endured such contradiction of sinners against himself, lest ye be wearied and faint in your minds.*

What was the joy set before Jesus? Some might say His joy was about us. Why do you think Jesus died on the cross? What comes to mind first when you think about that question? The most common answer is, "Jesus died to save us."

John 12:27-30 *Now is my soul troubled; and what shall I say? Father, save me from this hour: but for this cause came I unto this hour. Father, glorify thy name. Then came there a voice from heaven, saying, I have both glorified it, and will glorify it again. The people therefore, that stood by, and heard it, said that it thundered: others said, An angel spake to him. Jesus answered and said, This voice came not because of me, but for your sakes.*

In this passage we see that Jesus actually died to glorify God the Father. It was in obedience to His Father. When I was young, I remember looking through a kaleidoscope and turning it 'round and 'round, fascinated by the many different, beautiful patterns and colors. Those many dazzling designs are just like the glory of God! Throughout the Bible we see different pictures of God's glory, like how the psalmist says that the heavens declare the glory of God (Psalm 19:1). Just as creation is one facet of God's glory, Jesus dying for us is only one part of how He brought God glory. The main reason that Jesus went to the cross saying, "Not My will, but Thine" was His obedience to His Heavenly Father — God's glory was the center of Christ's life and death.

We are not the center, and that little tweak of making our salvation the center of the crucifixion can actually start us down the wrong path. If we think that it's only about us, we start thinking that Jesus suffered so that we never have to suffer, and this can lead to what our culture calls the "Prosperity Gospel," which is spreading like wildfire. People who believe this gospel think that we do not need to participate in the suffering of our Lord and that life is only about our entitlements and prosperity. This is so contrary to the Word of God — again, we are not the center. What did we learn in Luke 9:23? God says to deny self, take up your cross, and follow Jesus. Yes, there will be mountaintop experiences, but there will also be many rough circumstances to work through that the Bible says are for our good. These valleys help us to get our focus off the physical and back onto our spiritual relationship with Jesus. If you take a biblical viewpoint and understand that Christ suffered and died for you primarily to glorify the Father, then you will be willing to suffer and glorify the Lord as well. That's exactly what 1 Peter 2:21 says!

> **1 Peter 2:21** *For even hereunto were ye called: because Christ also suffered for us, leaving us an example, that ye should follow his steps:*

Just as our attitude colors our world, our perspective on why Jesus died shapes our outlook on and expectations of life. We must remember God and His glory are at the center of our salvation, not us. We are only here to bring glory to God — that's our purpose in life. We saw in Revelation 4:11 that we were created for God's pleasure. Again, in our Laodicean culture, this sometimes gets a little distorted, so we have to keep going back and realigning our thinking with this truth. The next verses also help us put God's glory in the center.

> **Isaiah 43:7, 10-11** *Even every one that is called by my name: for I have created him for my glory, I have formed him; yea, I have made him. [...] Ye are my witnesses, saith the Lord, and my servant whom I have chosen: that ye may know and believe me, and understand that I am he: before me there was no God formed, neither shall there be after me. I, even I, am the Lord; and beside me there is no saviour.*

Bringing glory to God is the only way we will truly have complete joy. We must remember that our lives must revolve around pleasing and glorifying God, and we must keep that in the center as we walk in His presence. There are so many examples of that principle in the Word — just do a word study on glorifying God. Look at all the ways that Jesus glorified God and how we are to glorify Him too — this includes going through the fellowship of His suffering. During one of our last chapters we will go deeper into the subject of suffering. It is both a mystery and a very important part in the life of a child of God. Although our current culture commonly rejects the notion of pain, God calls it a gift, and we will see this in a clearer light by the end of this book. Just start thinking about it now as you learn to develop a positive, thankful attitude of acceptance with joy!

When it comes to our attitude and expectations, we need to be careful of not becoming "bridezillas." There are a lot of movies and reality TV shows out there now about bridezillas — they're brides who are over-the-top and self-centered and they get upset when something isn't exactly the way that they like it. Remember, we are the bride of Christ, and our Laodicean culture has become (or can become) somewhat of a bridezilla. We must examine ourselves and heed the warning in Revelation 3.

> ***Revelation 3:17-19*** *Because thou sayest, I am rich, and increased with goods, and have need of nothing; and knowest not that thou art wretched, and miserable, and poor, and blind, and naked: I counsel thee to buy of me gold tried in the fire, that thou mayest be rich; and white raiment, that thou mayest be clothed, and that the shame of thy nakedness do not appear; and anoint thine eyes with eyesalve, that thou mayest see. As many as I love, I rebuke and chasten: be zealous therefore, and repent.*

Unfortunately, the blessings of God on this nation have turned into our curses and entitlements! When we toured Israel, we visited a home in Nazareth depicting the conditions in which Jesus grew up — a wooden shack with a few rooms and a dirt floor. In Capernaum, we saw the stone foundation of a home where Jesus is believed to have lived while ministering with His disciples. It had two rooms, each one about the size of a common living room. That is where God, the Creator of the Universe, chose to live on this earth. He was born in a barn with animals — that's where God the Father chose to send

His Son to this earth. The Lord could have done it any way He chose, and He could have even been born into a culture like ours, but He wasn't.

We need to remember how Jesus walked on this earth and let that shape how we see the purpose of our lives and our attitude towards the physical blessings we have. Sometimes we can get out of balance with trying to be perfect with all of our stuff — we strive for the perfect home, perfect clothes, perfect cars, and the list could go on. Don't get me wrong, it's okay to have nice things! We just can't get too focused on the physical.

The Lord warns us that when we are rich and increased with goods, we start thinking we do not need Him. He says, "[No, no.] I counsel thee to buy of me gold tried in the fire, that thou mayest be rich; and white raiment, that thou mayest be clothed, and that the shame of thy nakedness do not appear; and anoint thine eyes with eyesalve, that thou mayest see. As many as I love, I rebuke and chasten: be zealous therefore, and repent" (Revelation 3:18-19).

His plea to us is to not fall into entitlement. Just look at the life, suffering, and death of Christ and His attitude towards the things of this world and His circumstances. Don't make your life all about the physical things, make it about your relationship with Him. Don't put your salvation in the center of why Jesus died, put God's glory in the center of this and of everything as you learn to develop a positive attitude! As we've seen, a little tweak in our thinking can have a big impact on our attitude.

Perspective is everything, especially when we go through hard times. As always, the Word is the key to keeping God's glory in the center and also the key to seeing what we're going through from His eternal perspective. 2 Corinthians 4 is one of the greatest, most encouraging set of promises I read when I'm going through a hard time, especially these last two verses.

> *2 Corinthians 4:17-18 For our light affliction, which is but for a moment, worketh for us a far more exceeding and eternal weight of glory; while we look*

not at the things which are seen, but at the things which are not seen: for the things which are seen are temporal; but the things which are not seen are eternal.

Whatever we are going through is actually just a "light affliction" according to God. We usually don't think so at the time, and both Elijah and Job certainly didn't think so, but it truly is just a light affliction. Regardless of what we're going through, on God's timeline, it's only for a moment and it will give us an eternal weight of glory.

We have to keep focusing on the eternal, correcting bad attitudes, and casting down imaginations. The key to all of this is found in 2 Corinthians 10:3-5, which tells us to bring every thought captive to the obedience of Christ. We need to examine every thought and purpose to think with an attitude of thankfulness and contentment. This was thoroughly covered in the "Attitude vs. Action" lesson in Chapter 5.

Here are a few promises to apply:

> *Philippians 1:6* *Being confident of this very thing, that he which hath begun a good work in you will perform it until the day of Jesus Christ:*

> *Philippians 4:8* *Finally, brethren, whatsoever things are true, whatsoever things are honest, whatsoever things are just, whatsoever things are pure, whatsoever things are lovely, whatsoever things are of good report; if there be any virtue, and if there be any praise, think on these things.*

> *Ephesians 3:20* *Now unto him that is able to do exceeding abundantly above all that we ask or think, according to the power that worketh in us,*

> *Ephesians 5:19-20* *Speaking to yourselves in psalms and hymns and spiritual songs, singing and making melody in your heart to the Lord; giving thanks always for all things unto God and the Father in the name of our Lord Jesus Christ;*

These promises are awesome! We need to hold onto what God has said He would like to do instead of holding onto the discouraging thoughts. Replace the bad thoughts by meditating on all of the great things that He has promised you!

In Psalm 23 David said that his cup was running over. How did that happen for him, and how do we get that for ourselves? The answer is in Psalm 1, which tells us how to be blessed and have a merry heart. Through the illustration of a tree that is planted by the water of the Word, David shows us how to prosper and have leaves that never wither.

> **Psalm 1:1-3** *Blessed is the man that walketh not in the counsel of the ungodly, nor standeth in the way of sinners, nor sitteth in the seat of the scornful. But his delight is in the law of the Lord; and in his law doth he meditate day and night. And he shall be like a tree planted by the rivers of water, that bringeth forth his fruit in his season; his leaf also shall not wither; and whatsoever he doeth shall prosper.*

He begins by telling us not to go to the world for counsel. Go to the Bible and the counsel of the Word of God instead! If you want to be blessed and flourishing, then you need to be careful about where you go for counsel — don't seek it from the ungodly. 1 Corinthians 15:33 says, "Evil communications corrupt good manners." No matter how well you're doing, taking in evil communication can corrupt you.

Secondly, the psalmist tells us not to participate in sinful activities. In Psalms 51:10, David asks God to create in him a clean heart. Romans 8:1 tells us, "There is therefore no condemnation to them which are in Christ Jesus, who walk not after the flesh, but after the Spirit." Therefore, if you are in Christ (saved) and choosing to follow after the Spirit, and not the flesh, then there is no condemnation to you. So every time you find yourself starting to follow the flesh, you must simply repent — just ask for forgiveness and go back to following the Spirit.

The final and third warning is not to sit with the scornful. Don't hang with scorners — that includes murmurers, discouragers, or complainers. The Bible talks about what happens to a scorner, and it's not good news:

Proverbs 21:9 *It is better to dwell in a corner of the housetop, than with a brawling woman in a wide house.*

Proverbs 21:19 *It is better to dwell in the wilderness, than with a contentious and an angry woman.*

Proverbs 27:15 *A continual dropping in a very rainy day and a contentious woman are alike.*

Philippians 2:14 is a great verse to memorize if you find yourself murmuring or complaining — "Do all things without murmurings and disputings." All things! When you start murmuring and disputing, ask God to help you keep that verse in your heart and He will help you guard your heart from scorners and from becoming scornful.

The opposite of scorning and murmuring is developing a thankful attitude. In 1 Thessalonians 1:2-3 after Paul had just been beaten and imprisoned, he preached to the new converts in prison with him. He didn't even mention the tragedies that had happened in his life. He chose to focus outwardly rather than inwardly, and he prayed and gave thanks for those to whom he was ministering. He remembered what God had done in their lives and he remembered that God had a purpose for them. Paul simply practiced what he preached. After all, he had learned how to stay thankful in the midst of extreme trials.

The apostle John did the same thing in the book of Revelation. He had been exiled to the isle of Patmos and was penning the book of Revelation from horrible living conditions. This was an island for prisoners where evil men were condemned for life, and John was sentenced there because of his preaching. But when he introduced the book in Revelation 1, he never mentioned all the difficult circumstances he was going through. He wrote only words of encouragement to his brothers and sisters in Christ.

Neither John nor Paul talked much about their pain and suffering unless it was to teach us how to look past it. As we read their words, it seems like they didn't even think about the terrible circumstances of their lives. How did they do that? What was their key? They simply kept focusing on praying and ministering to others, leading people to the Lord, and making disciples. Their lives were all about God using them to reach someone else. They knew the Good News and desired to pass it on! This was the case with Elijah and Elisha, and it should be the case with us, too.

When it comes to being positive, this is the bottom line: we Christians are the only ones on the face of this earth that have the ability to truly be thankful and positive always! We are children of the living God! He is the Creator of the Universe, the King of kings, and the Lord of lords! You are an heir of God and a joint-heir with Christ, and we have His living presence with us 24/7! WOW, think about that. What more could we need or want?

> **Galatians 4:6-7** *And because ye are sons, God hath sent forth the Spirit of his Son into your hearts, crying, Abba, Father. Wherefore thou art no more a servant, but a son; and if a son, then an heir of God through Christ.*

In Genesis 15:1, God told Abram, "Fear not, Abram: I am thy shield, and thy exceeding great reward." And that's what He says to us, too. He is our shield and EXCEEDING GREAT REWARD! And not only that, He is also our HOPE. Now, the biblical definition of hope is very different from the way we use the word today. Biblical HOPE is placing trust in or having confidence in a sure thing, not something that "might be." Our hope is built on nothing less than Jesus' blood and righteousness — that means it's a FOR SURE deal.

> **Romans 8:24-25** *For we are saved by hope: but hope that is seen is not hope: for what a man seeth, why doth he yet hope for? But if we hope for that we see not, then do we with patience wait for it.*

> **Romans 15:13** *Now the God of hope fill you with all joy and peace in believing, that ye may abound in hope, through the power of the Holy Ghost.*

When David was going through tough times, he said something similar to himself in Psalm 43:5: "Why art thou cast down, O my soul? and why art thou disquieted within me? hope in God: for I shall yet praise him, who is the health of my countenance, and my God." In order to develop and keep a positive attitude, we must learn to think the same way. We must focus on the spiritual facts, not the physical realm, feelings, or circumstances. As we go through trials — and we will — we can't focus on the pit. Instead, we must cling to the Anchor of our souls. It is possible, ladies! Get into the habit of giving thanks and praising God, even in — and especially in — the difficult times.

Homework: An assignment for developing a positive attitude.
1. Pick at least one of these activities and do it:
   - Watch *Schindler's List*. Next time you're feeling down, watch it. See if you still feel sorry for yourself.
   - Watch *Soul Surfer*. It makes a good point about how God can turn horrible tragedies into something for good.
   - Visit a children's cancer ward.

2. Memorize and meditate on the verses and principles in this study.

3. Sing spiritual songs to the Lord. Psalm 100 says that we enter into the gates of the Lord when we're singing to Him. Let your life be filled with thanksgiving and praise.

4. Most importantly, begin a journal and write down five different things you're thankful to God for every morning. When I first started doing this, I was diligent to write down those five things every day, but by days four and five I was struggling to find five new things to write down! That was ridiculous. We have millions of things to be thankful for! When you begin to focus on your blessings, it becomes easy to find things to be thankful for. On the other hand, when you get so focused on the flaws, that's all you end up seeing. We must take a step back and see God. We can't let molehills become mountains. Whichever we choose to focus on, whether it be blessings or flaws, will determine our issues of life.

Questions to Consider:

1. Would those around you describe you as someone with a positive attitude?

2. Do you consider the cup half empty or half full? As followers of Jesus Christ, why can the cup always be full or even overflowing (as David described in Psalm 23:5)?

3. God's will for us is to be thankful _____ and _____ everything.

4. What should we do if we can't give thanks for something?

5. Why are we to keep (guard) our hearts with all diligence in Proverbs 4:23?

6. What does it mean to have a merry heart? What is the key to getting a merry heart?

7. What does it mean to be a scorner? What does God say happens to scorners?

8. In the book of Ruth, Naomi suffered much loss and returned to Bethlehem with a bitter outlook. How did she turn her attitude around?

9. Complete an assignment from the suggested homework. How did it go? How did it affect your attitude?

15

A Meek and Quiet Spirit

et me ask you a very serious question: do you want to please Jesus? Is pleasing Him the desire of your heart? If you answered with a yes, then you will want to pay special attention to our key text for this lesson:

1 Peter 3:1-7 Likewise, ye wives, be in subjection to your own husbands; that, if any obey not the word, they also may without the word be won by the conversation of the wives; while they behold your chaste conversation coupled with fear. Whose adorning let it not be that outward adorning of plaiting the hair, and of wearing of gold, or of putting on of apparel; but let it be the hidden man of the heart, in that which is not corruptible, even the ornament of a meek and quiet spirit, which is in the sight of God of great price. For after this manner in the old time the holy women also, who trusted in God, adorned themselves, being in subjection unto their own husbands: even as Sara obeyed Abraham, calling him lord: whose daughters ye are, as long as ye do well, and are not afraid with any amazement. Likewise, ye husbands, dwell with them according to knowledge, giving honour unto the wife, as unto the weaker vessel, and as being heirs together of the grace of life; that your prayers be not hindered.

We clearly see in these verses that, in God's eyes, a meek and quiet spirit is of great price. In fact, to God, this quality in ladies is priceless! So if pleasing God is something that you want to do, you must work on this characteristic. Although I still have a lot to learn in this area, I guarantee you that if you do not learn how to run your emotions through the Word of God, you will never develop a meek and quiet spirit.

Learning about having a meek and quiet spirit starts with first learning humility. Meekness cannot occur without humility because it is just controlled strength — the strength of God run through the boundaries of His Word. It's submission to God's will and not our own. We know about and often focus on the strengths that we have access to in the Lord, but we must also learn how to let His Spirit direct us within His boundaries so that they are controlled strengths. Jesus is the obvious person who personifies this attribute for us. He had all the strength of God, yet in His humility, He did not use this strength in pride. Rather, He humbled himself and was meek. Before Jesus, Moses was called the most meek man who ever lived on earth (Numbers 12:3) because he had access to a close and powerful relationship with God, yet he did not defend himself against Aaron and Miriam when they rose up against him (Numbers 12). Instead, he submitted himself to God's will.

Another thing to note as we begin learning this trait is that 1 and 2 Peter contain some of the greatest illustrations on learning submission and humility. The most amazing part about it is that when you look at Peter's life and first meet him in the gospels, you would never in a million years think of "humble" as an apt word to describe him. He was straightforward, blunt, and often put his foot in his mouth, yet he became a great example of true humility. It's totally amazing that when God chose to speak on submission, he took someone like Peter and changed him. He let him show the world who God was by taking this strong, stubborn, and self-willed man and teaching him how to follow the Lord in humility. That's exactly what He wants to do in our lives!

I remember when the Lord first started dealing with me on this subject; it was the first time that I had ever read 1 Peter 3:1-7. I was very fearful of people, I was a people-pleaser, and I was incredibly quiet. My motivation for being quiet was not that I was trusting in the Lord, but that I was afraid of what others might think — I was fearful of man. So when I read these verses, I initially thought that I had a meek and quiet spirit. As God started working on me, He began to teach me how to deal with all my fears and how to learn to be bold and walk in the light, first in my relationship with Him and then with others. That took ten to fifteen years as I began growing, and the more that I walked with Him, the more that I learned to be up-front with Him and with others. "If we walk in the light, as He is in the light…" 1 John 1:7 was the anchor verse He gave me to learn to confront my fears and walk past them to Him (into the light). He showed me that I was lying by not being up-front, direct, and assertive. This wasn't a simple task, and it took many, many years to learn.

It wasn't until He taught me how to bring things out into the open that He was able to teach me how to have a meek and quiet spirit. And ladies, that was very hard after having finally learned to speak up and say what's on my mind. Now don't get me wrong, there is a definite balance here. We have to keep in mind that there are times when God wants us to keep our mouths shut, and there are times when God wants us to speak up. The only way we can truly learn that balance and let it be motivated by our relationship with the Lord is by walking with Him. He is the only way we are going to learn it.

Another important word to note in these verses is "own." He says be in subjection to your own husband, not someone else's. This sounds fine, but what about those who are single or those whose husbands are not saved? For singles, the key is to recognize that the Lord is our husband and bridegroom. If you are a wife with an unbelieving husband, then you have to remember that this is a key text that you're going to want to glean from and live out, because you can actually reach your husband through your lifestyle as you fear and walk with the Lord. We should also mention here that this passage is not saying that you cannot wear jewelry or do your hair, it's only saying that those shouldn't be the emphases of your life. The emphasis should instead be on meekness to the Lord — not fearing man, but fearing God. We want to learn to be the bride of Christ, not a bridezilla. Life isn't all about us, it's all about Him.

A lot of times when I'm doing word studies, I like to start with Webster's 1828 Dictionary. Do you know that when Noah Webster wrote that dictionary, most of the examples he used were from Bible verses? So if you were to look up "meek," you would find the definition as "humble and submissive to God's will." You will also find Bible verses listed that help describe that word. Now, I'm not saying we use the 1828 dictionary instead of the Word, but it can be a helpful tool. I often use it and the definition found in my concordance when I begin looking at a word, and then I do a thorough study on the word by looking at every instance it is used in the Bible. That often gives me a good place to start.

I think we've laid out a good introduction on a meek and quiet spirit, so now let's walk through two key steps that the Lord used to teach me how to begin the process of growing in this area.

Step 1: We have to learn to trust in the Lord and not in anything (or anyone) else, especially not in an authority figure. There can be a tendency for us ladies to trust in authorities, and we can sometimes even put our authorities up on a pedestal. I know you acknowledge in your mind that your authority figure is not supposed to take the place of God, but we can lose sight of this and be easily deceived. Realize that everyone in this world and everyone you love (including yourself) is going to let you down at some point in their lives. No one is perfect. Again, the only things that are never going to let us down are the Word of God and the Lord Jesus Christ, and this is because they are perfect.

> **Romans 3:4** *God forbid: yea, let God be true, but every man a liar; as it is written, That thou mightest be justified in thy sayings, and mightest overcome when thou art judged.*

This verse tells us that everyone is a liar. I don't purposely want to lie or let anyone down, but I am made from sinful flesh. Some things I say, either intentionally or unintentionally, will not line up with what God says. This is why we need to correct ourselves with the Word of God.

> **Psalm 118:8** *It is better to trust in the Lord than to put confidence in man.*

We have to always remember that God is in control. No matter who your authority is, God is in control of them! The key isn't trusting the authority, the key is trusting God to work through the authority. That's what it has to always go back to! When I came out of an abusive marriage, I was terrified of men's authority and the idea of getting advice from a pastor terrified me! God began giving me some verses and challenged me to trust Him for my pastor's leadership. The first year that I began to call on my pastor for advice, my heart would be pounding hard, but the Lord taught me to stand on His Word and walk through the fear as I went in for help. We have to trust God for the authorities He gives us.

Here's another important thing to realize about this concept: we must trust God for our authorities' leadership even when they are wrong and even when they let us down. We've laid a great foundation in preceding chapters that will help us to correct the natural response from our flesh that wants to combat or dismiss our authorities when we think they're wrong. Instead, we need to lay down and die to self, get ourselves out of the way, pray, and let the Lord change them when they're wrong. We need to be trusting solely and completely in God, because He will always take care of you when you are seeking to follow Him. The first time I found this out was while I was married to my abusive husband. After turning to the Lord and trusting Him, He protected me from my husband's abuse. I desired my husband to turn around and be saved, but unfortunately that is not what he chose. After God gave him many opportunities to choose the right way, He finally removed my husband from my life and all the while used my authorities to protect me. So ladies, we have to realize that if we have learned to truly trust and obey God, we will learn how to be adorned with a meek and quiet spirit. This happens through submission and subjection, and it doesn't just happen overnight. If you trust and obey God, you will be adorned with a meek and quiet spirit which will produce subjection and obedience to all your authorities (even when they are wrong).

One time I taught a young married lady the verses from 1 Peter 3 and she asked me why I had the ability to counsel her on this subject since I was single. My answer was that we all have to learn subjection to authority, whether our authority be a husband, a boss, or a pastor. Even our male authorities have to learn subjection. Everyone has to learn it. Though a married woman may have more real life examples and ability to empathize through experience, God can use any mentor in your life to teach you subjection.

Step 2: Study out three key examples of meekness: Peter, Sarah, and Jesus. We've already looked at Peter's example, and if you're wanting to learn more about how to submit, prayerfully meditate on his writings and life. There is much for you to learn from Peter.

Peter writes about the other two examples in 1 Peter. One is Sarah, a lady who trusted in God despite her imperfect authority figure. The other is our Lord Jesus Christ. I've often heard ladies say that their authority is an exception to the rule — surely they are too imperfect and flawed to be covered by God's grace! We always think that we are the exception, but there are no exceptions to the Word of God! Everybody falls under this umbrella, and the more that we can believe God and trust Him, the more He can and will work through that ungodly authority by changing him or removing him. However, what often happens is that we get in the way and God is unable to step in. We have to learn to get out of the way.

In 1 Peter 3:6, Peter encourages us to learn from Sarah's example. Let's go back and examine Sarah's life and see how she trusted God despite her imperfect husband. For those who aren't married yet, you may be married someday, and that person is not going to be perfect. I'm sorry, but they will occasionally let you down, and they may sometimes be wrong. Prepare yourself for that truth. Remember this lesson and it will spare you lots of grief.

Sarah's story is detailed in Genesis 12-21 and she is also mentioned in Hebrews 11. Hebrews 11 is often referred to as the "Hall of Faith," and it lists godly men and women and how they trusted in the Lord by faith. I encourage you to go back and study out Sarah for yourself! Read about her — how did He teach her how to have a meek and quiet spirit? What did He need to take her through for her to learn? I began seeing that, even though Sarah was listed in God's Hall of Faith, she didn't always trust the Lord. Sarah went through a growth process just like we do. She is first introduced to us in Genesis 12.

> **Genesis 12:1-5** *Now the Lord had said unto Abram, Get thee out of thy country, and from thy kindred, and from thy father's house, unto a land that I will shew thee: and I will make of thee a great nation, and I will bless thee, and make thy name great; and thou shalt be a blessing: and I will bless them that bless thee, and curse him that curseth thee: and in thee shall all families of the earth be blessed. So Abram departed, as the Lord had spoken unto him; and Lot went with him: and Abram was seventy and five years old when he departed out of Haran. And Abram took Sarah his wife, and Lot his brother's son, and all their substance that they had gathered, and the souls that they had gotten in Haran; and they went forth to go into the land of Canaan; and into the land of Canaan they came.*

So we notice right off the bat that Abram begins obeying God, but it's only partial obedience because he wasn't supposed to take Lot with him. As he obeyed, Sarah followed. She left her home and all her friends and family, but we already see a subjected spirit in her as she follows her husband as he follows the Lord. Let's move on and look at Abraham and how he let Sarah down. It's easy to think that the amazing people in the Bible never had problems, and we can tend to put these people on pedestals. However, it is often that the more the Lord uses a person, the more problems they have had to work through.

Here is Abraham, this great father of the faith, and yet he tells Sarah to lie about her relationship with him out of fear for his own life. We see him giving her to another man to protect his own life — talk about great leadership. How many of you married ladies would like your husband to give you to another man? He was afraid that other men would see her beauty and kill him in order to get her, so he told them that she was his sister instead of his wife. This was a half truth, because she was actually his half-sister, but he still didn't want her to tell the whole truth. The sad thing is that he actually did this two times!

Here is this great prophet whom the Lord uses mightily and whom the Lord calls His friend. God is showing us how Abraham learned to trust Him through a painful growth process. Sarah submitted to him and God intervened, stopping the whole ordeal. Even though her authority was messing up big time, God honored her submission and protected her.

Let's read about one of these instances.

> **Genesis 20:2-7** *And Abraham said of Sarah his wife, She is my sister: and Abimelech king of Gerar sent, and took Sarah. But God came to Abimelech in a dream by night, and said to him, Behold, thou art but a dead man, for the woman which thou hast taken; for she is a man's wife. But Abimelech had not come near her: and he said, Lord, wilt thou slay also a righteous nation? Said he not unto me, She is my sister? and she, even she herself said, He is my brother: in the integrity of my heart and innocency of my hands have I done this. And God said unto him in a dream, Yea, I know that thou didst this in the integrity of thy heart; for I also withheld thee from sinning against me: therefore suffered I thee not to touch her. Now therefore restore the man his wife; for he is a prophet, and he shall pray for thee, and thou shalt live: and if thou restore her not, know thou that thou shalt surely die, thou, and all that are thine.*

Now don't you think that really let Sarah down? I mean, if you were putting your husband on a pedestal, it wouldn't be difficult for him to fall from the pedestal after something like that. Most of us would have expectations of a husband that would never do something like that. Wouldn't it be difficult and almost impossible to follow him here? Think about being in that kind of situation. However, Sarah followed and obeyed. This is where she laid down and died to self, and this is also where God came through for her and protected her. When I've read through this, sometimes it seems like Sarah actually learned to submit and be in subjection to God before Abraham did. You see the two of them growing together in their obedience and God intervening to set things right. If Sarah hadn't obeyed, we might not be reading about them. When her husband let her down, she trusted God and He came through for her. It's a great story to hold on to with hope when our authorities let us down or do something that doesn't seem right. Keep in mind, too, that we don't know everything — we might not agree with what they are doing, but it may turn out to be the right thing to do in the end. Sarah didn't fix the wrongdoing of her husband and she didn't try to teach him. Instead, she died to self and let the Lord take care of it for her. When your authority makes a mistake, trust God. Get out of the way and let God fix it, not you.

However, Sarah wasn't perfect either. We'll see that she faced another difficulty that taught her submission. We all have areas where God is seeking to grow us, and Sarah struggled with this next difficulty just as many of us ladies do when we try to fix a situation through manipulation. We saw where she obeyed and let God come through in the previous illustration, but this next area revealed the need for her growth. God had promised Abraham and Sarah a son, but she was far too old — or so she thought. When she didn't see the promise being fulfilled right away, she took control instead of just waiting on God's perfect timing. She, like Abraham, had much to learn. That's why Proverbs 31:30 is so good for us to remember: "Favor is deceitful, and beauty is vain: but a woman that feareth the LORD, she shall be praised." God's favor is the only favor under which you want to operate. It is never about controlling situations through our earthly relationships or the favor of man. Another way we women can be manipulative is by our looks — we know that they can open doors for us, but those really aren't the doors you should be opening.

A great assignment that teaches us to develop a meek and quiet spirit is comparing the differences between the foolish woman of Proverbs 7 with the virtuous woman of Proverbs 31 like we did back in chapter 12. The foolish woman trusts in her looks and manipulation and is cunning and deceptive, which is very different from the qualities of the virtuous woman. Don't be a bridezilla. Choose to be a virtuous woman.

Sarah knew the promise that God had told Abraham, but she hadn't learned this important proverb. So she decided to take things into her own hands and suggested that Abraham have a child through her handmaid Hagar (Genesis 16:1-2). She came up with her own idea on how to fix the problem and Ishmael was born. Sarah's solution only complicated matters, and to this day, Hagar's offspring have been trouble for Sarah's offspring, Israel. That's how bad it can get for us when we try to control the situation. But when she finally put it into God's hands, He provided her with a son. Sarah just had to learn to submit both to God and to her husband in every circumstance and situation. She was a real person with real problems just like us, yet as she yielded to God, she learned how to trust Him and not her family, herself, or her husband.

The other great example of meekness that Peter writes about in 1 Peter 3 is Jesus. The very first word of that chapter is very important, and that word is "Likewise." That means that we need to take into consideration everything he just said in the preceding chapter because it applies here as well. Since the preceding chapter was all about Jesus, learn from the example of Jesus as He went to the cross. There is so much to be said for the encouragement in these verses when you're going through a really hard time and you don't understand why. Chapter 2 is a great, great source of comfort because it details what our Lord and Savior Jesus Christ went through — it's all about dying to self in obedience to God the Father. Jesus is one of the greatest examples of a meek and quiet spirit.

The next two words of chapter 3 are "ye wives." This means that it applies to all of us, whether single, married, male, or female. As believers we are all part of the bride of Christ.

> ***1 Peter 2:13-25*** *Submit yourselves to every ordinance of man for the Lord's sake: whether it be to the king, as supreme; or unto governors, as unto them that are sent by him for the punishment of evildoers, and for the praise of them that do well. For so is the will of God, that with well doing ye may put to silence the ignorance of foolish men: as free, and not using your liberty for a cloke of maliciousness, but as the servants of God. Honour all men. Love the brotherhood. Fear God. Honour the king. Servants, be subject to your masters with all fear; not only to the good and gentle, but also to the froward. For this is thankworthy, if a man for conscience toward God endure grief, suffering wrongfully. For what glory is it, if, when ye be buffeted for your faults, ye shall take it patiently? but if, when ye do well, and suffer for it, ye take it patiently, this is acceptable with God. For even hereunto were ye called: because Christ also suffered for us, leaving us an example, that ye should follow his steps: who did no sin, neither was guile found in his mouth: who, when he was reviled, reviled not again; when he suffered, he threatened not; but committed himself to him that judgeth righteously: who his own self bare our sins in his own body on the tree, that we, being dead to sins, should live unto righteousness: by whose stripes ye were healed. For ye were as sheep going astray; but are now returned unto the Shepherd and Bishop of your souls.*

No matter what we are going through, we will never have it as bad as Jesus. But in spite of all of this, He was sinless! He was accused left and right and bore all of our sin on His shoulders, but He did not open His mouth. It is often more difficult for us to submit and have a quiet and meek spirit when we feel like we are being wronged unfairly. But even though Jesus actually was right, He didn't open His mouth in defense. He could have said a lot of things in the moment, and He could have easily rationalized or argued His way out of this situation, but He instead chose to just trust and obey God. He surrendered and submitted and let God the Father take control of the whole situation. To be clear, Jesus was not a doormat — He knew how to speak up, and there were plenty of times when He spoke His mind and said what needed to be said at God's direction. But at this time He was to be silent, and He remained that way. God in the flesh was silent, was judged by the world, and took all of our sin upon Himself. This is recorded for us in all four gospels.

> **Matthew 27:11-14** And Jesus stood before the governor: and the governor asked him, saying, Art thou the King of the Jews? And Jesus said unto him, Thou sayest. And when he was accused of the chief priests and elders, he answered nothing. Then said Pilate unto him, Hearest thou not how many things they witness against thee? And he answered him to never a word; insomuch that the governor marvelled greatly.

The mark of a person truly trusting in God is their ability to keep their mouth shut during a trial, even when (and especially when) they are right.

> **Proverbs 10:19** In the multitude of words there wanteth not sin: but he that refraineth his lips is wise.

> **Proverbs 13:3** He that keepeth his mouth keepeth his life: but he that openeth wide his lips shall have destruction.

There are numerous verses where the example of our Lord and Savior was bold and forthright. Likewise, there are many instances where Jesus was right and said nothing. Absolutely nothing. Believe me, the Lord wants to teach each of us how to do that, too. That is meekness; that is controlled power. We must look to Jesus' example.

> **Hebrews 12:2-4** Looking unto Jesus the author and finisher of our faith; who for the joy that was set before him endured the cross, despising the shame, and is set down at the right hand of the throne of God. For consider him that endured such contradiction of sinners against himself, lest ye be wearied and faint in your minds. Ye have not yet resisted unto blood, striving against sin.

Realize that the mark of a person that truly trusts in God is their ability to have His strength under submission to His Word. It's their ability to keep their emotions within the boundaries of the Bible, and this will ultimately be reflected in their words. A lot of times our emotions get us messed up here. What I've learned to do when I think I hear from God is to wait and see if the Lord is really in it, because if I can't wait, then there's a good possibility that He's not behind it. If I absolutely can't wait, that's a warning signal to me that it might be under the control of my emotions. That's been one little test I've learned over the years to see if God is in something. I pray to God about it and wait instead of jumping to action. If He's not in it then I don't want to continue anyway.

We've learned so much from Peter, Sarah, and Jesus. In addition, we can learn much from Paul's writings. He tells us that tribulations teach us to trust in God rather than others or ourselves. In 2 Corinthians 1:8-10 he writes about being left for dead so that he would learn to trust in God and not himself. The Lord may sometimes have to allow difficulties in our lives so that we learn to trust Him! We should lean on God's strength instead of our own, and as we learn to operate in God's strength, we learn to obey Him and to discern when He wants us to speak and when He needs us to hold it in. This teaches us to operate by the strength of the Lord instead of by our flesh or our passion. Meekness is strength under control, and it is accomplished by focusing on Him.

> ***Philippians 2:12-13*** *Wherefore, my beloved, as ye have always obeyed, not as in my presence only, but now much more in my absence, work out your own salvation with fear and trembling. For it is God which worketh in you both to will and to do of his good pleasure.*

Paul is not talking about losing our salvation; he's actually talking about the tribulation that we're going through and how God uses it for good. God's Spirit lives inside us, and what we have to learn is how to work out that salvation. We need to be getting our flesh out of the way and be adorned in the Lord's Spirit so that people see Him and not us. We need to allow Jesus to come out through our brokenness. We are the temple of the Holy Spirit, and we can work out our salvation by allowing Christ to have control instead of our flesh. Our flesh gets in the way of letting God work through us, so we have to work it from the inside out and allow tribulation to conform us into people who are submitted to and crucified with Christ.

> **Galatians 2:20** *I am crucified with Christ: nevertheless I live; yet not I, but Christ liveth in me: and the life which I now live in the flesh I live by the faith of the Son of God, who loved me, and gave himself for me.*

This is a great memory verse about this subject and has helped me get through so many difficult times. It reminds us that we need to allow God to do all things through us — remember, it is His faith that lives inside you! We don't want to do it with our faith, we want to do it with His faith. Oftentimes during those rough valleys, our faith can be so small that it is easy to surrender to Him and ask Him for His faith to work through us. Jesus Christ lives in us, and He wants to work the new creature to the outside. His faith is accessible to you.

God wants us to be meek and quiet, and this can only come through surrender to Him in every situation as well as submission to the authorities He has given us. He has given us great examples through Peter, Sarah, Jesus, and Paul that we can turn to when we are struggling. In the end, we need to allow Him to work through us and speak through us and put aside our own desires, objections, and persuasions. Surrender to Him at all times — whether it be a mountaintop or a valley — and let Him do all things through you. These are the characteristics of a meek and quiet spirit, and this is how we can please the Lord.

Questions to Consider:

1. What is the first quality we must learn before we can develop a meek and quiet spirit?

2. The world often equates meekness with weakness. How does God define meekness?

3. Who are our three key examples from 1 Peter 2 & 3, and how did they develop and display a meek and quiet spirit? What else have you learned from their lives?

4. Have you ever done a word study? If not, take a moment to search online for Webster's 1828 Dictionary and a Bible concordance resource like Strong's or Blue Letter Bible. Bookmark these sites for easy future access and then practice using these tools by doing a quick word study on the word "meek" as laid out in the chapter.

5. Is there any authority figure you're putting on a pedestal? Is there anyone or anything you're trusting in besides the Lord? What does the Bible say to do?

6. What do you do when your authority figure is wrong? What is the biblical way to respond?

7. What are the only two things that will never let us down?

8. "The mark of a person truly trusting in God is their ability to _____ during a trial."

9. According to Philippians 2:12-13, how do we work out our own salvation with fear and trembling?

10. Write down Galatians 2:20 and commit to memorizing it this week.

16

Learning from Failure

Over the years I have learned a lot from Peter in the Bible, as he often shows us what not to do. God has chosen to record many of his infirmities and then show us how he was transformed! I think one of the greatest experiences Peter ever had was when he walked on the water with Jesus (Matthew 14:28-31). This happened on the Sea of Galilee, which I've actually been able to visit in person! When we started out on the boat it was stormy, but then it calmed down, the clouds broke up, and the sun shined through. And that happened on two separate trips! It was literally the most peaceful place I've ever been on earth. Oftentimes when we think about Peter and Jesus on the water, the main thing we remember is that Peter sank! Whenever we consider him getting out to walk on the water with Jesus, we always emphasize that he failed.

Oftentimes God will ask us to do things and we won't want to do them because we think we're going to fail. Even something so easy as opening your mouth and telling your friends about Jesus can be so hard! With that in mind, there is a lot we can learn from Peter and his example. Here's something we should consider rather than focusing on his failure: there were 12 disciples in the boat and only one of them tried to follow Jesus and walk on water. Nobody talks about that. They were all in there and only Peter got up and attempted to be with Jesus, and he was even successful for a moment! He walked on the water with Jesus!

> **Proverbs 24:16** *For a just man falleth seven times, and riseth up again: but the wicked shall fall into mischief.*

We can all experience walking on the water in the sense of rising above the circumstances and the difficulties of our life as we connect with the Lord and walk in His presence. The Word of God says that in the world we have tribulation, but in Jesus we have peace (John 16:33). So when we're going through those hard times, we need to be like Peter and be willing to take that first step forward onto the waves with Jesus. Maybe we'll fail initially, but we just have to keep getting back up. Sooner or later, we learn. So the next time you think of Peter and the guys in the boat, focus on the fact that he believed God and was willing. After all, all that matters to God is our willingness. Realize, too, that when He asks us to do something, the first step is trying to follow through with it regardless of any fear. Proverbs 24:16 is a great promise for us to remember when the fear of failure creeps in.

Who is just? Jesus. Who do we have? Jesus. The more we walk in His righteousness and justification, the more that we get to experience Jesus' righteousness picking us back up when we fall. We can get beyond fear of failure and let Him teach us through the fear. One of the ways that the enemy gets us down is discouragement rooted in fear of failure. Did you know Jesus was never discouraged?

> **Isaiah 42:4** *He shall not fail nor be discouraged, till he have set judgment in the earth: and the isles shall wait for his law.*

When I read that, I was blown away! The One who lives inside of my imperfect self is never discouraged. He actually wants to live His life through me, and I just have to surrender my life as a living sacrifice (Romans 12:1). I have to die to my flesh and let Him live through me. No matter what happens, He will never be discouraged — no matter what I am facing, even if it is my huge fear of public speaking, He wants to do it all through me. So how could I ever be discouraged?

I promise you that anyone that has accomplished anything for the Lord will have had many disappointments and failures. Let's go back to the iceberg example — all we see is the tip above the surface of the water, but we don't know about the large foundation below it. Our relationship with the Lord is like the iceberg because people can see the tip of it, but only you can see all the struggles He took you through to build the solid depth and foundation beneath the "water." If God is going to use you, there are going to be some failures and obstacles. The key is that no matter how many times you are knocked down by the world, the flesh, or the devil, you've got to get back up. Ephesians 6 says to stand, stand, stand!

Romans 5:3-5 talks about how we can "glory in tribulations" because those tribulations produce patience, experience, hope, and shamelessness in us, each one building upon the other. As we have more experience with suffering, we can take comfort in the fact that those experiences are growing our hope in Christ! We have this hope of God inside of us (Romans 15:13), so if our flesh gets bogged down, we need to let Him raise us up.

Abraham is a great illustration of this in Romans 4. Consider all the tragedy and pain he went through while waiting for God to fulfill His promises. Just study him out and look through all that he and Sarah went through. He stuck with the Lord no matter what happened, and he shows us how to walk by faith and be persistent.

If God has called you to do something (and He has), then He has called you to let Him accomplish something through you to the glory of God. He wants to accomplish it but the enemy wants to stop it, so you will be hit, and you will be hit hard. Everyone loses, so we need to learn not only how to lose, but how to lose well. We need to learn to "eat crow" — I don't know if that's something this generation has heard of, but "eating crow" means that you are being humbled. In the spiritual sense, I have eaten a lot of crow! Peter was also someone who ate a lot of crow. Learn to eat crow, and learn to like crow. We will always experience different forms of failure, but remember to hold on — in the end, God will pick you up! No matter what you're going through, God says that our light affliction is only for a moment (2 Corinthians 4:17) and that He will always make a way out (1 Corinthians 10:13).

We often make our difficulties seem larger than they actually are, and we are often our own worst critics. We need to remember that we will never have it as bad as Jesus did, and He lives inside us! Think about the fact that Jesus had the cross — the whole cross — and Paul just had a thorn (2 Corinthians 12:7). Look at the comparison between the two — on that scale, our cross is a tiny splinter. We're all going to carry some form of that cross and bear the burden as we fellowship with the Lord (Luke 9:23).

Here are some good points to consider as we face difficulties. First of all, problems serve as a wake-up call, and criticism can help you check yourself. Don't take it too personally — remember Ecclesiastes 7:21-22. We should always investigate criticism and see if there is any truth in it by comparing our lives to the Word of God. We also need to ask God what He is trying to teach us. For example, pain teaches us patience and helps us to be more sensitive to others (Romans 5:3-4). Sorrow will bring repentance and mercy, and it will help us relate more to people (2 Corinthians 1:3-7). Disappointment keeps us humble and kills pride. Fear overwhelms to produce repentance, which leads to righteousness. Difficulties will come one after another to teach us to depend on the Lord and have no confidence in the flesh, and this will allow God to use us to reach others more effectively. That's why all this adversity is happening in our lives — all these things in our lives work together for good to help us be conformed to the image of the Lord Jesus Christ (Romans 8:28-29). In this chapter we are going to learn from John Mark. John Mark was one of my favorite people in the Bible as I was growing up in the Lord. Like Peter, he was a great source of encouragement for me. He failed profoundly, but God still used him to write the book of Mark. The interesting thing is that if we look at John Mark's life from the perspective of what the Lord had for him to do, we can see how God prepared him to write the book, as the gospel of Mark is one of the greatest books in the Bible about being a servant. Writing a book with a focus on servanthood requires a great degree of humility, so the Lord had to prepare him and take him through a lot of things to get him to the point where he could write it.

> **Acts 12:11-12** *And when Peter was come to himself, he said, Now I know of a surety, that the Lord hath sent his angel, and hath delivered me out of the hand of Herod, and from all the expectation of the people of the Jews. And when he had considered the thing, he came to the house of Mary the mother of John, whose surname was Mark; where many were gathered together praying.*

This is where John Mark is first introduced in 42 AD. If you remember the story, James had been killed, Peter had been thrown in jail, and the church was under great persecution. All the church was praying at Mary's house, and she had a son named John Mark. An angel came and rescued Peter, leading him out of the prison. When this happened, Peter knew the church would be gathered at Mary's house, so he immediately went there. This means this young man John Mark was there to see everyone praying and see God answer that prayer, and it also means that he was brought up around many great men of God. He was seeing all that was going on with the disciples and how God was moving in and through them.

Throughout our Bible we will see John Mark referred to in multiple ways, such as John Mark, Mark, and Marcus. In 1 Peter 5:13, Peter called John Mark "Marcus" as well as "my son." Paul called Timothy "my son" even though he wasn't his physical son because he was his spiritual son and disciple. So based on what Peter says in 1 Peter 5:13, John Mark was probably discipled by him — and who better to learn from about overcoming failure than Peter?

Emotional Victory

There are four gospels, and three were written by apostles who were the direct disciples of Jesus. But not the book of Mark! It was written by Peter's disciple, which is pretty interesting. Peter was a discipler, and God chose his disciple to communicate some of the truths that God showed Peter. Acts 12:25 is when we see John Mark starting to minister. It doesn't say his exact age, but it's obvious that he was younger when he began ministering to Barnabas and Paul. They were in Antioch, which was the hub of Christianity and also the place where the believers were first called Christians (Acts 11:26). This was the place to be to make disciples.

This was also where the first missionaries were sent out. According to Acts 13, Paul and Barnabas got sent out in 45 AD, and John Mark went along to minister to them. Think about that! This was a great, great time for him — he was now a young leader, he had been discipled, and he was going out with the two great men Paul and Barnabas on their first missionary journey to spread the gospel. But as they came to the first town, something went wrong. Something pretty drastic happened that caused John Mark to go home, though we don't really know the specifics of what it was (Acts 13:13). This was one of the huge failures of John Mark, and it ended up really sticking with him. The fracture was also severe enough that it really affected the ministry team, which we'll go over soon. The church was small, growing, and together in unity, so everybody knew about this failure. Mark was eating crow.

The next time we pick up John Mark's story is seven years later in Acts 15:36-39, and we're going to see what Paul says about the situation. Most failures are forgotten after a few months or years, but we're talking seven years later. John Mark's previous failure was so severe that on Paul and Barnabas' next missionary journey, Paul did not want Mark to go with them. Barnabas, the encourager and also Mark's uncle, wanted to give him another chance. But Paul wouldn't hear of it — in his mind, this guy had messed up, failed, and "ran home to mama." He hadn't completed what he was supposed to complete. The contention over this decision was so strong between Paul and Barnabas that it split their missionary team.

They ended up parting ways — Barnabas took Mark and Paul took Silas. Now there were two teams, which was actually a great thing because there were more people out spreading the gospel. But think about the disappointment John Mark had to face and overcome — he would have known about the contention, and he would have known that the mighty leader Paul didn't want anything to do with him. Think of the heartache of what this kid had to go through. Now, also remember that God was preparing him to write the book of servanthood. He was taking him through the journey of all these ups and downs and difficulties to grow and teach him a great deal.

> **Philippians 1:6** *Being confident of this very thing, that he which hath begun a good work in you will perform it until the day of Jesus Christ.*

This verse teaches a principle that can also be found in the book of Mark. No matter how far you think you've gotten down and no matter who is against you (even if it's a great leader), if you're still here on this earth, God wants to keep working within you and use you. Even Paul didn't see this in John Mark at this point. But John Mark still learned how to overcome what others thought of him and how to not let his failures define him. He learned to stay fixed on God and His promises, and all the while, he was being prepared to write the beloved book of Mark!

It is interesting to watch for principles he learned from Peter, his discipler. Next time you read Mark, remember that background and look for things Peter would have had to pass on to him. Think about what the Lord had to take him through to get him to the place where he could write the book. The Holy Spirit of God which was writing the book of Mark through him had to take him through some major ups and downs. Let's look at some of what he learned from Peter.

> **Mark 14:35-38** *And he went forward a little, and fell on the ground, and prayed that, if it were possible, the hour might pass from him. And he said, Abba, Father, all things are possible unto thee; take away this cup from me: nevertheless not*

what I will, but what thou wilt. And he cometh, and findeth them sleeping, and saith unto Peter, Simon, sleepest thou? couldest not thou watch one hour? Watch ye and pray, lest ye enter into temptation. The spirit truly is ready, but the flesh is weak.

We see that it wasn't only Peter sleeping, but Peter was the one that was singled out for it. That detail isn't mentioned in any other gospel but Mark. There are times when you alone are singled out for a special lesson from the Lord, and Peter may have warned John Mark of this.

Ladies, sometimes we get singled out and might think that it is very unfair. John Mark might have been wondering the same thing throughout his difficulties. But He remembered what Peter said and realized that there are some lessons that can only be learned by experience. He didn't quit and he didn't give up, and he was able to do this by focusing on dying to self and waiting on God's timing to deliver him (see 1 Peter 4:12-13). These lessons prepared him to allow God to write the book through him.

> **Mark 8:31-33** *And he began to teach them, that the Son of man must suffer many things, and be rejected of the elders, and of the chief priests, and scribes, and be killed, and after three days rise again. And he spake that saying openly. And Peter took him, and began to rebuke him. But when he had turned about and looked on his disciples, he rebuked Peter, saying, Get thee behind me, Satan: for thou savourest not the things that be of God, but the things that be of men.*

We also see that in Mark 8:31-33 that there was something in Peter's character that still needed changing because he had not yet completely come to the end of self. In order to do that, Peter had to learn who he really was in the flesh, not who he thought he was or wanted to be. Sometimes we, like Peter, want to serve God and love Him with all of our heart, but we fail Him because we can't do that in the flesh. Our flesh fails us and fails God, and Peter had to learn this hard lesson. His flesh was getting in the way, and this was one of those occasions of needing to eat crow. Peter had to fail himself and God in order to realize that he couldn't do it. He took his eyes off Christ and got distracted by the size of the waves. The waves were stronger than his flesh and he sank (Matthew 14:28-31). He had to realize that he couldn't have confidence in the flesh, and while he may have already known that in his head, his heart had to catch up with his head through experience.

In Mark 14:26-31 Peter professed his love for Jesus, but Jesus pointed out that he was still going to deny him three times. Peter's flesh was not strong enough to face Jesus' arrest and trial, and we all know what happens afterward. Mark writes about it later on in the chapter:

> **Mark 14:72** *And the second time the cock crew. And Peter called to mind the word that Jesus said unto him, Before the cock crow twice, thou shalt deny me thrice. And when he thought thereon, he wept.*

Peter saw his sin, understood it, was sorry, and repented. That is godly sorrow. Peter knew that in his spirit, he had no desire to deny Christ because he loved Him! But his flesh was too weak and incapable and he ended up failing. God had to reveal to him that he was still operating in the flesh. He had to learn to come to the end of self. That's exactly what God did in Mark's life, and that's what He's going to do in our lives. Peter could have explained these experiences many times, but some lessons can only be learned by going through them. We have to experience them and go through them to learn how to let God work through us.

> **Acts 15:39-40** *And the contention was so sharp between them, that they departed asunder one from the other: and so Barnabas took Mark, and sailed unto Cyprus; and Paul chose Silas, and departed, being recommended by the brethren unto the grace of God.*

After seven years, John Mark tried again! He had to wait on God's perfect timing, but finally he and Barnabas went on another missionary journey. Consider what would have happened if John Mark had taken Paul's rejection to heart and had let it defeat him. Fortunately, instead of doing that, he was moving forward, learning proper lordship, and waiting on God's timing. We don't know all that John Mark went through during those seven years, but clearly God was preparing him to write his gospel. He had to learn to hear and see God through his failings and Paul's rejection. John Mark wrote the book around 57 AD, and it reveals to us how John Mark found victory: he focused on who he was in Christ as a servant instead of what others thought of him. He didn't find victory through how great he was — he knew that his flesh would only fail and that in it dwelt no good thing (Romans 7:18).

> **Mark 9:33-35** *And he came to Capernaum: and being in the house he asked them, What was it that ye disputed among yourselves by the way? But they held their peace: for by the way they had disputed among themselves, who should be the greatest. And he sat down, and called the twelve, and saith unto them, If any man desire to be first, the same shall be last of all, and servant of all.*

In this passage, the disciples were arguing about who was going to be the greatest and were really focusing on how great they were instead of how great God was. Just like them, we need to learn that our flesh is rotten and can be very deceptive. This will take lots of humbling and eating crow. God loves us and wants to do great works through us, but He can't do that as long as our flesh is in the way. The really amazing thing is that eventually Paul changed his mind about John Mark! He saw what God did through him in the book of Mark and he began acknowledging him in his letters in places like Colossians 4:10. He called him a fellow laborer in Philemon 1:24, and his closing words in the book of 2 Timothy 4:11 (written near the end of his life) were for Timothy to bring John Mark to him because he was profitable! Isn't that amazing? Paul totally changed his mind about John Mark. Mark suffered failures and rejection, but he stood back up and saw past the failure, which allowed God to greatly use him.

We, too, have to remember to get back up when we fail. When I try, I fail. But when I believe, He succeeds. We will all fail, but God never fails us

(Deuteronomy 31:6). We have to keep getting up and trusting the Lord while having no confidence in our flesh. The Lord has a purpose behind every obstacle we go through, and He knows what it will take to bring us to the end of ourselves. Don't let the difficulty, disappointment, or failure keep you down. That's exactly what the enemy desires — to knock us down and keep us down. Failure is a great opportunity for learning and growing. After all, winning isn't always victory and losing isn't always defeat. Just look at the cross! At first glance the cross looks like a terrible defeat, yet it ended up being God's greatest victory! Sometimes God will even allow everyone to fail us and it will seem like we have no one but Him. When that happens, we need to remember the simple phrase, "but God!" We fail, "but God!" God is sufficient, and we can see that in places like 2 Timothy 4:16-17.

If you want God to use you, don't be surprised when you face failure along the way. There will be times of much tribulation, and you may not understand what the Lord is doing. Looking back, there are plenty of times in my life where it seemed like I had failed hugely. One example is how I came to work for MBT. Several years before that point I had a corporate job as a senior programmer analyst. It was 30 hours a week, full benefits, lots of vacation time, and great money. The Lord started leading me to consider leaving programming to work for a non-profit organization. Then, lo and behold, our company announced that it was downsizing and offered a benefit package depending on tenure to retire. The package and timing seemed so perfect and of the Lord, so after also checking with my authorities, I decided to take it. Leaving that job was a big step for me. I'm not one to take risks, but the Lord was leading and I had peace. It took some time, but just as I was getting to the end of my finances, a job at the Billy Graham Crusade office opened up! It was a sixty-five percent decrease in pay and zero benefits, but the Lord showed me how to make it work. Then, after six weeks, a job opened up at my church, KCBT. It was part-time pastor's admin and part-time counselor — a perfect fit. It was all starting to make sense, and many of my previous questions about direction seemed to fall into place.

Emotional Victory

At the time, there was a ministry out of KCBT that started up called KCBT Midtown. This was a group of about 60 members from KCBT who started meeting for services to do outreach in the Midtown area. Initially this ministry was only on Sunday nights, but it grew to where we were also meeting on Sunday mornings. I loved attending there and wasn't at KCBT services much, other than for my job. Sam, who was a pastor at KCBT and over KCBT Midtown, ended up needing an admin. One day HR called me in and said, "You know, we've been noticing how much you love Midtown, and we've been needing to do some moving around here. Sam needs an admin, so we've decided to move you there." That's how I was told. I had no idea that they would decide to move me there — there was no preparation, no asking, and no reasoning.

Now remember, I originally had a career as a principal analyst. I had achieved something in the world's sense, so becoming a secretary was a big adjustment. While the job title for the church was "administrative assistant," it was basically just another name for "secretary." Believe me, people treat a secretary very differently than a principal analyst, and I had to learn that the hard way. I wasn't given the opportunity to provide input or opinion, and I wasn't used to being treated that way, especially not by my manager. I was floored, but what could I say? I'd left the security of my long-time job and now was a secretary for a church, and it was devastating for me at the time. I had nothing against Pastor Sam, I just wasn't looking to be transferred and have different job duties. I was content in my current job, but I accepted the move. By that time, I had learned a little about just keeping your mouth shut and dying to self, but I still cried my eyes out for a week or two. I was eating crow again, and lots of it. It seemed like such a failure. But looking back, I see God was dealing with my tendency to draw security and identity from my job. He was also showing me that there were elements of pride that needed to be dealt with. However, at the time, I had no idea what the Lord was doing. Why was there a sudden move? What was going on?

At that point I could have left and tried to go back into programming, but I knew that that was not how the Lord was directing. I really did feel like a total failure. Part-time counseling was no longer part of the job, which was the biggest disappointment. But today I look back and think "Praise the Lord!" I get goosebumps just thinking about it. It was one of the greatest things that ever happened in my life as far as God redirecting me. At the time it seemed like a huge failure, but that was just because I couldn't see the road ahead.

Back then, Midtown Baptist Temple was still just KCBT Midtown and there was no intention of planting another church through this ministry. But God had other plans — it was just a year later that KCBT decided MBT needed to be an independent church plant. It was only two weeks before we became a church that the board decided they had enough funding to hire me if I wanted the job. I gratefully accepted and have been here ever since. I knew it was where the Lord wanted me. I had questioned all of my decisions and felt like a failure, but what had seemed like such a failure was actually God's hand moving me to a huge victory!

There are so many other stories I could share about how God can take devastating experiences and perceived failures and turn them completely around, and I say that as an encouragement to you if you're going through a hard time. It may end up being something God uses to lead you into His perfect will and prepare you for what's coming and what He wants to do in your life. God is for you and He loves you. There is an enemy that wants to convince you that He is against you, but He is not! He is your Heavenly Father — the greatest Father you could ever have — and He has a purpose for your life. Whatever difficulty you're facing in your life might just be preparation for you to accomplish some special work He's called you to do. Be like Peter and John Mark, persevere, and keep your eyes on Christ. Remember that your flesh will only ever lead to failure, so choose to surrender to God and let Him work through you. And when you fail — because you will fail — trust God for the strength and grace to stand back up and move forward in faith.

Emotional Victory

Questions to Consider:

1. Who was John Mark?

2. Who was John Mark's discipler, and what lessons did John Mark learn from him?

3. What work did God call John Mark to do? How did the Lord prepare him for the task?

4. What was John Mark's failure? How did he overcome the failure and Paul's rejection? What was Paul's ultimate conclusion about John Mark?

5. "Failure is a great opportunity for learning and growing. After all, winning isn't always victory, and losing isn't always defeat." What is our greatest example of this paradox?

6. Recall a time you failed. How did you respond? What did the Lord teach you through it? How do you see Him working it together for good like Romans 8:28 describes?

7. Is fear of failure a factor in your life? What will you apply from this chapter to help you overcome that fear?

8. What is the key to overcoming any failure or fall?

17

Suffering

So far we've covered a lot of territory and laid a solid foundation, and as we move to this next topic of suffering, one thing I want to emphasize is that we need to pull from all the principles and lessons that we've already been through. Just like we talked about in the beginning, these lessons are building one upon another, and they also work with the Biblical Discipleship material. I recommend you go back to the appendix of this book and get familiar with the basic principles of discipleship and mentorship and make sure you have laid that foundation. In other words, whenever you're going through a season of suffering, I would not recommend opening this book and going straight to this chapter (or any other chapter, for that matter). Instead, start at the beginning and lay a base to work from. This is how God works, and as He says in Isaiah, He builds precept upon precept, principle upon principle, here a little and there a little (Isaiah 28:10).

I'd like to begin this chapter with a word of testimony. Over the last 35 years God has provided victory in Jesus through a number of avenues. When I was 27 years old, I experienced the first Valentine's Day as a single woman that I'd had since I was 14 years old. At this time I had not yet learned how to be content or how to rest in the reality that Jesus completes me (Colossians 2:10) and is with me always (Matthew 28:20). That year, for the first time in over a decade, I was without a boyfriend or husband and I was desperately praying for help. Of course, my prayers were for help in the form of a guy miraculously showing up at the front door, but the Lord had other plans. I happened to pick up *Foxe's Book of Martyrs* and, by God's grace, turned to the chapter about Lady Jane Grey. God used her story to touch me like no other — at the young age of 17, she and her husband were martyred for the cause of Christ on February 12th. Here I was crying over not having a beau to celebrate Valentine's Day with, when on nearly the same day hundreds of years earlier, Lady Jane had been executed for the cause of Christ. Needless to say, God used her story to bring me to His reality. The letter she wrote to her sister the night before her execution still moves me to tears and to my knees every time I read it. After that week, whenever I would start to feel sorry for myself, I'd remember Lady Jane and read her story. God showed me how to find great victory through her testimony. The following is the letter she wrote to her sister:

> A Letter written by the Lady Jane in the end of her New Testament, the which she sent unto her Sister Lady Katherine the night before she suffered death.

> *I have here sent you, good sister Katherine, a book: which although it be not outwardly trimmed with gold, yet inwardly it is more worth than precious stones. It is the book, dear sister, of the law of the Lord. It is His testament and last will, which He bequeathed unto us wretches, which shall lead you to the path of eternal joy. And if you with a good mind read it, and with an earnest mind do follow it, it shall bring you to an immortal and everlasting life. It will teach you to live, and learn you to die. It shall win you more, than you should have gained by the possession of your woeful father's lands. For, as if God had prospered him, you should have inherited his lands, so if you apply diligently this book, seeking to direct your life after it, you shall be an inheritor of such riches, as neither the covetous shall withdraw from you, neither the thief shall steal, neither yet the moths corrupt. Desire with David, good sister, to understand the*

law of the Lord your God. Live still to die, that you (by death) may purchase eternal life. And trust not, that the tenderness of your age shall lengthen your life. For as soon (if God call) goeth the young, as the old: and labour always to learn to die, defy the world, deny the devil, and despise the flesh, and delight yourself only in the Lord. Be penitent for your sins, and yet despair not. Be strong in faith, and yet presume not. And desire with Saint Paul, to be dissolved and to be with Christ, with whom even in death there is life. Be like the good servant, and even at midnight be waking, lest when death cometh and stealeth upon you like a thief in the night, you be with the evil servant found sleeping, and lest for lack of oil ye be found like the five foolish women, and like him that had not on the wedding garment, and then ye be cast out from the marriage. Rejoice in Christ, as I trust I do. Follow the steps of your master Christ, and take up your cross, lay your sins on His back, and always embrace Him. And as touching my death, rejoice as I do (good sister) that I shall be delivered of this corruption, and put on incorruption. For I am assured, that I shall for losing of a mortal life, win an immortal life. The which I pray God grant you, send you of His grace to live in His fear, and to die in the true Christian faith: from the which (in God's name) I exhort you, that you never swerve, neither for hope of life, nor fear of death. For if ye will deny His truth to lengthen your life, God will deny you, and yet shorten your days. And if you will cleave to Him, He will prolong your days to your comfort and his glory. To the which glory God bring me now, and you hereafter, when it pleaseth Him to call you. Fare you well (good sister) and put your only trust in God, who only must help you.
—published 1563

Lady Jane's story, along with others' in *Foxe's Book of Martyrs*, set me on the path to learning how to overcome my physical surroundings and sufferings through the Word of God. How did these martyrs of the past carry on in victory? They were able to learn how to let the spiritual kingdom of God become more of a reality to them than the physical kingdoms of this world.

There are many kinds of suffering ranging from minor inconveniences to extreme seasons of loss and pain, but what exactly is suffering? Two definitions that cover any kind of suffering are: (1) experiencing something you don't want, or (2) wanting something you don't have. These descriptions cover any kind of suffering that we face. Also, keep in mind that the reasons behind all of our difficulties as Christians — including our sufferings, our problems, and our trials — break down into three categories:

1. **God is dealing with our sin.** We have an issue that He's trying to address (Hebrews 12:5-11). He's saying, "Come now, and let us reason together" (Isaiah 1:18) and deal with this to make it align with biblical principles.

2. **He's trying to grow us up.** God's perfect will for every Christian on the face of this earth is to become more like His Son Jesus Christ (Romans 8:28-29). This comes through suffering because Jesus Christ Himself endured suffering (Isaiah 53:3-7), and if we're being conformed to His image, we must also suffer (Philippians 1:29, 3:9-10; 2 Timothy 3:12).

3. **Your difficulty has someone else's name on it.** In other words, we are going through a hard time because He wants to use what we're going through in somebody else's life (2 Corinthians 1:3-4). He's preparing us to be used by Him to edify our brothers and sisters of Christ and also reach the lost more effectively.

Now the amazing thing about God is that He often uses all three of these together to grow us up and perfect us as only He can do.

Another thing about suffering is that it comes in many different forms. There are minor inconveniences, like losing a set of keys, and there are extreme seasons of pain and loss, like when I watched my mom suffer from Alzheimer's. When I see people suffering, I often wonder what God sees. I think about all the pain and suffering out there, like kids being severely abused or Christians being tortured, and I wonder how God sees and handles it all.

The longsuffering of our Lord is truly baffling to me. He not only allows it, He also works through it to offer His plan of salvation to just one more because

His will is for all to be saved (1 Timothy 2:4; 2 Peter 3:9). He is longsuffering and waiting for each soul to turn back to him. Right now we're going through the COVID-19 pandemic and there's a lot of difficulty and suffering going on through that. We just see a tiny bit, but God sees it all and He's developing His longsuffering in us. There will be times of extreme loss and affliction in our lives as we fellowship with His suffering.

We have to begin looking at the idea of our suffering through the lens of the physical and spiritual kingdoms mentioned in previous chapters. 2 Corinthians 4:4 talks about how the god of this world is blinding people to the truth, and the chapter also talks about the ministry of suffering. Starting in verse 8, it talks about how "we are troubled on every side, yet not distressed; we are perplexed, but not in despair." It continues to go back and forth with this element of suffering in the flesh on one hand and resting in the treasure of God on the other. 2 Corinthians 4 is a great chapter to meditate on when you're going through difficult times, and I've camped there many times throughout my life.

Continuing with verse 16: "For which cause we faint not; but though our outward man perish, yet the inward man is renewed day by day. For our light affliction…" I want to emphasize that God says what we are going through is a light affliction. Looking at it in terms of eternity, He says "one day is with the Lord as a thousand years" (2 Peter 3:8), and so our time here is but for a moment. We have to hold on to that because this is how we look at it from God's point of view. He operates through an eternal, spiritual kingdom during our age, but we can get so easily caught up in the physical. 2 Corinthians 4 continues on to say that "our light affliction, which is but for a moment, worketh for us a far more exceeding and eternal weight of glory; while we look not at the things which are seen, but at the things which are not seen: for the things which are seen are temporal; but the things which are not seen are eternal." We have to keep focused on the things which are not seen. That means being focused on the eternal — the Kingdom of God. The physical will end soon and pass away, never to be seen again. But the eternal, spiritual kingdom lasts forever, and our suffering and afflictions work for us and bring us exceeding eternal rewards! Think about that and let it sink in. We live in a sin-stricken world, a vale of tears. There is wickedness and evil, and it's all around us. But when we look at things through the new man and through God's Word, we can become sanctified and protected from the snare of the devil (1 Peter 5:8-10; 2 Timothy 2:24-26). Then we have the ability through Jesus to rise above the physical and walk on the water with Him.

Suffering is also a paradox. The first questions we start wondering when we suffer are, "Why God? Are you there, God? Do you love me, God? Why am I going through this, Lord? How could this be happening? How could a loving God let this happen?" And yet He whispers back, "Trust Me." He says, "I AM that I AM." Look at Job and what he went through and you'll see that God didn't coddle Job. He simply said, "I AM." He has a reason and purpose for whatever we're going through, and that's what we have to keep our focus on. We have to keep Him in the center.

I have been through a rough season over the last seven or eight years as we watched my mom slowly slip away from us as she battled Alzheimer's. First we watched her begin losing her mind — it was just small at first and very frustrating for her and for others. Then the disease began changing her personality, and some of her close friends and family just couldn't handle being around her anymore. It was too hard for them to see this beautiful woman — who was normally so meticulous about things like her dress, her house, and her relationships — lose control and change into someone we didn't know. Eventually she seemed to be gone from us forever, and as hard as it was to watch, God always provided the grace to get through each new difficulty. During the last year of her life she lost the ability to go to the bathroom, then she didn't know how to walk, then she didn't know how to talk, and then she didn't know how to feed herself. Towards the very end she'd forgotten how to swallow and went for 13 days without food. This was during the pandemic, so we couldn't go see her for about a week when the pandemic started, but we were able to return when she stopped eating. I think that was one of the hardest times, and during this time, the Lord led me to messages on suffering. Two days before mom passed they stopped us from going in because they found COVID-19 in her place. This meant that she didn't have anyone there but hospice and the nurses, and this was heartbreaking to me. Through all the adversity, these messages from the Lord became great sources of comfort and I'd like to share a few things that I remember from them. First of all, I realized that suffering is not for nothing! This phrase is a fabulous reminder and it is so true. The second lesson was another important point — for the Christian, suffering is not in vain. God has a plan and is trying to work something out in us. We may not be able to do anything about our suffering, but we can certainly do something with it. The following are some of the pointers on how to do that. We have gone over some of the following principles through a different light in this study, but they are always good to re-emphasize as we pass through the deep waters of our sufferings.

1. **Accept it.** In order to move through it, you have to accept it and rest on the promises of the Lord. My mom had Alzheimer's and was dying. Initially I wanted to fix it, but eventually I had to accept it. Ask God what He is trying to accomplish or teach you. He won't always answer right away, but He says that it is the honor of kings to search out a matter (Proverbs 25:2). When I think of "accepting it," I always go back to the phrase "acceptance with joy" from *Hinds' Feet on High Places*. This phrase helped me tremendously while my mom was physically dying. Joy is not the absence of difficulty in our lives; joy is the presence of God. If we can grab hold of the fact that God is here with us, then we can have victory! Hebrews 12:2 says that Jesus, "for the joy that was set before him endured the cross, despising the shame." He had joy even through the cross. Again, this is a mystery and a paradox — how is that possible? It is possible if you first learn to accept suffering with joy by dying to our flesh and following after Jesus in the Spirit.

2. **Thank Him.** This goes hand in hand with acceptance. We've already gone over how God's will for our lives is that we give thanks (1 Thessalonians 5:18). We are to thank Him in and for everything, acknowledging that He is in

control and knows what's best. When we trust Him, it brings peace in our life. In Hebrews 13:15 it even says that He is pleased with the sacrifice of our praise. It's a sacrifice to praise God when you're going through a hard time, but through thanks we are acknowledging that He's in control and He knows best.

3. **Offer it back to God.** The Bible says suffering is a gift, and what do we do with our gifts? We give them back to God to use for His glory. In ministry we often think of gifts like singing or preaching and how it is easy to offer them back to God. But our suffering? This is a total shift in our mindset, because in our minds gifts are good things and suffering doesn't seem to be a good thing at all. But Romans 12:1-2 says that it is only reasonable to give God our lives as living sacrifices. To offer our suffering back to God as a gift looks like acknowledging that our lives are living sacrifices, so we will suffer willingly in order to bring glory to God. That is our gift of suffering. For a long time singleness was suffering for me, yet He used it to teach me things that I have now used to mentor hundreds of girls. If I hadn't been willing to offer this suffering back to Him, He could not have used it. He has let me be a co-laborer with Him all over the world and see numerous lives changed through the gospel and discipleship! Through suffering He rescued me from the dump and began changing me and putting a song in my mouth so that I could share these principles with others. We are transformed and transfigured by the cross. By suffering.

> *2 Corinthians 1:3-7* *Blessed be God, even the Father of our Lord Jesus Christ, the Father of mercies, and the God of all comfort; who comforteth us in all our tribulation, that we may be able to comfort them which are in any trouble, by the comfort wherewith we ourselves are comforted of God. For as the sufferings of Christ abound in us, so our consolation also aboundeth by Christ. And whether we be afflicted, it is for your consolation and salvation, which is effectual in the enduring of the same sufferings which we also suffer: or whether we be comforted, it is for your consolation and salvation. And our hope of you is stedfast, knowing, that as ye are partakers of the sufferings, so shall ye be also of the consolation.*

We all will be called to sufferings, ladies. This "Prosperity Gospel" that's promoted in the Laodicean culture we live in is out of the pit of hell — it is not at all what God says. If we're following Jesus, it is promised to us that we're going to suffer, and suffering is a good thing! It transforms us — He uses it to bring life out of death and beauty out of ashes. Out of pain we better realize God's love for us, because knowing the Lord and having the "peace that passeth understanding" is an indescribable blessing that can only come through suffering (Philippians 4:6-7).

There was a blessing of joy in helping my mom. There was a blessing of joy in having our prayers answered or a new solution arrive when we were at the end and didn't know what to do next. My brother and I became so much closer during this time, which was a huge blessing because it allowed me to invest in him and speak truth into his life. God used that whole situation in so many ways, and I got to know the Lord in a much deeper way through the fellowship of His sufferings. All of this came out of pain. He is able to transfigure and transform something terrible into something good as only He can.

The cross, at first glance, looks like the most horrific event in history. It's terrible! But then you look at it through the lens of what He did for us, it's the best. It's awesome and spectacular — thanks be unto God for His unspeakable gift! So suffering is not for nothing. Let's look into the paradox and mystery of suffering by looking at the life of someone in the Bible who went through a great deal of suffering: the apostle Paul. Paul penned the book of Philippians, which is a great book on joy in the midst of suffering that also lines right up with the book of Job.

> ***Philippians 3:7-9*** *But what things were gain to me, those I counted loss for Christ. Yea doubtless, and I count all things but loss for the excellency of the knowledge of Christ Jesus my Lord: for whom I have suffered the loss of all things, and do count them but dung, that I may win Christ, and be found in him, not having mine own righteousness, which is of the law, but that which is through the faith of Christ, the righteousness which is of God by faith:*

We see here that Paul suffered the loss of all things so that he could win Christ. We suffer to win, because when we suffer loss, we win Christ! It's true that there are some troubles that we may never ever understand on this side of eternity, but I guarantee you that God always has a reason behind it. Though we might not know that reason now, someday we'll see it.

> **Philippians 3:10** *That I may know him, and the power of his resurrection, and the fellowship of his sufferings, being made conformable unto his death;*

All of Philippians 3 is worth meditating on, but you should spend a lot of time on this verse, as it shows why Paul was so willing to suffer the loss of all things. He simply said, "That I may know Him." If you recall chapter 12 on romantic relationships, you'll remember that the word "know" in the Bible represents a very intimate relationship similar to that between a man and his wife. Paul goes on and breaks down "knowing Him" into two parts: the power of His resurrection and the fellowship of His sufferings. We like the first part — the power of His resurrection — because it is so exciting to be filled with God's power and see it work in and through us. But the second part — the fellowship of His sufferings — is much harder.

All of the people in the Bible went through sufferings. The more that they suffered, the more that they saw the power of His resurrection in their lives. There is a balance between these two things — suffering leads us to die to our flesh, and that death allows us to experience the power of God resurrecting and quickening us. Jesus wants us to fellowship with Him through His sufferings — just think about all the sufferings that He went through. Even before He got to the cross and the wrath of God was poured out upon Him, "He came unto his own, and his own received him not" (John 1:11). He was totally rejected and "wounded in the house of his friends" (Zechariah 13:6). He was even rejected by His Father — on the cross He cried, "My God, my God, why hast thou forsaken me?" (Matthew 27:46). He wants us to fellowship with Him in that suffering, and what a privilege. I think that's why He calls it a gift — because it is such a privilege to get to grow closer to our Savior by sharing in His sufferings. And then, "being made conformable unto His death," we die daily so that He can live through us (1 Corinthians 15:31).

Let's look deeper into some biblical facts about suffering in the life of a Christian. If you've been a Christian for any length of time, I'm sure you are acquainted with grief and loss and suffering. You must keep in mind that as a Christian, you are either getting ready to go through a storm, you are in a storm right now, or you are coming out of a storm. That's part of the cycle of life, and we are constantly being conformed to His image in that way. Let's look at Isaiah 53 and Ecclesiastes 7 to see this principle in action.

> **Isaiah 53:3-5** *He is despised and rejected of men; a man of sorrows, and acquainted with grief: and we hid as it were our faces from him; he was despised, and we esteemed him not. Surely he hath borne our griefs, and carried our sorrows: yet we did esteem him stricken, smitten of God, and afflicted. But he was wounded for our transgressions, he was bruised for our iniquities: the chastisement of our peace was upon him; and with his stripes we are healed.*

This is our Lord — He was rejected, He was despised, and He was a man of sorrows. If we are being conformed to that image, then we're going to be transformed by going through trials that take us through the fellowship of what He went through. The only way to get through that is by denying self, picking up our cross, and following Him (Luke 9:23).

There are some weeks where our church hosts multiple funerals over the course of just a few days. Despite the sorrow and season of loss, it's always comforting when we know that they're on their way to heaven! Even in spite of this joy, the loss can sometimes seem devastating in the moment. Ecclesiastes 7 is always a good place to rest when times like that come. It paints a completely different picture of how we should think when we go to a funeral. In fact, it paints an ironic picture between times of sorrow versus times of laughter or amusement.

> *Ecclesiastes 7:1-4 A good name is better than precious ointment; and the day of death than the day of one's birth. It is better to go to the house of mourning, than to go to the house of feasting: for that is the end of all men; and the living will lay it to his heart. Sorrow is better than laughter: for by the sadness of the countenance the heart is made better. The heart of the wise is in the house of mourning; but the heart of fools is in the house of mirth.*

It seems strange to us that it's better to go and face death than to go to a party. Why is this true? Mainly because death is where we are all going to go. Barring the rapture of the church, we are all going to die eventually, and a funeral actually helps us consider living the right way. It is good for us to accept that fact and think about what's coming. We aren't going to live forever, and our days are numbered (Job 14:1-2, 5; Psalm 90:12). We Christians will all stand before the judgment seat of Christ (2 Corinthians 5:10). Are you ready? Do you live your life with that in mind? That is a key to helping us have victory through suffering. Disciplers and mentors help instruct us in how to grow up and prepare for the judgment seat, and that is why discipleship is so very important.

We have to realize that there's not going to be blessing in our life without suffering. We also have to realize that we are going to be tried by the things that we love. It's not really a trial if you don't care about it, so we will be tried by the things that we love and the things that we fear. You see that over and over in the lives of the characters of the Old Testament — just look at Abraham and Isaac. Abraham's mind was always on the promise of God and how He hadn't seen it fulfilled in his life yet. And even after God had fulfilled the promise of giving him a son, what does He ask of him later in Genesis 22?

> *Genesis 22:1-2 And it came to pass after these things, that God did tempt Abraham, and said unto him, Abraham: and he said, Behold, here I am. And he said, Take now thy son, thine only son Isaac, whom thou lovest, and get thee into the land of Moriah; and offer him there for a burnt offering upon one of the mountains which I will tell thee of.*

He asks, "Who do you love more: me or your son?" There was no question in Abraham's mind — God was on the throne, not his son. Hebrews 11:17-19 tells us that Abraham was willing to sacrifice Isaac because he believed God's promise so much and knew He could raise his son from the dead. Those 25 years of fellowship and trials helped him see where he was at spiritually and where he needed to grow. God knew what was possible through his belief, and so over time He helped him work it out. And God wants to do the same in us! When God's not on the throne of our hearts and other things take up that place, God will put us through storms to teach us how we can put Him back in His rightful place in our lives.

> **Hebrews 2:10** *For it became him, for whom are all things, and by whom are all things, in bringing many sons unto glory, to make the captain of their salvation perfect through sufferings.*

The Bible's very clear that we are made "perfect through sufferings." It says that Jesus is our captain and that He was made perfect (mature/complete) through suffering. If we are following Him, the same will be true of our lives. Suffering works in our lives to perfect, stablish, strengthen, and settle us.

> **1 Peter 5:10** *But the God of all grace, who hath called us unto his eternal glory by Christ Jesus, after that ye have suffered a while, make you perfect, stablish, strengthen, settle you.*

Our spiritual growth process will have times of deep suffering, and a lot of that will bring out the impurities of our flesh. I once got to go see gold mines when I was in South Africa, and what they would do is melt the gold down so the impurities within the gold would rise to the top to be scraped off. They knew it was pure when they could see themselves in the gold, and that's exactly what happens in our lives spiritually. We go through the trials to take away the impurities that are buried so deep in our heart and in our flesh that only God can see them. When we go through this suffering, those impurities come out onto the surface so that they can be cleansed and dealt with by the

Word of God. Ultimately, this rough and tedious process happens so that we are more conformed to Christ — so that the Lord can see His image in us.

Purging and pruning are other functions of suffering that help us bring forth fruit. John 14-17 are some of the richest chapters in the Bible because they are the last words Jesus gave to His disciples before He went to the cross, and in John 15, He says that if you're bringing forth fruit, He's going to prune or purge you so you can bring forth even more fruit. In other words, He's going to cut off some of the dead stuff in your life that's holding you back from the fruit He wants you to bear. My dad had two green thumbs and every plant or bush he attempted to grow grew beautifully, especially his rose bushes! His secret was in his pruning or purging — not only would he prune or purge a little every spring and autumn, but every once in a while he would do a "heavy-hitter" pruning. The timing for this pruning was different for every bush depending on the budding and maturity of the tree.

I remember coming home from school and seeing a little nub in the place of what had been a big, beautiful bush just that morning. We kids would laugh and say, "Daddy's been pruning again!" Initially we thought the bush was a goner, but soon the new branches and buds would be popping out of that bush and it would become bigger and more beautiful than ever. Sure enough, that's what the Lord has often said to me after going through a rough season. I needed a heavy-hitter pruning that would help me grow some new fruit! And what do you do to get going again after a good purging? Nothing! Just be still and just abide in the Vine. That is your only responsibility. So if you've been fruitful in the past and all of a sudden you find yourself going through a rough time and unable to move forward, maybe God's doing a little (or a lot of) purging in your life. If that is the case, do nothing but sit back, wait, and abide!

The story in Daniel 3 is another great resource when dealing with trial. Remember Shadrach, Meshach, and Abednego? They were thrown into the fiery furnace for worshipping God instead of the world's idols. Talk about a trial! Yet they were still able to walk with Jesus in that fire (Daniel 3:25). They were thrown in with ropes tied around them and they came walking out without the ropes! The only thing the fire did to them was to burn off the oppression that was in their lives. As contrary as it seems, suffering and trial can do this because they free us up to walk closer with Jesus.

Joseph also went through a great deal of suffering and is a great picture, or type, of the Lord Jesus Christ. I'm going to point out a few things about Joseph as we look at what happened to him. God had a plan for Joseph's life, just as He does for us all. At a very early age of 17 years old, Joseph was given dreams from God about what that plan was (Genesis 37). No one else saw them but Joseph, and it was these dreams that sparked the trial in his life. God has a burden for you too, and there might be suffering involved in seeing it come true.

> **Galatians 6:4-5** *But let every man prove his own work, and then shall he have rejoicing in himself alone, and not in another. For every man shall bear his own burden.*

We all have a purpose God wants to accomplish through us, and the only way you will realize it is through growing in your relationship with Him. He and He alone can tell you. God did the same thing in the lives of Samuel and Moses.

> **1 Samuel 3:19-21** *And Samuel grew, and the LORD was with him, and did let none of his words fall to the ground. And all Israel from Dan even to Beersheba knew that Samuel was established to be a prophet of the LORD. And the LORD appeared again in Shiloh: for the LORD revealed himself to Samuel in Shiloh by the word of the LORD.*

> **Acts 7:24-25** *And seeing one of them suffer wrong, he defended him, and avenged him that was oppressed, and smote the Egyptian: for he supposed his brethren would have understood how that God by his hand would deliver them: but they understood not.*

God wants to accomplish a specific work through you, but He can only do that if you grow in your relationship with Him. While God communicated with Joseph and other people in the Old Testament through dreams, signs, and miracles, now that we're in the church age, God speaks to us through His Word. He's going to give each one of us a vision through our personal time with Him as we study and walk with Him in His Word. He wants to show you why He has you here and direct you into the purpose or good work He wants to accomplish through you. Habakkuk gives us great insight into developing a vision of God.

> *Habakkuk 1:2* O Lord, how long shall I cry, and thou wilt not hear! even cry out unto thee of violence, and thou wilt not save!

> *Habakkuk 2:2-3* And the Lord answered me, and said, Write the vision, and make it plain upon tables, that he may run that readeth it. For the vision is yet for an appointed time, but at the end it shall speak, and not lie: though it tarry, wait for it; because it will surely come, it will not tarry.

When He gives us a task or a purpose, He says to first cry to Him for it, then to write it down, and finally to wait (and that's usually the hardest part). This task or purpose always has an appointed time — like we mentioned earlier, Joseph was first shown the vision at the age of 17. Shortly after telling his family what God had told him, he was betrayed and thrown in a pit by his jealous brothers, then carted off to Egypt and sold as a slave to Potiphar, an officer of Pharaoh. He worked for Potiphar for years, and despite his blameless testimony and his work prospering Potiphar's household, Joseph was put in prison after being falsely accused of a crime he didn't commit. While in prison, he helped Pharaoh's chief butler (a fellow prisoner) by accurately interpreting his dream. When the butler was released from prison and restored to his position, he promised to remember Joseph and get him out too... but he forgot. After two more years in prison, the chief butler remembered Joseph when Pharaoh had a dream no one could interpret. So finally, at the age of 30, Joseph was released from prison and stood before Pharaoh. Just as before,

God gave him the accurate interpretation for Pharaoh's dream, and Pharaoh rewarded Joseph by making him second in command over all of Egypt, which was the most powerful nation in the world at that time!

> *1 Thessalonians 5:24* Faithful is he that calleth you, who also will do it.

This kid went through so much difficulty while waiting for God to fulfill His vision. It was approximately 13 years from the time Joseph received the vision to the time he got out of prison. Then there were 7 years of plentiful harvest and 2 more years until his brothers showed up. In total, Joseph waited 22 years for the vision that God had given to come to pass. For Abraham, it was 25 years before his promised seed was born. For Moses, it was 40 years before he delivered Israel from Egypt. There are so many great illustrations in the Old Testament of this process of growth. This process often includes us trying to do it ourselves or letting someone else help us do it until we finally learn to die to self, wait on God, and let Him do it.

Here are some things that we can glean from what Joseph learned. As mentioned earlier, we first have to learn to wait, because learning how to wait will also help us learn contentment and submission. We've already discussed this in several previous chapters. Suffering will be a big part of learning to wait because it requires learning to surrender and die to self. This is such a paradox — God has a work for us, but we must labor to rest (and die), as we learned in the chapter on grace.

Like Joseph, we must also learn to deal with pride. Paul, one of the greatest Christians that ever lived, tells us in 2 Corinthians 12:6-10 that "lest I should be exalted above measure…there was given to me a thorn in the flesh." We're all going to have a thorn, but we still need to carry our cross and stay humble before the Lord. Joseph had to learn that too when he was dealing with his brethren and realizing that God also had a plan for them. Just because Joseph had God's vision for his life didn't mean Joseph himself was the center. God is the center, and God has a plan for every single person in His Body. No one is better or worse, because He has a different plan and different gifting for each one of us. It's our job to get with Him and find out what that is. There is nothing quite like suffering to cut us down to size and reveal to ourselves who we truly are in the flesh.

Joseph also had to learn how to trust in God more than his earthly father and not put confidence in man (Psalm 118:8). I can identify with that. When my mentor and father in the Lord fell from grace, I was faced with one of the hardest crossroads of my life as I had to make the decision to walk away from him. It was clear that he was not following Christ, and that meant that I shouldn't be following him (1 Corinthians 11:1; Romans 16:17-18). You cannot put someone, no matter who they are to you, above the Lord. Joseph had such a close relationship with his father, but God obviously had to take Joseph out of that situation so he could learn how to trust in his Heavenly Father more than his earthly father. There may be things in our lives that He has to remove so that He can teach us to trust in Him wholly.

One of the greatest keys in Joseph's life was his relationship with the Lord. In the midst of the many tragedies Joseph went through, we always read: "And the Lord was with him." That is so amazing! As you think on that fact, here is the next amazing thing to consider: God didn't stick with Joseph because he was "so special." Joseph was no different than us — he was just a regular, imperfect sinner. The key to Joseph's life is that God was so special to him — God was so real to him that Joseph never walked away from Him. We all have that decision to make.

Unfortunately, what usually happens when the hard trials come is that we give up on God, even though 1 Corinthians 10:13 tells us God will always show us a way out if we just stick with Him. It's our choice and our free will to decide whether we will stay with the Lord through the trial, and it all hinges on whether we choose to walk away from Him or toward Him when the going gets tough. For everything that Joseph teaches us, I think that is one of the greatest things – the Lord was always with him because he never walked away from God, no matter how bad the circumstances seemed.

We also see that Joseph prospered in the midst of trials and difficult circumstances. He knew God's principle found in Joshua 1:8, which is the only time that the word "success" is used in your Bible. Shouldn't we find out what God says about success if we want to be successful? He's the one we should really ask. If this is the only place in the whole Word of God that the word "success" is used, I would say it is an important verse to show us how to be successful.

> **Joshua 1:8** *This book of the law shall not depart out of thy mouth; but thou shalt meditate therein day and night, that thou mayest observe to do according to all that is written therein: for then thou shalt make thy way prosperous, and then thou shalt have good success.*

This verse tells us that we need to hold fast to God and His Word so that we can meditate on it and observe to do it. We can only be successful if we stick with God. Another passage we have touched on is in Psalm 1, where it talks about how to be prosperous. We have concentrated mainly on the first verse of Psalm 1, which tells us what not to do, but let's look at the next two verses. In these verses God talks about delighting in the law of the Lord, just like in Joshua 1:8. The outcome is prospering, fruitfulness, and life.

> **Psalm 1:1-3** *Blessed is the man that walketh not in the counsel of the ungodly, nor standeth in the way of sinners, nor sitteth in the seat of the scornful. But his delight is in the law of the Lord; and in his law doth he meditate day and night. And he shall be like a tree planted by the rivers of water, that bringeth forth his fruit in his season; his leaf also shall not wither; and whatsoever he doeth shall prosper.*

Those are two great sets of verses to apply to our lives. Joseph applied both of these principles to his life, and that's why the Lord was with him. This kid had to have been totally sold out in order to have stuck with the Lord through 22 years of trials. His faith in and love toward God would not have been developed or revealed had it not been for the difficult trials he faced. You can tell that he loved the Lord and always put Him first.

What will it take for you to walk away from the Lord? That's what the enemy is searching for, and there are people who are no longer at our church because he found that spot. There are pressure points in our lives, and the enemy is after those points. That's why we have to learn to deny self, pick up our cross, and follow the Lord so that Jesus can live His life through us. We must remember God always gives us a way out of any temptation. The last verses I'd like to look at pertaining to Joseph are in Psalm 105, Genesis 50, and Philippians 3. These are all great principles Joseph learned. Let's first look at Psalm 105:

> **Psalm 105:11-21** *Saying, Unto thee will I give the land of Canaan, the lot of your inheritance: when they were but a few men in number; yea, very few, and strangers in it. When they went from one nation to another, from one kingdom to another people; he suffered no man to do them wrong: yea, he reproved kings for their sakes; saying, Touch not mine anointed, and do my prophets no harm. Moreover he called for a famine upon the land: he brake the whole staff of bread. He sent a man before them, even Joseph, who was sold for a servant: whose feet they hurt with fetters: he was laid in iron: until the time that his word came: the word of the Lord tried him. The king sent and loosed him; even the ruler of the people, and let him go free. He made him lord of his house, and ruler of all his substance:*

This passage says that God sent Joseph before them. We look at the circumstances of Joseph's life and blame the brothers for what he went through, but God clearly says that He was the one who designated this trial. It is the same way in our lives — there is an appointed time that the Lord will accomplish the task or purpose He has for you, but before that, the word of the Lord is trying you. The Lord tried Joseph through the attack of the enemy. The enemy doesn't want God's plan for your life to come true, so attack will come. However, God will use that attack for good by proving you until His appointed time.

Joseph's story continues in Genesis 50. After Joseph's father died, his brothers were all scared that Joseph was going to hurt them because they remembered what they had done to him. Fortunately, Joseph had learned that God had a purpose for all those trials because he believed that "all things worked together for good to them that love God" (Romans 8:28).

So here in Genesis 50:18 it says, "And his brethren also went and fell down before his face; and they said, Behold, we be thy servants." With their father dead, his brothers likely thought that Joseph would seize the opportunity to finally exact vengeance. We see Joseph's response in verses 19-20: "And Joseph said unto them, Fear not: for am I in the place of God? But as for you, ye thought evil against me; but God meant it unto good, to bring to pass, as it is this day, to save much people alive." Joseph understood that God was in control, and he was able to forgive them. He did not put himself in the place of God to judge because the Lord allowed it to happen. Joseph, like Job, was portraying unconditional love and total forgiveness toward others who treated him unfairly. That's God's love which can only be obtained through fellowshipping with Him.

Another thing that we can learn as we study out Joseph's life is how he dealt with his past. In psychology they always talk about digging up the past and working through it, but that's not what God says. In Philippians 3 it says, "forgetting those things which are behind, and reaching forth to those things which are before." When God was ready for Joseph to deal with his past, God brought his past to him. Do you see that? Joseph didn't go looking for his past and try to dig it up. Instead, he trusted the Lord and followed what He was doing in his life. God brought the past to him when he was mature enough and at a place in his life where he would be able to deal with it. This is a good reminder for us that we are to "forget those things which are behind." Now, if the Lord brings it to your face and you need to deal with it, you just need to deal with it. But otherwise, we don't need to go digging it up to pity ourselves or dwell on the past.

> ***Philippians 3:13-14*** *Brethren, I count not myself to have apprehended: but this one thing I do, forgetting those things which are behind, and reaching forth unto those things which are before, I press toward the mark for the prize of the high calling of God in Christ Jesus.*

> **Romans 8:15-18** For ye have not received the spirit of bondage again to fear; but ye have received the Spirit of adoption, whereby we cry, Abba, Father. The Spirit itself beareth witness with our spirit, that we are the children of God: and if children, then heirs; heirs of God, and joint-heirs with Christ; if so be that we suffer with him, that we may be also glorified together. For I reckon that the sufferings of this present time are not worthy to be compared with the glory which shall be revealed in us.

As we experience loss and suffering, we need to take to heart Joseph's example and fill the void in our soul with God. Suffering and grief can open up a void in our heart, so we need to choose to fill that void with the presence of the Lord. As He tells us in Psalm 126:5-6, our sorrow can be turned to joy. God uses the picture of a mother in labor to help illustrate this important principle — the labor can be horrible, but after birth, there is the joy of a child! There is sorrow in the night, but joy comes in the morning.

> **John 16:21** A woman when she is in travail hath sorrow, because her hour is come: but as soon as she is delivered of the child, she remembereth no more the anguish, for joy that a man is born into the world.

This is an old hymn that I love and got me through so many trials over the years. It's called "When We See Christ / It Will Be Worth It All." It's fabulous, and I encourage you to listen to the song. There's coming a time when all of the suffering that we faced will be worth it, when He's going to right every wrong, and He's going to make plain and clear why we're going through what we're going through.

When We See Christ / It Will Be Worth It All

Oft times the day seems long, our trials hard to bear,
We're tempted to complain, to murmur and despair;
But Christ will soon appear to catch His Bride away,
All tears forever over in God's eternal day.

Refrain:
It will be worth it all when we see Jesus,
Life's trials will seem so small when we see Christ;
One glimpse of His dear face all sorrow will erase,
So bravely run the race till we see Christ.

Sometimes the sky looks dark with not a ray of light,
We're tossed and driven on, no human help in sight;
But there is one in heav'n who knows our deepest care,
Let Jesus solve your problem – just go to Him in pray'r.

Life's day will soon be o'er, all storms forever past,
We'll cross the great divide, to glory, safe at last;
We'll share the joys of heav'n – a harp, a home, a crown,
The tempter will be banished, we'll lay our burden down.

Let us look to the Lord as we await His return. Suffering in the life of a child of God takes us directly into our next subject: the joy of the Lord!

Emotional Victory

Questions to Consider:

1. What is the 2-part definition of suffering?

2. What are the 3 possible reasons for our suffering?

3. "You will be tried by the things that you _____ and _____."

4. Why is suffering a gift from God? What do He want us to do with this gift?

5. Are you suffering or going through a storm now? Have you tried accepting it, thanking Him for it, and giving it back to God?

6. Can you recall a time in your life when God brought you through a hard season and allowed you to suffer? What did God teach you from that season, and how did He use it to grow you?

7. What do the illustrations of gold mines and rose bushes show us about the process and results of suffering?

8. According to Habakkuk 2:2-3, what are we to do with a vision from God?

9. Can you relate to Joseph? What have you learned from his life?

18

The Joy of the Lord

How were the early disciples of Jesus able to jump with joy when they were persecuted for the cause of Christ? How did our forefathers burn at the stake and sing with joy? How did Stephen pray as the Pharisees stoned him? What is the source of this kind of joy? I'd like to mention *Hinds' Feet on High Places* again — if you haven't read it, you should. It's actually a requirement in the "Emotions Study" class I teach. As I've mentioned in chapters prior, there's one phrase in the book that has stuck with me through the years: "acceptance with joy." That is a great phrase to live by as a Christian, and I think that's how Joseph lived his life. He accepted with joy anything that came his way because he knew that God was in control and that all things worked together in his life for good, which is the promise to all Christians in Romans 8:28. Anyone that knows Jesus has direct access to the joy of the Lord.

What we are going to start seeing in this chapter is that this joy has nothing to do with our circumstances and everything to do with our personal relationship with the Lord. Joy is not the absence of suffering, but the presence of God. A song that comes to mind as we begin this chapter is "I've got the joy, joy, joy,

joy down in my heart, down in my heart down in my heart to stay!" Do you know that sense you get when you are totally right with God? That's the joy that we are talking about! It is a connection with the Lord that's available even when we're going through tough things. I guarantee you that Joseph had joy in his life even through those 22 years that he was separated from his earthly father and in a strange land. Look back over your life and ask yourself if you have ever experienced this joy of the Lord. If you've experienced it, you won't forget it. You must now understand it is always accessible to us, and if you've lost it, you can get it back!

To lay a solid biblical foundation, we've looked at developing a positive attitude as well as giving thanks in and for everything. Before we spend much time on joy, we now need to add another layer to our foundation, and that is examining our mission and our growth as a Christian. This layer will help us learn how to capture and keep the joy of the Lord in our lives! One thing the early Christians knew and embraced was the privilege of being a co-laborer with Christ, and we too have that same great opportunity!

If you've gone through the Biblical Discipleship lessons, you'll know that God's will for each one of His children is to become more like Jesus (Romans 8:29). He desires for us to be conformed to the image of His Son who was the first among many brethren. The moment we accepted Jesus as our Savior, we were predestined to become like Him!

So if that's our ultimate goal, then we need to look at the biblical pattern of Jesus' life and ministry. About twenty years ago there was a key phrase amongst Christians — "What would Jesus do?" This phrase sounded like a good thing to ask yourself, but what the Lord started impressing on me at that time was that I shouldn't stop there. He wanted me to go one step further and ask, "What did Jesus do?" In other words, what was His ministry all about? Where did He get His joy from? That's what we are going to look at here. In order to find the "joy of the Lord," we need to first examine the ministry of the Lord.

His main ministry was spending three and a half years with his disciples, sharing His relationship with God the Father with them, and teaching them how to know God. His goal is clearly defined in John 17, which is an incredibly rich passage! I would recommend meditating on that chapter as you read this lesson.

> **John 17:4** *I have glorified thee on the earth: I have finished the work which thou gavest me to do.*

Jesus prayed this to God the Father before the cross, and He was saying in this verse that He completed the work that God gave Him to do. In the Bible we can see that there were at least two great works that God had for Jesus, and the one we most commonly think of is His work on the cross, since that's how we have access to the Father. But here in John 17 He lays out another work, and as you spend time reading and meditating on that chapter, you'll see what it was. He says that the work He finished before the cross was teaching His disciples how to know the Lord. His other work was in discipling, mentoring, and teaching His disciples how to connect with the only true God! Though Jesus was preparing to leave, His disciples were able to pass that work on to others just like Jesus had done with them because they now knew how to connect with the living God. They were to continue to teach His words to others and disciple others as He had discipled them. This work was finished before the cross! He introduced this work in John 4 and finished it here in John 17.

> **John 4:34** *Jesus saith unto them, My meat is to do the will of him that sent me, and to finish his work.*

We know that we are called to do the same work, and we can gain further insight into this work in passages like John 15:16, 21:15-17, Colossians 3:16, Ecclesiastes 11:1, and 2 Timothy 2:2.

> **John 14:12** *Verily, verily, I say unto you, He that believeth on me, the works that I do shall he do also; and greater works than these shall he do; because I go unto my Father.*

That's it! That's His great work! If you can capture the vision, burden, and mission of discipleship, it will carry you far in your relationship with God. We are all called into this ministry of reconciliation, this mentoring, and this feeding of God's sheep. Becoming a discipler is our life's goal if we are committed to becoming more like Jesus, and it brings true joy into our lives. Some will look at this verse in John 14 and say it's referring to all the miracles or the healings of Jesus, but He clearly defined for us what His work was in John 17. His earthly ministry wasn't so much about the miracles and healings and feedings as it was about teaching His disciples. How can we do greater works than He did? The answer is that He did it for three and a half years, but we have the opportunity to do it for many more years. The verse isn't talking about the miracles and healings, unless you define the miracle and healings as mentoring. If you look at all the miracles and healings He did, then you will see that every time He was doing something miraculous, He had at least one of His disciples with Him. While He did reach the masses, His focus was always on teaching the disciple how to reach and teach others — after all, the purpose of the miracles was to prove the words that He was speaking. His disciples were able to see all of these things, and that grew their faith in Jesus' message and deity.

Jesus' focus was on the few, and His work was to connect with the disciples and help them minister to others. Interestingly, if we look at His model, we see that He had twelve different disciples with twelve different personalities. Each one of them had a purpose, and He dealt with each of them differently. We can use this example as a blueprint for mentoring others, and we can learn a lot about how to disciple simply by studying Jesus' life and the people that He discipled. He spent about three and a half years with them, and while three of the men (Peter, James, and John) became closer to Him than the rest, they all had purpose. Though they did contend with one another about who was the "greatest," the reality wasn't that any one of them was better than the other; they simply had different gifts and ways that God wanted to use them and grow them up. At the same time, they each decided how far they would go with Jesus, just like us. Each of us can decide how close we will be in our relationship with the Lord and how much we will let Him use us. Think about Andrew and Peter, for example. Peter was one of the three who were closest to Jesus, and yet if it hadn't been for Andrew, Peter wouldn't have even been there to begin with. God has a different purpose for each of us, and we have to understand that as we work with people. Everybody's different, but we all have a purpose in God's plan.

The Bible says that there are seven stages of spiritual growth that we and our disciples will grow through. When we accepted Jesus as Savior, we were born again, and we began growing spiritually as others invested in us. Spiritual growth is pictured or illustrated by our physical growth, and the Bible lays out the details for each of these stages. You'll go deeper into these stages in the Discipleship 2 (D2) materials and classes, but for now, let's just list them here. These stages can be similar to a yardstick for our growth, and just as a parent uses different boundaries and guidelines to teach a child as he grows, we can learn how to be Christ-like mentors as the people we're mentoring begin to grow.

Seven Stages of Spiritual Growth

	Spiritual	Physical	Tree
1	Repentance	Baby	Grounded
2	Enlightenment	Little Child	Settled
3	Ministry Training	Child	Not Moved Away
4	Leadership Development	Young Man	Rooted
5	Reevaluation & Separation	Father	Built Up
6	Leader	Elder	Stablished
7	World Vision	Aged	Abounding

Regardless of whether or not you're a discipler, this list helps give us vision for ourselves and for those we mentor. The first person you want to counsel or disciple is yourself. We all want to get to a place where we learn to let the Lord teach us how to deal with our problems as they arise so that we can then turn around and help someone else get through theirs. That's what we are here for, and that's how we glorify the Lord.

So we start out when we are born again as a spiritual baby, then we're a spiritual toddler, then we're a child, then we're a young man, a father, elder, and aged. Colossians 1-2 talks about our growth like a tree which gets grounded, settled, rooted, built up, stablished, and abounding. In D2 you'll go deeper into the definitions of those stages, but for now, let's just realize that we are all somewhere on this continuum.

Ask yourself where you are at in this process, and then as you move forward and begin the work of helping others, ask God to help you understand where they are. That's the first question I ask the Lord as I begin discipling someone, and this wisdom helps tremendously when you're working with people. Are they saved? Are they even born again? If they are, then are they a babe in Christ? Where do we start? How do I meet them where they are at and help them grow in their relationship with God?

After all that, we are now ready to begin talking about the joy of the Lord. This joy began in your life after you were saved and became a babe in Christ. It's often referred to as your "first love," and it was present on the day you met Jesus and surrendered your life to Him. From there it continues as you grow with Him, stay connected with Him, and allow Him to remain on the throne of your heart! As you let the Lord use you and live His life through you, you will experience this joy of the Lord! He lives inside of you, His joy resides there, and He wants you to experience it and walk in it!

God is preparing you to be a co-laborer with Him and mentor others just as Jesus did. Jesus' earthly life and ministry help us see exactly where His joy came from, and we are going to see that it has to do with having spiritual babies and raising them up. The people that we minister to and mentor are God's kids, and He loves them and wants help for them more than any of us do. If we can remember that as we are ministering to His kids, then we will be miles ahead. We have to stay connected with Him because we're not necessarily going to know how to help them using our own logic and wisdom. But He does, and He wants it even more than we do. If we can just remember that they are His children and He wants to help them grow up and stay connected with Him, then He will give us what we need as we ask. That reminds me of a verse God gave me when I first began discipling:

> **John 15:16** *Ye have not chosen me, but I have chosen you, and ordained you, that ye should go and bring forth fruit, and that your fruit should remain: that whatsoever ye shall ask of the Father in my name, he may give it you.*

I recommend you ask God to give this verse to you — write your name in all the spots that say "ye" and "you"! God chose you and ordained you... why? For you to go and bring forth fruit (evangelism) and that your fruit would remain (discipleship)! He goes on to say that as you do this (take care of HIS kids), He will give you whatsoever you ask in His name. In other words, He's going to take care of all your needs as you take care of His kids! As He was teaching me this principle, He allowed some good friends of mine to help enlighten me with the depth of its meaning. My friends were married with children and were planning their will. They asked if I would consider watching over and raising their children if anything were to happen to them. I prayed and agreed. Later, after their will was completed, I learned that if I needed to step in as guardian, their children (and I) were pretty much set for life and all our monetary needs were covered. Were they taking care of those needs because of our great friendship? NO! It was because I was raising their kids and they wanted to make sure I had everything I needed to do that. And ladies, that's exactly what Jesus is saying to us here — "Take care of My kids. Show them who I am. And I will take care of everything you need to do that!" I encourage you to claim that principle as you disciple.

And remember, you are taking care of God's kids! Look out for them just like Paul and Timothy did.

> **Philippians 2:20-21** *For I have no man likeminded, who will naturally care for your state. For all seek their own, not the things which are Jesus Christ's.*

> **Acts 20:28-32** *Take heed therefore unto yourselves, and to all the flock, over the which the Holy Ghost hath made you overseers, to feed the church of God, which he hath purchased with his own blood. For I know this, that after my departing shall grievous wolves enter in among you, not sparing the flock. Also of your own selves shall men arise, speaking perverse things, to draw away disciples after them. Therefore watch, and remember, that by the space of three years I ceased not to warn every one night and day with tears. And now, brethren, I commend you to God, and to the word of his grace, which is able to build you up, and to give you an inheritance among all them which are sanctified.*

We must let Jesus love them through us. His love will always be better for them than our fleshly love, and whether you are a mom to them or a big sister just helping them grow, realize that that's what we are here for. Letting Jesus live and love through us is what will bring us joy. Let's see what the Bible has to say about this, starting in Nehemiah 8:

> **Nehemiah 8:10** *Then he said unto them, Go your way, eat the fat, and drink the sweet, and send portions unto them for whom nothing is prepared: for this day is holy unto our Lord: neither be ye sorry; for the joy of the Lord is your strength.*

First of all, we must see that our strength is found in the joy of the Lord that lives in us and is available to us. Next, we see in Nehemiah that this joy is a choice. He says "neither be ye sorry." God gives us the same principle in John 14:1 when Jesus says, "Let not your heart be troubled." There are areas in our lives where we choose our attitude and we stand at crossroads and decide which direction to go. If we go down the hill the wrong way it will just snowball and get worse, but if we're going the right way, then righteousness can snowball and get better. We have to make the choice that we're not going to let our hearts be troubled, because this is the first step in reclaiming joy. We should desire to be like Joseph, who chose to trust in God's Word regardless of his circumstances. After all, those who love God's law will not be offended (Psalm 119:165). That choice — His joy — will become our strength.

Next, we see in John 15 that finding and fulfilling the joy of the Lord in your life comes by bearing fruit! We meditated on John 17 to learn what Jesus' work was, and now let's learn from and meditate on John 15 to see where this joy comes from:

> **John 15:11** These things have I spoken unto you, that my joy might remain in you, and that your joy might be full.

If His joy is to remain in us, and if our joy is to be full, then we need to know the things that He has spoken unto us. We can even find "these things" in verses 1-10 of the chapter, so let's go back and see what these things are!

> **John 15:1-10** I am the true vine, and my Father is the husbandman. Every branch in me that beareth not fruit he taketh away: and every branch that beareth fruit, he purgeth it, that it may bring forth more fruit. Now ye are clean through the word which I have spoken unto you. Abide in me, and I in you. As the branch cannot bear fruit of itself, except it abide in the vine; no more can ye, except ye abide in me. I am the vine, ye are the branches: He that abideth in me, and I in him, the same bringeth forth much fruit: for without me ye can do nothing. If a man abide not in me, he is cast forth as a branch, and is withered; and men gather them, and cast them into the fire, and they are burned. If ye abide in me, and my words abide in you, ye shall ask what ye will, and it shall be done unto you. Herein is my Father glorified, that ye bear much fruit; so shall ye be my disciples. As the Father hath loved me, so have I loved you: continue ye in my love. If ye keep my commandments, ye shall abide in my love; even as I have kept my Father's commandments, and abide in his love.

The things that will lead to us having full joy are all about bearing much fruit! Do you see that? We glorify God by bringing forth much fruit, and fruit, as you know, is offspring. A married couple will have children and these children are their fruit. There are many ways we can see bringing forth fruit, but the Bible clearly talks about three ways to bring forth fruit, and they're all connected with our joy and the joy of the Lord in us. Let's look at these three ways of bearing fruit.

First of all, we know that one type of fruit is the fruit of the Spirit:

> **Galatians 5:22-23** But the fruit of the Spirit is love, joy, peace, longsuffering, gentleness, goodness, faith, meekness, temperance: against such there is no law.

Love, joy, peace... we can clearly see what the fruit of the Spirit is. This form of fruit is the fruit of the Spirit in our lives as we deny self and follow the Spirit instead of our flesh. This is the fruit we begin growing as new Christians, and this fruit gives us access to the joy of the Lord. If you are a Christian you have at least tasted this joy, and the only way to keep it is to keep growing and dying to self by choosing to walk in the Spirit.

Another way Paul explains we can bear fruit is through our giving:

> **Philippians 4:15-17** Now ye Philippians know also, that in the beginning of the gospel, when I departed from Macedonia, no church communicated with me as concerning giving and receiving, but ye only. For even in Thessalonica ye sent once and again unto my necessity. Not because I desire a gift: but I desire fruit that may abound to your account.

Giving produces fruit to our account, which we can also see in 2 Corinthians 8:1-12. When we think of giving we usually think of money, but when God thinks of giving it's not just about our money. It's about our time, our talent, and our treasure all wrapped into one. It's our heart and our life, and God wants both of those things! God wants your heart!

> ***Proverbs 23:26*** *My son, give me thine heart, and let thine eyes observe my ways.*

Think about it. What is your attitude toward giving? Jesus said it's more blessed to give than to receive (Act 20:35). We are becoming more like Him as we grow, and His character is all about giving. If you have truly given Him your heart, it will be reflected in your giving.

The third and main principle of bearing fruit in the life of a Christian is spelled out for us here in John 15. It is the reproduction and growth of life in Christ, and this looks like discipleship. That's why He's left us here on this earth to invest our spiritual lives into the lives of those around us, and John 15 says that's where our joy comes from. We need the first two fruits (fruit of the Spirit and fruit of laying down our life through giving) in order to reach this third fruit bearing phase. Study John 15 and John 17 and you'll see that they're full of the work of the Lord and the joy of the Lord. As we become more like Jesus, we are to fulfill that same work and have access to that same joy! As you connect with Him and begin to know Him in a personal way and also see people born again and invested in, you will find the joy of the Lord. That's what He wants to do through us. Let's look at God's awesome call in this verse again:

> ***John 15:16*** *Ye have not chosen me, but I have chosen you, and ordained you, that ye should go and bring forth fruit, and that your fruit should remain: that whatsoever ye shall ask of the Father in my name, he may give it you.*

He chose us and ordained us to go and bring forth fruit that would remain! The only way our fruit can remain is through mentoring and discipling. Just as we needed help from our parents when we were born the first time, we need help to grow after being born again. That is what the local church is for! That's why we are here, and that's where our joy comes from.

When I first read about fruit in the Bible long ago, I remember thinking that I should study physical fruit and see if the Lord would give me a better understanding of this fruit-bearing process. I decided to study fruit trees, and I found that it commonly takes about three years for a fruit tree to really produce much fruit. That made me think of the disciples and how Jesus spent three and a half years with them before He sent them out on their own. Once a fruit tree starts producing, it will start to gradually abound if it's getting the right nourishment. And of course, the seeds begin falling to the ground so that they can grow into fruit trees that will bring forth abundant fruit. It's such a great picture for us, and it is also laid out in the Bible for us in Psalm 1:

> **Psalm 1:3** *And he shall be like a tree planted by the rivers of water, that bringeth forth his fruit in his season; his leaf also shall not wither; and whatsoever he doeth shall prosper.*

We all have seasons and we all have a different kind of a fruit. Most fruits take three years to be produced, but there are some that take even longer. This goes back to God making each one of us different — these differences mean that we can't compare ourselves with other people. He has gifted you for a specific task or work, and He's going to tell you what that is as you spend time with Him and grow. Part of that work is discipleship.

If you see that and you're not bearing fruit, then one of the greatest prayers that you could ever read is Hannah's prayer. In the Old Testament the focus was on raising physical babies, and in the New Testament our commission is to raise spiritual babies. For those of you who have physical babies, you are to be discipling them and bringing forth spiritual babies too! Again, it all goes together, and God uses it all in His purpose for each one of us. Hannah desperately wanted to have children, but she was barren. Finally, according to her prayers, God granted her a child: Samuel. You can find her story and her prayer in 1 Samuel 1-2, and it is the greatest prayer that you can pray to the Lord asking to bring forth fruit. She prayed to the Lord and was then given the peace to stand up, walk away, and trust God for the result. She didn't rehash it and turn it over and over in her mind, she simply entrusted it to the Lord. Use her example to help you to learn how to turn it over to God, get up, and walk away from it in faith. I encourage you to pray her prayer from your heart if you want to bring forth fruit.

Another good illustration for moms who have physical kids is Micah 6:4. Moses' parents were some of the best because they ended up raising three leaders in Israel: Moses, Aaron, and Miriam.

> **Micah 6:4** *For I brought thee up out of the land of Egypt, and redeemed thee out of the house of servants; and I sent before thee Moses, Aaron, and Miriam.*

More mentions of Amram and Jochebed, the parents of Moses, Aaron, and Miriam, are in Exodus 6:20, Numbers 26:59, and 1 Chronicles 6:3. The Bible doesn't say a lot about them, but what it does say is pretty powerful, and you can tell a lot about their lives and how they raised their children. There are so many great illustrations that you really have to get into and search out to let the Lord show you how to be a good parent, discipler, and mentor.

> **Proverbs 31:16** *She considereth a field, and buyeth it: with the fruit of her hands she planteth a vineyard.*

This is another verse you may want to remember. In it, the virtuous woman plants her vineyard one field at a time. This isn't mass production, this is discipleship, and this must happen one at a time. It eventually produces masses, but that's never how it starts out. We must begin spending time teaching them individually how to know the Lord and connect with the living God.

At the end of our lives we should want to be able to look back and see how God was glorified through our fruit bearing. Our joy is tied to our fruit, but sometimes the works of the flesh can steal away this joy. When this happens, we need to focus instead on the fruit that God wants: the fruit of the Spirit, the fruit of giving, and the fruit of discipleship. These are the only fruits that will produce the joy of the Lord in our lives!

Questions to Consider:

1. True or false: Joy is the absence of suffering in the presence of God.

2. What is God's ultimate perfect will for every believer, as outlined in Romans 8:29?

3. What did Jesus do? What was His main ministry, as seen in John 17?

4. How can we do greater works than Jesus?

5. Review the Seven Stages of Spiritual Growth chart and examine your life. Where do you think you are on the continuum?

6. When does the joy of the Lord begin in the believer's life? How does it grow?

7. When was the last time you experienced the "joy, joy, joy, joy down in your heart"? Do you have it now? If not, how can you get it back?

8. What are the three ways to bear spiritual fruit? What kind of fruit is growing in your life?

9. Examine Hannah's prayer in 1 Samuel 1:10-19. Are you desperate to bear fruit? Can you turn it over to God like she did? Have you tried?

19

Mentorship

The true mark of discipleship is whether a person develops a vision to use their own life to make disciples and invest the things they've learned into others. Our church's discipleship ministry program ends with an emphasis on becoming a disciple by making disciples, and that's how we're ending here. We want to present the vision of being a discipler before every individual and ask them to begin praying about bringing forth fruit, realizing that this will produce the joy of the Lord and glorify God! In the end, that's why we're really here on this earth. We were saved and discipled so that we can then invite others to do the same — to evangelize and disciple. Our strength is found in the joy of the Lord, and it is connected to making spiritual babies, which means seeing people born again and then maturing them in Christ through discipleship.

Naomi was just an ordinary woman, but she was greatly used to mentor Ruth. Just like we saw how God brought together Isaac and Rebekah to bring forth fruit for His glory, we can also see how God brought together Naomi and Ruth to bring forth the fruit of discipleship. Let's walk through Naomi's story. I would recommend reading through the book of Ruth before reading this chapter, and as you study it, instead of looking at Ruth and examining how God prepared her, look at Naomi and study how God used her. We can learn so much from Naomi about being a mentor. Naomi wasn't perfect, but God still used her to teach Ruth how to have a relationship with Him. God used her in spite of her infirmities, just like the Lord can use us!

It's good to realize that Naomi and Ruth lived around the time of Deborah and Gideon in the book of Judges and this was a time when "every man did that which was right in his own eyes" (Judges 17:6, 21:25). This was a time just like today — it's a time when every man is doing what he thinks is right instead of using an absolute authority. Discipleship is contrary to this because it means submitting to the authority of your mentor, the Bible, and God. After reading the book of Ruth from the Bible, let's walk through these principles we see in Naomi's life.

First of all, we see that her husband took her from the place of blessing. For Naomi this place of blessing was Bethlehem, and for us it is the local church. There was a famine in the land, so Naomi's husband took her and the whole family from Bethlehem-judah to Moab (Ruth 1:1). Naomi submitted and followed her husband, leaving all of her friends and family. God still had a plan for them even though they were not following His perfect will (1:3-5). Somewhere along the line, God brought Ruth across this family's path and she married one of Naomi's sons. We know that God had a plan for Ruth to become a part of the Jewish nation, so He chose to weave Ruth and Naomi's lives together to accomplish this plan. Unfortunately, this plan included the deaths of both their husbands. It was through those tragedies that God was able to work in Ruth and Naomi's lives to get them back to Bethlehem and back to the place of blessing. Their authorities were not following God's Word, so God moved in such a way that their wives could be in a right place with Him. Like we said when we talked about romantic relationships, God will always take care of whomever wants to do what is right. He promises to take care of us.

We see that Naomi was acquainted with grief, and it wasn't until her husband was removed from that authority position in her life that she was able to even consider going back to Bethlehem on her own. In the grief of losing two sons and a husband she moved toward God instead of away. In spite of her discouragement and bitterness over the circumstances, she chose God and moved toward His structure and place of blessing (1:6-7).

The other godly, amazing thing about Naomi is that she gave her daughters-in-law the same choice. She told them that they didn't need to go back with her. She didn't try to control them or make them feel sorry for her and stay with her. She understood that they had a free will and was ready to go back alone, even though they were the only family that she had left (1:8-14). Ruth, as we all know, chooses to stay with Naomi. Why is that?

> **Ruth 1:15-17** And she said, Behold, thy sister in law is gone back unto her people, and unto her gods: return thou after thy sister in law. And Ruth said, Intreat me not to leave thee, or to return from following after thee: for whither thou goest, I will go; and where thou lodgest, I will lodge: thy people shall be my people, and thy God my God: where thou diest, will I die, and there will I be buried: the Lord do so to me, and more also, if ought but death part thee and me.

Ruth had somehow seen God in Naomi's life, and even though Naomi was just a regular, imperfect person, she had a relationship with the Lord. This is exactly what we want to see between a mentor and someone that they are mentoring: a connection where the disciple can see the reality of the mentor's relationship with God. Obviously, Naomi cared about Ruth. They had lived together for many years and had also gone through extreme loss together. Somehow Ruth was able to see beyond their relationship to see Naomi's relationship with God, and this caused her to desire to have the same thing that Naomi had. As a mentor or discipler, that is what you want your disciple to see.

There are so many biblical principles here that we can look at. Naomi humbles herself and returns to Bethlehem, and Ruth accompanies her (1:19). Upon their return, Naomi sees herself as a total and complete failure. She calls herself Mara, which means "bitter" (1:20-21), even though she was standing on the threshold of blessing. She had fruit standing beside her and she didn't even realize it. Matthew 7:20 says that "by their fruits ye shall know them," and that can apply to spiritual fruit. Ruth was the spiritual fruit of Naomi's life, and she was also the only woman called "virtuous" in the Bible (Ruth 3:11). Ruth's presence and character were a great indicator of Naomi's faithfulness and of God's goodness. But in spite of this blessing, Naomi was struggling to view her life through God's eyes as she humbled herself and returned home. We need to view our lives through the Lord's eyes and we need to see what He sees. What did God see in her? God saw David's great-great-grandma.

In chapters 2 and 3, Naomi counseled Ruth through the law and helped her develop a relationship with Boaz, who was a picture or type of Christ. Galatians 6:7-9 says, "Be not deceived; God is not mocked: for whatsoever a man soweth, that shall he also reap. For he that soweth to his flesh shall of the flesh reap corruption; but he that soweth to the Spirit shall of the Spirit reap life everlasting." This chapter continues on to give the key we can learn from Naomi's life: "let us not be weary in well doing: for in due season we shall reap, if we faint not." Naomi reaped the blessing because she didn't faint and she didn't give up. She kept seeking God and sharing that with others.

In summary, had Naomi not submitted to her husband and followed him despite his disobedience, she would not have known Ruth or returned to Bethlehem. Had she not sown righteousness, she would not have reaped her grandson, Obed, or her great-great grandson, king David (Ruth 4:17, 21-22). She went from bitterness to joy and from following the flesh to following the Spirit. God wants us to be mentors not according to our own wisdom, insight, or strength, but according to His Word and His power. Capture the vision of sharing your relationship with others by teaching them who the God of the Bible is, and be fruitful by making disciples of the Lord Jesus Christ.

Questions to Consider:

1. What is the true mark of discipleship?

2. To what and to whom are we to submit as we are being discipled?

3. How and where did Naomi and Ruth meet?

4. Why did Ruth choose to stay with Naomi after the deaths of their husbands?

5. Is your relationship with God evident in your daily life? Do others want to follow you?

6. When Naomi returned to Jerusalem, she was struggling to see her life from God's perspective. Consider your past week, month, and year. What has been your focus? Is it on the physical or spiritual; the temporal or eternal; the difficulties or blessings?

7. What is the key to Naomi's (and our) reaping of blessing in Galatians 6:7-9?

8. Had you ever considered the book of Ruth from Naomi's point of view? What have you learned from her life and example as a mentor?

9. Have you been discipled yet? Are you discipling or mentoring anyone? After reading this chapter, what's your next step? If you're curious to learn more about the lifelong process of discipleship, please see the appendix for more information.

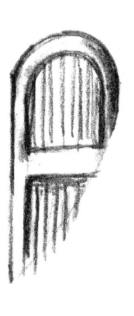

20

Closing Principles

In closing, let's review some of the important principles that we've covered throughout this book.

1. **We have to believe the Bible.** I can't stress this enough because we have the certainty of the words of truth (Proverbs 22:20-21). The major attack of our age and in our culture is the same attack that was on Eve, and that is whether or not we have the words of truth AND if we're going to believe them. That is the constant attack of the enemy, and that's why we have so many different Bible translations out there. The devil wants to take your Bible from you, and he is succeeding in much of the world today. If he can get the Word away from you then you'll have no foundation for growth. We have to know that we have the certainty of the words of truth, and each one of us should search out that subject for ourselves. You must know that you have God's very words in your hand and His Word will be the authority in your life — not a Bible scholar, not a Bible critic, not your mom or dad, and not your feelings.

There will always be instability and uncertainty when you have more than one authority (James 1:8). This is what most religions do — the Mormons have the Book of Mormon and the Bible; Catholics have the Council of Trent, the Pope's word, and the Bible, just to name a few. Any time you have more than one authority you have to choose which one to believe, so in the end you become the final authority. The difference between Bible-believers and any other faith in the world is that we have one Bible and one authority. That means you need to believe it and become accountable to it! Much of the Bible is not hard to understand, it's just hard to believe. Do you believe you have the words of the living God? If you don't yet, then find them and search them out. God has preserved His words, and He tells us that we can know the certainty of His words.

Up until 50 years ago, most Christians used the King James Version (KJV). The first revision, the Revised Version (RV), was created in the late 1800's, and the American Standard Version (ASV) in the early 1900's. That's when this questioning of the authority of the Word of God and babbling over versions began. Since the invention of the printing press in 1440 and the publishing of the King James Bible in 1611, the Bible exploded onto the scene and changed the course of missions and history. God promised those in the Philadelphian church age that He would give them the key of David and that He would set before them an open door that no one could close (Revelation 3:7-8)! This was all because they had little strength (in themselves), kept His Word, and didn't deny His name! Study it out for yourself and know that the Bible you hold in your hands is the preserved Word of God for you in your language. God promises that (Psalm 12:7), and you should believe on that promise.

Don't listen to ungodly counsel to solve your problems. Instead, get your counsel from God! We often seek advice that agrees with how we are feeling, but don't do that! Remember Psalm 1:1-3. Know God, know His Word, and know that you have it. Ask God what He says about a subject using "book, chapter, verse." Do a word study or ask a Bible-believing mentor or pastor for help. One set of verses we went over when we looked at confidence and security was Jeremiah 9:23-24, and I think that is a passage that we need to remember. It's about knowing God, being in His presence and in an intimate relationship with Him, being sure of what He said, and running our emotions through the boundaries of His Word.

Jeremiah 9:23-24 Thus saith the LORD, Let not the wise man glory in his wisdom, neither let the mighty man glory in his might, let not the rich man glory in his riches: but let him that glorieth glory in this, that he understandeth and knoweth me, that I am the Lord which exercise lovingkindness, judgment, and righteousness, in the earth: for in these things I delight, saith the LORD.

"Let him that glorieth glory in this, that he understandeth and knoweth me." God delights in us knowing Him, and the only way we are going to do that is through His Word.

2. **We have to develop balance and consistency in everything.** Proverbs 11:1 says that "a false balance is an abomination to the LORD," so that means that there needs to be balance in everything. We talked about spirit, soul, and body and how they all ripple together, so there needs to be balance and consistency in our personal walks. We need to make the spiritual — rather than the physical — the foundation in our lives. As Paul explains in 2 Corinthians 13:5, we need to be constantly examining ourselves to ensure that we're building our lives upon the right foundation.

There are certain areas I look at first when I examine myself, and whenever I have a problem, I check these areas first to see if there's something I can immediately adjust. If I'm counseling someone, these are the first places I look in their lives. The first and most important area is the question of their salvation. If they are saved, have they been discipled? If they have been discipled, do I see the four goals operating in their life? Remember that these are the four goals: established in worship, established in the Word, established in the local church, and established in ministry. The last one will even automatically take care of itself if you're established in the first three!

So examine yourself and look at your life — are you established in the four goals of discipleship that are in our Biblical Discipleship lessons? That establishment takes place through the three things that Jesus replaced Himself with: the Word, the Spirit, and the church. Some of the solutions to our problems can be very simple, especially when someone first comes looking for counsel, because you need to be established and balanced in these three areas with which Jesus replaced Himself. Biblical Discipleship also includes lessons over each of these three things, so some questions you may have can be addressed there. Are you reading the Bible regularly, are you walking in the Spirit and under God's control, and are you plugged into and serving at a good church? If any one of those things gets out of balance then the whole mix will be messed up.

It's small issues in the basics that can quickly get us away from God. To avoid going through the motions, we have to examine ourselves and each other to ensure we're not out of balance.

3. **Life is a cycle.** We are going to go through seasons of trials and blessings. We will never be problem-free, but we can be triumphant. Ecclesiastes 3 talks about a time and a season for every purpose under heaven and details 28 phases of life's cycles.

Cycles of Life

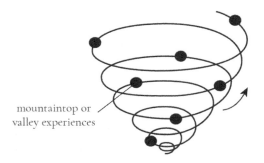

As we grow in Christ, we move outward and upward through the cycles of life. Along the way, we will hit up against trials of adversity and prosperity. During those times, we can fall down and even backslide (which is why we need to examine ourselves regularly), or we can stand strong in Christ and move forward in faith by running our emotions through the Word of God.

Closing Principles

Our life is full of cycles in an upward motion or growth process. We will hit up against something hard, get victory, keep going, and then hit against the next hard thing. At any time we can start going down or backwards, and many seasons of blessing or trial can actually be crucial crossroads that determine our future direction. We can fall far back, but at some point we have to start moving forward in this cycle of life. God gives us the principles we need to get through these cycles without violating His Word. That's what this book helps us do — to run our emotions through the Word of God without violating His principles.

As you recall, the Bible shows us many different characters and how God dealt with them and their emotions. In Acts 7:20-40 we see that God started working in Moses' heart long before he ran into the wilderness. He was already beginning to reveal to him His purpose and call and was still trying to work it out. When Moses first recognized the nation of Israel, he saw that the Hebrews were under extreme suffering, and what did he do? He tried to fix it himself in the flesh, similar to Abraham and Sarah. They all got calls from the Lord and initially tried to fix it or do it themselves. Moses did this by killing an Egyptian who was harming a Hebrew brother. Another Hebrew brother witnessed it and accused Moses of murder, which caused Moses to fear and run for his life. He ended up spending 40 years in the wilderness, but the thing to see as we read through Acts is that God didn't cancel Moses' plan when he tried to do it in the flesh. What God did in the wilderness was to teach him how to run his strong emotions through the Word of God and be balanced. That's what He's doing in the school of the wilderness, and that's what He wants to do with us. He's giving you a vision of what He wants to accomplish in your life, and He's teaching you how to walk with Him through the trials of the wilderness.

We see that Moses did not become emotion-free. For instance, after he went up and got the tablets from God and saw the nation of Israel sinning, he was so filled with anger and emotion that he broke them. He had an emotional outburst even after learning in the wilderness. The 28-phase cycle from Ecclesiastes 3 includes our emotions because, after all, our emotions are God-given. God's going to use them, but at the same time, we can't let them control us and we can't stuff them and deny them. Let's look at what God says about Moses through this journey:

> **Acts 7:20-29** In which time Moses was born, and was exceeding fair, and nourished up in his father's house three months: and when he was cast out, Pharaoh's daughter took him up, and nourished him for her own son. And Moses was learned in all the wisdom of the Egyptians, and was mighty in words and in deeds. And when he was full forty years old, it came into his heart to visit his brethren the children of Israel. And seeing one of them suffer wrong, he defended him, and avenged him that was oppressed, and smote the Egyptian: for he supposed his brethren would have understood how that God by his hand would deliver them: but they understood not. And the next day he shewed himself unto them as they strove, and would have set them at one again, saying, Sirs, ye are brethren; why do ye wrong one to another? But he that did his neighbour wrong thrust him away, saying, Who made thee a ruler and a judge over us? Wilt thou kill me, as thou diddest the Egyptian yesterday? Then fled Moses at this saying, and was a stranger in the land of Madian, where he begat two sons.

The thing I really want us to see is that when Moses killed the Egyptian in verse 24, God was already working in his life to make him into a deliverer for Israel. It's just that he wasn't supposed to do it himself — he was supposed to wait on God. God often begins revealing His plan to us early in our walk with Him, but then He's waiting on us to stop trying to do it ourselves. He uses the wilderness to teach us how to let Him do it through us. That often takes lots of time and growth spurts, as well as lots of lessons on balance and the consistency of running everything through the boundaries of the Word of God.

4. **Jesus recognizes the feelings of our infirmities.** Hebrews 4:15 is a fabulous verse to claim when you are going through a really rough spot. It talks about how Jesus is intimate with each of our struggles because He came in the flesh and was tempted as we are.

Hebrews 4:15 *For we have not an high priest which cannot be touched with the feeling of our infirmities; but was in all points tempted like as we are, yet without sin.*

When nobody else is there for you, when you feel rejected, and when nothing else is working out, go to Jesus. He can be touched by the feeling of our infirmities. Whenever someone doesn't understand or doesn't care to understand your feelings, Jesus wants to hear them. Talk to the Lord and let Him be your best friend. Proverbs 18:24 says that a friend "must shew himself friendly: and there is a friend that sticketh closer than a brother." That friend that "sticketh closer than a brother" is Jesus! Jesus is the friend of sinners and the friend of the lowly, and He wants to be a friend of you.

5. **God uses relationships.** Ministry runs on the rails of relationships. We've looked at anger and forgiveness, and we've learned that those two things are often used by the devil to disrupt our relationships. Why? Because God uses relationships. In Luke 5 you see John and James, two brothers, as well as Peter and Andrew, two brothers. Those two sets of brothers were partners in business, and after Jesus called them, He didn't separate them. Instead, He called them and used them together mightily by building upon the relationships they had already established.

If the enemy can get in there and stop some of your relationships, he knows God's not going to be able to use you as well. That's why dealing with our emotions and our relationships is so, so important. Whether they be discipleship, family, or marriage relationships, God wants to use them. There are so many interpersonal connections that were used by God, and that's why 1 John 1:7 is so important for us to apply to our lives.

1 John 1:7 *But if we walk in the light, as he is in the light, we have fellowship one with another, and the blood of Jesus Christ his Son cleanseth us from all sin.*

This verse says that if you are walking with God, instead of hiding in the darkness and dishonesty like Adam and Eve, He can make your relationships right. So if I'm having difficulty in a relationship, I need to get with God and figure out why. I need to ask where I am not walking in light with Him. What principle am I not applying? 1 John 1:7 clearly says that He takes care of our relationships ("we have fellowship one with another") AND He cleans us ("the blood of Jesus Christ His Son cleanseth us from all sin"), WHEN we walk in the light. All we have to do is stay right with Him and be open, honest, and out in the light with Him. That's why spending time in the presence of God is so important. Spend time with God and get everything out in the open with Him. Then apply the biblical principles He gives you and He will be faithful to take care of your relationships. The closer the relationship is, such as marriage, the more God has to be in the center. Anytime difficulty arises, go to the Lord, look at His principles, and ask what needs to be brought into the light.

Remember, too, that relationships, like everything else, have cycles and seasons. You may have a springtime season with a best friend and be very fruitful, but that may not be forever. Similarly, just because you go through a winter with a friend doesn't mean that there's anything wrong in the relationship. Sometimes we make mountains out of molehills.

Also realize that if you get really close with some people, you might end up focusing on their faults instead of their positive qualities. The moon is an awesome picture of this — a full, bright moon shining in the night sky looks absolutely beautiful from our view on earth. However, if we were to fly to the moon in a rocket ship, we would see that its surface is marred and scarred. It might be easy to start focusing on the craters and imperfections and forget about the beauty of the moon itself. Sometimes we do that in our relationships with people. We can get so close that we only focus on their flaws, and when we notice that happening, we just need to take a giant step back and see them as God sees them.

6. **Practice keeping a positive attitude.** Focus on the blessings we have in Christ and on the presence of God in your life. We have hope because we have Jesus! We have access to the Creator of the Universe! Of all the people in the world,

we Christians are those who should be walking in an attitude of acceptance with joy! We should be thankful! I mean, if you really believe Romans 8:28, and you love God, shouldn't you be different from those without the Lord who don't have any real hope?

Unfortunately, this is why we are under so much attack. The enemy wants to steal our joy and get us focused on this world — on the physical instead of on the spiritual. We are here to share that hope with others, but he doesn't want that hope to shine from our countenances for other people to see.

We can give thanks in and for everything, but complaining NEVER helps with this. After all, the Bible tells us to "do all things without murmurings and disputings" (Philippians 2:14). Develop an attitude of thankfulness rather than complaining, and let God pass His hope on to others through you! We've had many lessons on being thankful throughout this book, and the list of verses in your Bible that back this up are never-ending. The battle is in your mind, so focus on the positive rather than the negative.

> *Philippians 4:8* *Finally, brethren, whatsoever things are true, whatsoever things are honest, whatsoever things are just, whatsoever things are pure, whatsoever things are lovely, whatsoever things are of good report; if there be any virtue, and if there be any praise, think on these things.*

7. God has a list of qualities that He wants to see established in us. In Titus 2:3-5, we see a list of specific godly qualities and traits that the aged Christian ladies are to possess and pass on to younger ladies. This is just another passage showing us God's purpose for our lives, and my prayer is that God has begun helping you learn some of those characteristics through this study. We have touched on them throughout this book. Soberness is the first, foundational trait listed and it can be defined as "temperate, balanced, not drunk, not out of mind, not overpowered by liquors, passion, emotion, imaginations," etc. etc. etc. In short, being sober has to do with your state of mind. It is learning to have a sound mind by establishing our thoughts in the Word of God and casting down vain imaginations.

God began teaching me these characteristics through one-on-one biblical discipleship. As He continued that journey in my life, I began recording them in this study and passing them on. My prayer is that they have been a help to you in building your spiritual foundation. Several key passages on this process to remember are 2 Corinthians 10:3-5 and 2 Corinthians 1:3-4.

> **2 Corinthians 10:3-5** *For though we walk in the flesh, we do not war after the flesh: (for the weapons of our warfare are not carnal, but mighty through God to the pulling down of strong holds;) casting down imaginations, and every high thing that exalteth itself against the knowledge of God, and bringing into captivity every thought to the obedience of Christ;*

I do not want you to walk away from this study believing that your emotions and imaginations are only or always bad. Our imaginations and emotions are God-given and can be used for good, but they can also take us places outside of the boundaries of the Word of God and cause us much turmoil. We must learn to run our emotions and imaginations through the boundaries of the Word of God. Use your imaginations to see Jesus on that white horse splitting the sky open (Revelation 19:11-13) or to see God on the throne (Revelation 4:2-3)! Let that fuel your emotions to love the Lord thy God with all thy heart, mind, soul and strength, then give that love to someone else. If you are willing, God is able! He can transform you from the inside out.

> **2 Corinthians 1:3-4** *Blessed be God, even the Father of our Lord Jesus Christ, the Father of mercies, and the God of all comfort; who comforteth us in all our tribulation, that we may be able to comfort them which are in any trouble, by the comfort wherewith we ourselves are comforted of God.*

God wants to use what He has given you to assist, influence, and encourage others. Just like how Titus 2 talks about the aged helping the youth, in a big family, everyone helps someone younger than themselves! That's what discipleship and mentoring are all about, and that's how my church runs — every member is a minister! In fact, God taught me far more through mentoring others than when someone else discipled me at the very beginning. 2 Corinthians 1:3-4 says He allows us to go through tribulations so that He can comfort us. And then after we are comforted and know Him more intimately, He wants us to pass on the comfort that He gave to us to someone else!

I encourage you not to put this book on a shelf and forget about it, just like you shouldn't do with your discipleship workbook. Mentor others, help them through the Biblical Discipleship principles, and as you have the opportunity, share them with others. First apply these principles to your life, and then help another apply it to theirs — that's what Titus 2, Matthew 28, John 15, and 2 Timothy 2 tell us to do. Pass on what God has given you. That's what discipleship is all about, and that's what Jesus did. This is the ministry of reconciliation that God has given to each of us (2 Corinthians 5:18), and this is how the Lord transformed my life from a broken young lady to who I am today in Christ. Remember that Satan, the world, and your flesh all want you running in emotional circles so that you're incapable of serving the Lord effectively. Choose to submit your mind, heart, soul, and strength to the authority of Christ today.

> **Psalm 73:25-26** *Whom have I in heaven but thee? and there is none upon earth that I desire beside thee. My flesh and my heart faileth: but God is the strength of my heart, and my portion for ever.*

We began this journey with my search for the perfect father, which was followed by a desperate hunt for the perfect husband as I tried to fill the void in my heart. As we end, please understand that it was through the words of the living God I found both! The Word of God has all the answers you are looking for if you come to it with a seeking and believing heart. We have access to the perfect Heavenly Father and His Son, our Bridegroom Jesus Christ. Please know, dear sister, you have the same access to find them, too.

Appendix: Biblical Discipleship Overview

Matthew 28:18-20 And Jesus came and spake unto them, saying, All power is given unto me in heaven and in earth. Go ye therefore, and teach all nations, baptizing them in the name of the Father, and of the Son, and of the Holy Ghost: teaching them to observe all things whatsoever I have commanded you: and, lo, I am with you alway, even unto the end of the world Amen.

Matthew 28:18-20 is a foundational set of verses for Bible-believing churches. This Great Commission was given directly to the apostles and the local church by the Lord Jesus Christ Himself. At the center of the commission is the command to "teach all nations," which is the call to make disciples. He was commanding the apostles and the church to make disciples of Him from every nation and to teach them the things they had been taught (2 Timothy 2:2). God has also given that mission to you today. If you're a disciple of Jesus, a "learner" or follower of the Lord, He's saying to you — "Go and make disciples."

Making disciples begins by preaching the gospel, which is "the power of God unto salvation to everyone that believeth," because no one can become a disciple of the Lord Jesus Christ without first becoming a believer in the

Lord Jesus Christ (Romans 1:16). When we receive Jesus Christ as our Savior by grace through faith, we are born again and need to begin growing in our relationship with God through the lifelong process of discipleship.

Just like a physical baby needs help growing, we need help growing up spiritually. Before Jesus left this earth, He not only left His followers with a mission, He left behind the three things needed to accomplish it: the Word of God, the Holy Spirit, and the local church. And these are the same three things we individually need to grow spiritually! At our church, Discipleship 1 (D1) is the first step after salvation to help the new believer get grounded in these keys to our relationship with God. We use the material published by Living Faith Fellowship, *Biblical Discipleship*, as a tool to accomplish this goal.

D1 begins with the young believer being matched with a mentor through whom he or she can see firsthand how to walk with the Lord. The mentor serves as a role model as well as a teacher and walks the disciple through 18 lessons of foundational doctrines and helps them get established in the Four Goals of Discipleship. While D1 does have a clear academic component, it goes far beyond any class, curriculum, Bible study, or program. Biblical discipleship (in the D1 setting and beyond) is all about having a moment by moment, day by day walk with Christ through obedience to His Word and being conformed to His image (John 8:31; Romans 8:29).

After completing D1 and maturing through the first 3-4 stages of spiritual growth, the disciple enters the classroom setting for Discipleship 2 (D2). This is a two-semester class that covers topics that every disciple needs to know to move forward in making disciples themselves, such as character and spiritual qualities of a godly man/woman, the seven stages of spiritual growth, the philosophy of discipleship, how to disciple, and how to study the Bible.

After that, the disciple is ready to disciple others and attend Living Faith Bible Institute (LFBI), an accredited institute that offers a 4-year program of study towards an Associate of Divinity degree. Degree or not, LFBI is for every local church member! These courses train believers to rightly divide the Word of God and equip them to live it out, lead, and be launched into a lifetime of following, loving, obeying, and serving the Lord Jesus Christ (2 Timothy 2:15; Mark 12:30-31).

Understanding that discipleship is to be the primary focus of the believer, we need to purpose in our hearts by the grace of God to follow Christ wholeheartedly and single-mindedly (Psalm 9:1, 119:34). The idea sounds simple, but it won't always be easy in reality. There WILL be trials, temptations, and distractions. However, by determining in advance that the Lord Jesus Christ is and will always be preeminent in His rightful place on the pedestal of our hearts and wills, we decide any suffering will not stop us from following the Lord all the days of our lives.

> ***Acts 20:24*** *But none of these things move me, neither count I my life dear unto myself, so that I might finish my course with joy, and the ministry, which I have received of the Lord Jesus, to testify the gospel of the grace of God.*

The purpose of the Biblical Discipleship lessons is to establish believers in the foundational doctrines of the faith and in the Four Goals of Discipleship, which the believer will continue to grow in for the rest of their lives. The following key values ensure that the foundational doctrines and critical goals are established.

The Values of Discipleship

> **2 Timothy 2:2** And the things that thou hast heard of me among many witnesses, the same commit thou to faithful men, who shall be able to teach others also.

1. **Sound doctrine is a priority.** (*"And the things..."*)
One of the ultimate goals of discipleship is to equip faithful believers with sound doctrine. Biblical doctrine will always center on following the Lord Jesus Christ.

2. **Discipleship is a teacher-student relationship.** (*"...that thou hast heard of me..."*)
There must be a disciple for it to be discipleship. This will normally happen one-on-one; however, it is possible to accomplish discipleship with two or three people, as long as there is only one teacher, and the rest are students. Discipleship is not simply a Bible study, or two individuals spending time together. It is focused on teachers pouring their lives and the Word of God into their students.

3. **Accountability is critical.** (*"...among many witnesses..."*)
Discipleship requires the close relationship between the teacher and the student. However, discipleship cannot be carried out in isolation. There must be accountability from others who are able to witness the process and identify that the four goals are being accomplished.

4. **Teaching must be repeatable.** (*"...the same commit thou..."*)
Sound doctrine is presented in a way that is simple to understand and easy for a disciple to teach another disciple.

5. **Discipleship requires faithful believers.** (*"...to faithful men..."*)
Discipleship is built upon one disciple of Jesus entering into a relationship with another believer who has been found to be faithful.

6. **Disciples reproduce disciples.** (*"...who shall be able to teach others also."*)
The reason we commit "these things" unto faithful believers is so that they can teach others to do the same — make a disciple that will make more disciples.

The 4 Goals of Discipleship

1. **Established in the Worship of God:** The focus of your life

    John 4:23 *But the hour cometh, and now is, when the true worshippers shall worship the Father in spirit and in truth: for the Father seeketh such to worship him.*

2. **Established in the Word of God:** The authority of your life

    1 Thessalonians 2:13 *For this cause also thank we God without ceasing, because, when ye received the word of God which ye heard of us, ye received it not as the word of men, but as it is in truth, the word of God, which effectually worketh also in you that believe.*

3. **Established in the Local Church:** The context of your life

    1 Timothy 3:15 *But if I tarry long, that thou mayest know how thou oughtest to behave thyself in the house of God, which is the church of the living God, the pillar and ground of the truth.*

4. **Established in the Ministry:** The purpose of your life

    1 Peter 4:10 *As every man hath received the gift, even so minister the same one to another, as good stewards of the manifold grace of God.*

Brief Overview of the Lessons

Lesson 1: Salvation

Receiving Jesus Christ as your personal Savior is the most important decision you will ever make in your lifetime. This simple decision of childlike faith carries profound significance for all of eternity.

Key word: Relationship

Key questions answered: What does it mean to be born again? How does salvation affect my relationship to God?

Key purpose: To briefly explain what took place in your life when you received Jesus Christ as your personal Savior and how that decision has changed your standing with God.

Key point: Our relationship with God is now a perfect father and child relationship.

Memory verses:

> ***Ephesians 2:8-9*** *For by grace are ye saved through faith; and that not of yourselves: it is the gift of God: not of works, lest any man should boast.*

> ***John 1:12-13*** *But as many as received him, to them gave he power to become the sons of God, even to them that believe on his name: which were born, not of blood, nor of the will of the flesh, nor of the will of man, but of God.*

Lesson 2: Eternal Security

It is important to understand and know that your relationship with God is an eternal one. When you accepted Jesus Christ as your Savior, God gave you eternal life and the security of an eternal relationship with Him. Being saved means that you have eternal life, and having eternal life means that you are saved.

Key word: Security

Key question answered: Is my new life in Christ going to last forever?

Key purpose: To know that the security of your relationship with God is based upon nothing other than the finished work of Jesus Christ.

Key point: Our birth is irreversible.

Memory verses:

> *John 6:37* All that the Father giveth me shall come to me; and him that cometh to me I will in no wise cast out.

> *1 John 5:13* These things have I written unto you that believe on the name of the Son of God; that ye may know that ye have eternal life, and that ye may believe on the name of the Son of God.

Lesson 3: The Ordinances

Various religious denominations teach many things concerning the ordinances of baptism and the Lord's Supper. The Bible teaches that the Lord Jesus Christ gave His church these ordinances to commemorate His death, burial, and resurrection. It is important to understand that the ordinances of baptism and the Lord's Supper are not essential to your salvation, but they are important to demonstrate your obedience to the Lord after your salvation.

Key word: Obedience

Key question answered: What is the importance of baptism and the Lord's Supper in my life?

Key purpose: To give the Bible's clear and definite teaching on the two ordinances given to the church.

Key point: Baptism is the first act of obedience for a believer, and the Lord's Supper is a remembrance of Jesus Christ's death until He comes.

Memory verses:

> **Acts 8:36-37** *And as they went on their way, they came unto a certain water: and the eunuch said, See, here is water; what doth hinder me to be baptized? And Philip said, If thou believest with all thine heart, thou mayest. And he answered and said, I believe that Jesus Christ is the Son of God.*
>
> **1 Corinthians 11:26** *For as often as ye eat this bread, and drink this cup, ye do shew the Lord's death till he come.*

Lesson 4: Holy Spirit

The Holy Spirit of God took up permanent residency within you on the day that you received the Lord Jesus Christ as your personal Savior. The Holy Spirit is God's personal presence in your life, and He desires to make you holy as you learn to walk with Him. This third person of the Godhead is often misunderstood and ignored in Christianity.

Key word: Indwell

Key question answered: What is the role and function of the Holy Spirit in my life?

Key purpose: To give you a basic understanding of the true work of the Holy Spirit of God in your life.

Key point: The Holy Spirit dwells within you.

Memory verses:

> *1 Corinthians 6:19-20* What? know ye not that your body is the temple of the Holy Ghost which is in you, which ye have of God, and ye are not your own? For ye are bought with a price: therefore glorify God in your body, and in your spirit, which are God's.

> *Galatians 5:22-23* But the fruit of the Spirit is love, joy, peace, longsuffering, gentleness, goodness, faith, meekness, temperance: against such there is no law.

Lesson 5: Word of God

What makes Christianity unique is its claim to an absolute written authority from God. The Word of God is essential to your growth in the grace and knowledge of Jesus Christ. The Bible sets a standard by which we are to conform our life. In its pages, we see how God governs the details of our lives in every way.

Key word: Infallible

Key questions answered: Do I have God's Word today? What is the significance of the Bible in my life?

Key purpose: To acquaint you with the basics of the Bible, and to learn how it relates to your everyday life as the guide to your personal walk with Jesus Christ.

Key point: Every experience in your life, physical or spiritual, should be judged by the infallible standard of God's Word. The Bible is the absolute final authority in your life as a believer.

Memory verses:

> *2 Peter 1:21* For the prophecy came not in old time by the will of man: but holy men of God spake as they were moved by the Holy Ghost.

> *2 Timothy 3:16-17* All scripture is given by inspiration of God, and is profitable for doctrine, for reproof, for correction, for instruction in righteousness: that the man of God may be perfect, throughly furnished unto all good works.

Lesson 6: Prayer

Your personal relationship with the Lord Jesus Christ cannot grow without having proper communication. The two basic elements of spiritual survival for a Christian are the Word of God and prayer. God speaks to you as you read the Bible, and you speak to God through prayer. Your relationship with God will only be as strong as your dependence upon prayer.

Key word: Communication

Key question answered: How important is prayer in my life?

Key purpose: To teach you how to cultivate an effective and intimate prayer life.

Key point: Prayer is the communication from the heart of a believer to God.

Memory verses:

> ***John 14:13-14*** *And whatsoever ye shall ask in my name, that will I do, that the Father may be glorified in the Son. If ye shall ask any thing in my name, I will do it.*

> ***Philippians 4:6-7*** *Be careful for nothing; but in every thing by prayer and supplication with thanksgiving let your requests be made known unto God. And the peace of God, which passeth all understanding, shall keep your hearts and minds through Christ Jesus.*

Lesson 7: The Local Church

God established the family, the civil government, and the local church as three unique institutions on the earth. Each one has been ordained with leadership, blessings, and accountability. God has commissioned the local church to carry out His purposes in reaching the lost and perfecting the saved. It is important to understand that God's plan for your life can only be fulfilled when you are connected with the local church.

Key word: Edification

Key question answered: What is the purpose of the local church?

Key purpose: To explain the importance of the local church in the everyday lives of believers.

Key point: God intends for the local church to educate, equip, and edify the saints of God for the work of the ministry.

Memory verses:

> ***Ephesians 4:11-12*** *And he gave some, apostles; and some, prophets; and some, evangelists; and some, pastors and teachers; for the perfecting of the saints, for the work of the ministry, for the edifying of the body of Christ.*
>
> ***1 Corinthians 12:27*** *Now ye are the body of Christ, and members in particular.*

Lesson 8: Other Christians

You entered into God's family through a spiritual birth when you trusted Jesus Christ as your Savior. You now have a spiritual family with many brothers and sisters who are saved through the death, burial, and resurrection of Jesus Christ. This lesson will guide you through the special relationship you have with your spiritual family.

Key word: Fellowship

Key question answered: What is my relationship to other Christians?

Key purpose: To give you a clear understanding of how the body of Christ operates as a family unit.

Key point: You must have a personal relationship with Jesus before it is possible to have proper fellowship with other believers.

Memory verses:

>*John 13:35* By this shall all men know that ye are my disciples, if ye have love one to another.

>*1 John 1:7* But if we walk in the light, as he is in the light, we have fellowship one with another, and blood of Jesus Christ his Son cleanseth us from all sin.

Lesson 9: The Family

Our worship and service to God begins within the home, and that is where we will discover our most important of all human relationships. God has entrusted certain responsibilities to each family member that enable us to enjoy a healthy and happy home to the glory of God.

Key word: Responsibility

Key question answered: What are your specific biblical responsibilities within the family?

Key purpose: To teach you how to function biblically within your family.

Key point: God uses your role in the family as an illustration of what it means to be a member of God's family.

Memory verses:

> *Ephesians 6:1-4 Children, obey your parents in the Lord: for this is right. Honour thy father and mother; (which is the first commandment with promise;) that it may be well with thee, and thou mayest live long on the earth. And, ye fathers, provoke not your children to wrath: but bring them up in the nurture and admonition of the Lord.*
>
> *Ephesians 5:33 Nevertheless let every one of you in particular so love his wife even as himself; and the wife see that she reverence her husband.*

Lesson 10: Dealing with Sin

Perhaps the greatest challenge for any believer is the battle we have with sin. This truth is not always evident to a young Christian, but as you grow in Christ, you will realize more fully the intensity of this struggle.

Key word: Overcome

Key question answered: How do I overcome sin in my life?

Key purpose: To help you learn to overcome your sin nature and walk in the Spirit of God as He intended.

Key point: If you have true godly sorrow concerning your sin, repentance will follow naturally.

Memory verses:

>**Romans 6:11** *Likewise reckon ye also yourselves to be dead indeed unto sin, but alive unto God through Jesus Christ our Lord.*

>**Psalm 119:11** *Thy word have I hid in mine heart, that I might not sin against thee.*

Lesson 11: Liberty in Christ

The New Testament is clear that as a saved person, you are not bound by the Old Testament law, you are bound by God's grace. Some believers abuse the grace of God by claiming liberty to do as they wish without consequences. Others measure the quality of their relationship with God by trying to keep self-imposed moral rules and religious traditions. This lesson establishes the lordship of Jesus Christ as the biblical principle that protects you from abusing your liberty in Jesus.

Key word: Freedom

Key question answered: Now that I am forgiven, how can my liberty glorify God?

Key purpose: To help you understand what your liberty in Jesus Christ is, and how it affects your daily life.

Key point: The liberty you have in Jesus Christ gives you freedom to do what is right, and to serve God fully and completely.

Memory verses:

> ***Galatians 5:13*** *For, brethren, ye have been called unto liberty; only use not liberty for an occasion to the flesh, but by love serve one another.*

> ***Romans 8:2*** *For the law of the Spirit of life in Christ Jesus hath made me free from the law of sin and death.*

Lesson 12: Will of God

If you want to be successful in life, then you must discover what God wants you to accomplish and then fulfill it. The true measure of success is not your social status, financial stability, influence, or fame; it is in the simple obedience to the will of God in your life.

Key word: Conformity

Key question answered: How do I find God's will for my life?

Key purpose: To reveal the will of God from the Word of God so that you can effectively conform your life to God's will.

Key point: You must be in conformity to the will of God before He will direct you in the specifics of your life.

Memory verses:

> *Romans 12:1-2 I beseech you therefore, brethren, by the mercies of God, that ye present your bodies a living sacrifice, holy, acceptable unto God, which is your reasonable service. And be not conformed to this world: but be ye transformed by the renewing of your mind, that ye may prove what is that good, and acceptable, and perfect will of God.*

> *2 Peter 3:9 The Lord is not slack concerning his promise, as some men count slackness; but is longsuffering to us-ward, not willing that any should perish, but that all should come to repentance.*

Lesson 13: Giving

God is a giving God, and His will is for you to reflect His nature in your giving. It is important to understand that God owns everything, and He does not need your money. The way you give is an indication of your maturity as a believer. Giving is an act of faith and worship, and it demonstrates your love for God and His mission. This lesson will help you to understand your responsibility in the stewardship of your life and your resources.

Key word: Control

Key question answered: What does it mean to give, and what are my responsibilities to give?

Key purpose: To help you understand the nature of New Testament giving.

Key point: True New Testament giving concerns turning over complete control of your life and resources to Jesus Christ.

Memory verses:

> *2 Corinthians 9:7* Every man according as he purposeth in his heart, so let him give; not grudgingly, or of necessity: for God loveth a cheerful giver.

> *Matthew 6:21* For where your treasure is, there will your heart be also.

Lesson 14: Money and Possessions

One of the greatest temptations that a believer can face is the tremendous amount of materialism in the world. We are misled to believe that success is measured by material wealth, when Biblical success is actually measured by following God's will. Many believers find themselves in harmful situations because of their attitudes toward money and possessions. The purpose of this lesson is to guide you in managing your resources by following Biblical principles.

Key word: Attitude

Key question answered: What should my attitude be toward money and possessions?

Key purpose: To teach from the scriptures how to be a biblical steward of God's resources.

Key point: To be content with the resources that God has entrusted you with.

Memory verses:

> ***Philippians 4:11*** *Not that I speak in respect of want: for I have learned, in whatsoever state I am, therewith to be content.*

> ***Luke 16:13*** *No servant can serve two masters: for either he will hate the one, and love the other; or else he will hold to the one, and despise the other. Ye cannot serve God and mammon.*

Lesson 15: Job and Employer

God will lead you to use your position within the workplace as a mission field to reach the lost with the gospel of Jesus Christ. Your job gives you the opportunity to build relationships with people that you would not normally have contact with. It is essential to your spiritual growth that you understand this area of responsibility in accordance with the Word of God.

Key word: Opportunity

Key question answered: What should my attitude be toward my job and my employer?

Key purpose: To help you be the type of employee or employer that God would have you to be in order to accomplish His mission in your workplace.

Key point: You should view your job as a mission field where God has placed you for His service and glory.

Memory verses:

> **Mark 10:44-45** And whosoever of you will be the chiefest, shall be servant of all. For even the Son of man came not to be ministered unto, but to minister, and to give his life a ransom for many.

> **Colossians 3:23** And whatsoever ye do, do it heartily, as to the Lord, and not unto men.

Lesson 16: The Lost World

The Bible commands God's people to be separate from the world, while at the same time reaching lost men and women for the Lord Jesus Christ. As you seek to rescue the lost, you will receive opposition from the world because it is contrary to God's eternal purpose. This lesson is focused on the importance of being an effective witness of the grace of Jesus Christ while overcoming the opposition you receive from the world.

Key word: Mission

Key question answered: What are your responsibilities toward the lost?

Key purpose: To reach the lost without compromising your walk with the Lord Jesus Christ.

Key point: Allow the actions of your life to demonstrate your love for God.

Memory verses:

> ***Romans 1:16*** *For I am not ashamed of the gospel of Christ: for it is the power of God unto salvation to every one that believeth; to the Jew first, and also to the Greek.*

> ***1 Corinthians 8:3*** *But if any man love God, the same is known of him.*

Lesson 17: Judgment Seat

The Bible is clear that all people will stand before God one day to face judgment. For the Christian, that judgment will be at the Judgment Seat of Christ where we are judged for our works and service to the Lord Jesus Christ. You should be looking for that day when you will be held accountable to Jesus Christ.

Key word: Service

Key question answered: What will I be held accountable for at the Judgment Seat of Christ?

Key purpose: To keep the believer focused on eternal matters by outlining our final accountability to the Lord Jesus Christ as His servant.

Key point: You will be judged as a servant of Jesus Christ.

Memory verses:

> **2 Corinthians 5:10** *For we must all appear before the judgment seat of Christ; that every one may receive the things done in his body, according to that he hath done, whether it be good or bad.*

> **Romans 14:12** *So then every one of us shall give account of himself to God.*

Lesson 18: Next Steps

The purpose of biblical discipleship is to reproduce spiritual sons of God. Now that you have been taught the basic doctrines found in God's Word, it is time for you to fulfill God's command to reproduce in others what has been reproduced in you.

Key word: Reproduce

Key question answered: Is it my responsibility to make disciples?

Key purpose: To impress upon you the commandment to make disciples.

Key point: You have the responsibility to reproduce your relationship with Jesus into another believer.

Memory verses:

> **2 Timothy 2:2** And the things that thou hast heard of me among many witnesses, the same commit thou to faithful men, who shall be able to teach others also.

> **John 17:4** I have glorified thee on the earth: I have finished the work which thou gavest me to do.

If you or your church have questions or would like more information about the discipleship material, process, or philosophy of ministry, visit www.lffellowship.com/biblical-discipleship.

Made in the USA
Coppell, TX
02 July 2021